990

RADIO PRODUCTION WORKTEXT

RADIO PRODUCTION WORKTEXT

Studio and Equipment

LYNNE GROSS

DAVID E. REESE

Focal Press

Boston   London

Focal Press is an imprint of Butterworth Publishers.

Copyright © 1990 by Butterworth Publishers, a division of Reed Publishing (USA) Inc. All rights reserved.

ISBN 0-240-80045-1

Library of Congress Catalog Card Number: 89-81283

Butterworth Publishers
80 Montvale Avenue
Stoneham, MA 02180

10 9 8 7 6 5 4 3 2 1

Printed in the United States of America

Contents

10 SIGNAL-PROCESSING EQUIPMENT 108

11 PRODUCTION SITUATIONS 120

Preface

This book is intended to give very practical information for those who wish to become engaged in radio production. It will also be quite helpful for those who are already producing for radio but wish to know more about equipment and production techniques. Overall, the book should be valuable to those enrolled in a formal radio production course as well as those who are studying on their own. Radio is a very competitive field and those with the most knowledge (and talent) stand the best chance of succeeding.

As the title implies, this isn't a book to just read, but rather a text that will become an integral part of your study and practice of radio production. Each chapter of the text is divided into an **Information section**, a section of **Self-Study Questions and Answers**, and a **Projects section**.

The Information sections are further divided into modularized units so that all the primary concepts can be easily learned. These concepts are illustrated with drawings and photographs that help the student grasp the specific ideas being presented.

The Self-Study Questions include multiple choice, true/false, and matching questions covering much of the material in the chapter. Answers, as well as suggested procedures for those who do not answer correctly, guide the student through this section. These questions are intended to be instructional, so that by the time the student has read the Information section and answered them all correctly, he or she will feel confident about knowing the information.

The chapter's Projects sections contain practical projects that should give the reader the hands-on experience needed for successful radio production. The importance of practical production experience should not be overlooked, and these projects should be viewed as a starting point for the developing radio production person. Additional hands-on work in the production studio is never wasted time and is highly recommended.

The book is organized primarily by equipment, but it does not deal strictly with a nuts-and-bolts approach. Techniques as well as mechanics are included within each chapter. In fact, the book is not intended to be technical. It is written in an easy-to-read style that should enable people without technical training to understand the nature and makeup of the radio process.

The first chapter introduces the reader to the layout and design of the radio production studio and describes briefly the equipment that is detailed in succeeding chapters. Chapters 2 and 3 introduce two of the basic sound sources used in production work, namely microphones and turntables. The center of all production work, the audio console, is presented in chapter 4.

Chapters 5 and 10 have varying degrees of relevancy to specific production studios, but both are important in understanding the overall production process. Digital broadcast equipment is introduced in chapter 5. Most production studios house at least a compact disc player or perhaps a digital audio tape recorder, and the future importance of digital technology in radio production is demonstrated in this chapter. Chapter 10 provides a survey of the most popular signal processing equipment employed in radio production work. The studio you are working with may not have much of this equipment, but as you work in radio production you will become exposed to more and more of it.

Chapter 6 looks at the audio tape recorders found in the production studio—the reel-to-reel, the cassette, and the cartridge, as well as the emerging DAT. The size of this chapter is attributed to radio production's heavy reliance on audio tape recording and playback. Chapter 7 is devoted to audio tape editing because this is a rather complex and frequently executed task in radio production work.

Often overlooked equipment is included in chapters 8 and 9. Monitor speakers and headphones are discussed in chapter 8, and chapter 9 surveys connectors, cables, and accessories that complement the major pieces of equipment in the production studio. The last chapter explains various production situations and provides production techniques that elaborate upon and synthesize points made in the main body of the text.

Appendix A provides some important concepts about the nature of sound, so many users of this text will want to read this before beginning the text. On the other hand, Appendix B provides two additional projects that can be appropriately tackled after completing the text.

Throughout the book, key terms are listed in **boldface**. These terms are explained in the text and definitions are also included in the glossary at the end of the book.

The authors are indebted to many people for their help and encouragement. Other members of the Communications faculties at John Carroll University and California State University, Fullerton, gave input to the project. People in the audio and radio industry—Nancy Pearlman, David Hurlbut, and Kevin Gross—also willingly gave of their time and their knowledge. Many helpful comments came from the reviewers—Professor Alan H. Frank of Curry College, Professor James B. Miskimen of James Madison University, and Professor David T. MacFarland of Kansas State University. We are also very grateful for the support given by the members of our families and by the editorial staff at Focal Press.

RADIO
PRODUCTION
WORKTEXT

The Production Studio

Information

1.1 INTRODUCTION

The room that houses the equipment necessary for radio production work is known as the **production studio.** If your facility has several studios, they may be labeled ''Prod. 1'' or ''Prod. B'' or maybe simply ''PDX.'' Most radio facilities have at least two studios; one, however, is usually delegated as the **on-air studio** and is used for the live, day-to-day broadcasting. The other studio or studios are production studios and are used for putting together programming material that is taped for playback at a later time. This includes such items as commercials, public service announcements, and station promotional announcements.

Today most radio work is done **combo,** that is, the announcer is also the equipment operator. Because of this, the equipment and operator are in a single studio, be it a production room or on-air room. In earlier radio days, the announcer was often located in a separate room (announce booth) adjacent to the studio that housed the equipment. Visual contact and communication were maintained via a window between the two rooms. An engineer was required to actually manipulate the equipment, and all the announcer did was provide the voice. Many larger market radio stations still use a similar announcer/engineer arrangement.

We should note here that anyone can be an announcer without a license; to broadcast combo, however, requires a license issued by the FCC. To be in charge of the station transmitter and make required station log entries, the operator must have, at least, a **Restricted Radiotelephone Operator Permit.** This permit is issued upon application to the FCC. The necessary form can be obtained at most broadcast facilities and can be completed after a brief orientation by the station engineer. A **General Radiotelephone Operator License** is also available from the FCC, but obtaining this license requires a thorough knowledge of engineering practices and broadcast law, and the applicant must pass an FCC examination.

Some stations also have a studio that is considered a **performance studio.** It houses nothing more than microphones and table and chairs. The output is usually sent to a production studio to be taped, although sometimes it is sent directly to the on-air studio. This performance studio is used for taping interviews, for discussions involving several guests, or for putting a small musical group on the air.

1.2 THE STUDIO MAP

Figure 1.1 shows a map of the typical radio production studio. Starting with various sound sources such as an announcer's voice, a CD, or a record, it shows routes that sound takes to ultimately be broadcast or recorded. The trip can be complicated because the sound can go through several changes along the way. For example, it can be dubbed or copied from phonograph record to reel-to-reel, or it can be **equalized.** The solid line shows sound being sent to the audio console, through **signal processing** equipment, and then to the transmitting system; this would be normal for an on-air studio. The broken line shows the sound being sent back to the various recorders after signal processing; this would be normal for a production studio. You'll learn more about all of this as you work your way through this text, but for now the diagram of Figure 1.1 provides a look at where you are headed.

The equipment shown is also representative of that found in the typical radio production studio. The **microphone** transforms the announcer's voice into an audio signal. It is not uncommon for a production facility to have one or more auxiliary mics for production work that requires two or more voices. Most production rooms also have two **turntables** so that more than one record can be played back-to-back or simultaneously. The modern production studio now includes at least one **CD** player as more and more recorded material for production use is available on this format. Tape recorder/player sources include **reel-to-reel, cassette,** and **cartridge** machines. In studios that are very up-to-date, these recorders may be **digital audio tape** recorders. The number of recorders found in the production room depends on the complexity of the studio and the budget of the station. All of this equipment feeds into the **audio console,** which allows the

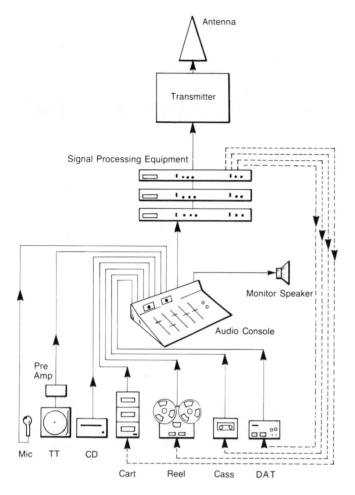

FIGURE 1.1   Studio map.

operator to manipulate the sound sources in various ways. Signal processing equipment (including **limiter/ compressor, harmonizer, noise-reduction, equalizer,** and **reverberation**) is usually put into the audio chain between the audio console and the transmitting equipment or recording equipment.

1.3 STUDIO LAYOUT

Almost all radio production studios use a U-shaped layout or some variation of it (see Figure 1.2). All the equipment needs to be within arm's reach of the operator and the operator needs to be immediately in front of the audio console. With the use of remote start/stop switches for equipment that must be out of convenient reach of the operator, all equipment manipulation does occur at the audio console once records have been cued or audio tapes threaded. Compare Figures 1.1 and 1.2 to see how the studio map translates into the actual production studio.

FIGURE 1.2   U-shaped studio design. (Courtesy of Arrakis Systems, Inc.)

1.4 STUDIO CABINETS AND COUNTERS

Studio equipment is often installed on and in custom-built cabinets and counters. A less expensive, but equally functional, approach is to lay out the studio using modular stock components. Audio cabinets have been designed that are expressly for turntables, tape decks, audio consoles, and other pieces of studio equipment. For example, the studio configuration shown in Figure 1.2 is composed of modular units. Studios can be designed to exactly fit the equipment a station has, and studios can even be expanded as new equipment is added. The cabinets are designed to provide easy access to the myriad of cables that are necessary to wire all the studio equipment together, yet maintain an attractive image for the look of the studio. Record cabinets are also available for production records and other recorded material that is kept in the production studio.

1.5 SOUND CONSIDERATIONS

There are several characteristics of sound that need to be considered in designing the radio production studio. Once a sound (such as an announcer's voice) is produced, it can be absorbed, reflected, or reinforced. In reality, a little of each usually occurs. Part of the sound is **absorbed** within the walls, ceiling, and flooring of the studio. Some of the sound is **reflected** back to the original source, perhaps off the glass surface of the windows in the studio. And sound can be **reinforced** by causing objects or surfaces within the studio to vibrate at the same frequencies as the original sound in a sympathetic fashion. In designing the radio studio, the goal is to manipulate these sound considerations to create a proper sound environment for production work.

1.6 REFLECTED VERSUS DIRECT SOUND

Another sound concept involves **reflected sound** and **direct sound.** When a sound is produced, the direct sound is the main sound that you hear. In a production situation, it is sound that goes directly from the announcer to the microphone. On the other hand, reflected sound that consists of **echo** and **reverberation** is considered indirect sound. This sound has bounced off or been reflected from one surface (echo) or two or more surfaces (reverb) before reaching the listener (see Figure 1.3).

In radio production, reflected sound reaches the microphone fractions of a second after the direct sound does because it has traveled an indirect route. We think in terms of reverb ring and reverb route, and the same concepts are true for echo, only to a lesser extent. **Reverb ring** is the time that it takes for a sound to die out or go from full volume to silence. **Reverb route** is the path that sound takes from its source to a reflective surface and back to the original source. A **live studio** has a long reverb ring and a short reverb route that produces a harder or more brilliant sound. A **dead studio** has a short reverb ring and a long reverb route that produces a softer sound.

Again, in the radio production studio, you want to control these factors to some extent through design considerations. One common studio design is a live end/dead end approach. The front of the studio (where the announcer and equipment are located) is designed to absorb sounds. This dead end quiets some of the equipment operation noise, picks up the direct sound of the announ-

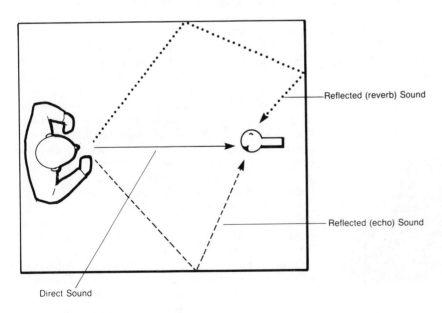

Direct Sound
Reflected (reverb) Sound
Reflected (echo) Sound

FIGURE 1.3 Direct versus reflected sound.

cer's voice, and absorbs the excess reflections that pass by the microphone from the live end. The live end adds a desirable sharpness to the sound.

1.7 STUDIO CONSTRUCTION MATERIALS

Part of these design considerations involve the actual construction materials used for the studio. Ideally, you want to keep outside (unwanted) sound from entering the studio and inside sound from escaping from the studio, except via the audio console. Radio studios utilize **soundproofing** to accomplish this. Doors are heavy-duty and tightly sealed; windows are usually double-glass with the interior pane slanted downward to minimize reflected sounds; and walls, ceiling, and flooring use special sound treatment materials. For example, studio walls may be covered with acoustically treated and designed panels that both absorb and trap reflected sounds (see Figure 1.4). Some stations use carpeting on the studio walls and some production studios have actually used egg cartons on the walls as sound treatment. (If you compare the design of an egg carton bottom with the design of the acoustic tile shown in Figure 1.4, you will see why some stations have gone the inexpensive egg carton route.) The purpose of soundproofing material is to give the studio a dead sound. Soundproofing absorbs and controls excess reverb and echo and produces a softer sound.

1.8 STUDIO SIZE AND SHAPE

The size and shape of a production studio can also determine how reflective the studio is. Any room that is highly reflective produces what is deemed a live sound. The radio production studio does not want to be overly reflective because the sound can be too bright and even harsh. Unfortunately, normal room construction often goes counter to good broadcast studio design. For example, studios with parallel walls (the normal box-shaped room)

FIGURE 1.4 Sonex acoustic tile. (Courtesy of Alpha Audio)

produce more reflected sound than irregularly shaped studios. The irregular angles produced by adjacent walls help break up reflected sound and control excessive reverb and echo.

The actual size of the production facility is partially determined by the equipment that must be housed in it. In constructing the radio production room, however, consideration should be given to the fact that when rooms are built with height, width, and length dimensions that are equal or exact multiples of each other, certain sound frequencies tend to be boosted and certain sound frequencies tend to be cancelled. Since this "peaks and valleys" sound is not desirable in the radio production room, this cubic construction should be avoided.

1.9 STUDIO AESTHETICS

There are some studio design considerations that can be categorized as the aesthetics of the production room. In general, the radio studio should be pleasant to work in; after all, the operator is confined to a rather small room for long stretches of time. For example, fluorescent lighting should be avoided. Not only does it tend to introduce hum into the audio chain, but it is a harsher, more glaring light than incandescent light. If possible, the studio lights should be on dimmers so that an appropriate level of light can be set for each individual operator.

Static electricity can be a problem in radio production studios because of the heavy use of carpeting. Most radio people do not enjoy getting shocked every time they touch the metal faceplate of a tape recorder. Also, some modern audio equipment has electronic circuits that can be disrupted by static discharges. If design factors can not keep the studio static-free, commercial sprays can be put on the carpeting or a static touch pad can be provided in the studio to keep static buildup at a minimum.

Stools or chairs used in the radio studio should be comfortable and functional. They must move easily because, even though most of the equipment is situated close to the operator, he or she must move around to cue records or thread tapes or select production music. The production stool must also be well constructed so that it does not constantly squeak if the operator moves slightly while the microphone is open. This may not be a factor for some production studios as they are designed for a stand-up operation. There is no stool, and the counters are at a height appropriate for the operator to be standing while announcing. This allows the operator to be more animated in his or her vocal delivery and actually provides a better posture for speaking than a sitting position.

Many radio production rooms are decorated with music posters or radio station bumper stickers and paraphernalia. Not only does this keep the studio from being a cold, stark room, but it also gives the studio radio atmosphere.

1.10 RADIO HAND SIGNALS

Radio **hand signals** don't play a major role in modern radio production; there are, however, situations when vocal communication is not possible and hand signals are necessary. For example, if an announcer and engineer are working an on-air show from separate rooms, they must be able to communicate with each other. There are also times when two announcers must communicate, but an open or live microphone in the studio prevents them from doing so verbally. People in a performance studio must be given hand signals because the open microphones prevent verbal communication. Because of situations like these, hand signals have evolved over the years to communicate some basic production information. (Many of these radio hand signals are used on a regular basis in the television studio.)

There is no universal set of hand signals, and only the more common signals are being presented here. You may find that your facility uses some that are different, uses some that are not given here, or doesn't use any at all. In any case, an understanding of these should prove helpful in some production studio situations. Refer to the drawings in Figure 1.5 to see how some of these hand signals are given.

The basic hand signals concern getting a program

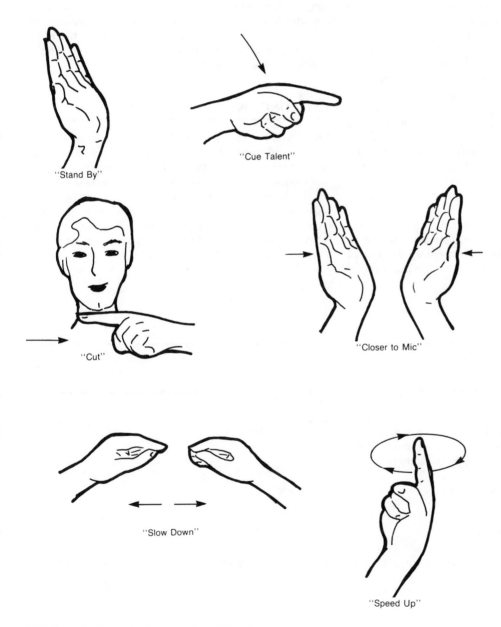

"Stand By" "Cue Talent" "Cut" "Closer to Mic" "Slow Down" "Speed Up"

FIGURE 1.5 Some basic audio hand signals.

started and stopped. The **stand-by** signal is given just prior to going on-air. It is given by holding one hand above the head with the palm forward. The stand-by signal is immediately followed by the **cue talent** signal. Meaning "you're on," this signal is given by pointing your index finger (using the same hand that gave the stand-by signal) at the person who is supposed to go on-air. At the end of a program, the **wrap it up** hand signal is given by holding both open-palmed hands in front of your chest and "rolling" them one over the other. The **cut** signal (index finger drawn across the throat) terminates whatever is happening at that moment and usually "kills" all live mics.

Several hand signals are used to give directions to the announcer regarding the microphone. An **open mic** signal is given by pointing the index finger at the microphone; it means that mic is "live" on-air. To get the announcer to move **closer to mic,** hold your hands in front of your chest with both palms facing toward each other and push them together or toward each other. To get the announcer to move **away from mic,** hold your hands in front of your chest with both palms away from each other and spread them apart or away from each other. To get an announcer to **give mic level,** hold one hand in front of you with palm down and thumb under the second and third fingers. Open and close the thumb and fingers in a "chattering" motion to indicate that the announcer should talk into the mic so that levels can be checked.

Hand signals are often used in the middle of a production to let the talent know how things are going or to convey some necessary information. To **speed up** the pace of a program, a signal is given by pointing the index finger

upward and rotating the hand in a circular motion in front of your chest. On the other hand, to **slow down** the pace (or perhaps stretch the reading of a script), both hands are held in front of the chest and moved apart as if stretching a large piece of taffy. If the program is **on the nose** (on time), an appropriate hand signal would point the index finger of one hand to your nose. Timing cues are given with the fingers. For example, to indicate that two minutes are left in the program you would hold up the index and second finger of one hand in front of you. The thirty-seconds-left signal is made by both index fingers forming a cross in front of you. To indicate that the talent should take a **station break,** you would hold both hands in front of your chest with fingers pointed away from you as if holding a brick and then make a motion as if breaking the brick in two. When everything is going fine, the radio hand signal is the traditional thumbs-up given with a clenched fist and extended thumb.

1.11 CONCLUSIONS

Unless you are building a radio facility from the ground up, it's probable that you will have little control over the construction of the studio; sound treatment is an important consideration, however, and some aspects of improving the sound environment can be put into practice in almost any situation. Completion of this chapter should have you in the radio production studio and ready to learn the procedures and techniques for operating all the equipment you see in front of you.

Self-Study

■ QUESTIONS

1. To work combo in radio means that the announcer _____.
   (a) has an engineer to operate the studio equipment for him or her
   (b) operates the studio equipment and also announces
   (c) works at two different radio stations

2. Which type of studio is least likely to contain an audio console?
   (a) on-air studio
   (b) production studio
   (c) performance studio

3. Sound produced in the radio studio that causes objects or surfaces within the studio to vibrate sympathetically is said to be _____.
   (a) absorbed
   (b) reflected
   (c) reinforced

4. In the radio production studio, sound that has bounced off one surface before reaching the microphone is _____.
   (a) echo
   (b) reverberation
   (c) direct sound

5. Reverb ring in the production studio refers to _____.
   (a) the circular route reflected sound takes before it reaches the mic
   (b) the time it takes reflected sound to go from full volume to silence
   (c) just another common name for echo

6. The use of carpeting on the walls of some radio production facilities is an example of _____.
   (a) an inexpensive way of decorating the studio
   (b) soundproofing the studio
   (c) producing a live sound in the studio

7. Studios with parallel walls produce less reflected sound than irregularly shaped studios.
   (a) true
   (b) false

8. Most production studios use a U-shaped layout because _____.
   (a) this places equipment within easy reach of the operator
   (b) such a configuration must use incandescent lights rather than fluorescent lights
   (c) this necessitates custom-built cabinets

9. The radio hand signal indicated by holding your hands in front of your chest with both palms facing away from each other and spreading them apart means _____.
   (a) move away from the mic
   (b) stretch out what you are reading
   (c) wrap up what you are saying

10. Which hand signal almost always follows immediately after the stand-by hand signal?
    (a) cut
    (b) station break
    (c) cue talent

11. If you hold up the index, second, and third fingers of one hand in front of you, the announcer knows _____.
    (a) there are thirty seconds left in the program
    (b) there are three minutes left in the program
    (c) to move three steps closer to the microphone

12. As a final test of this chapter, match the items in the first list (1, 2, 3 . . .) with the choices in the second list on page 8 (w, l, m . . .) and then select the correct set of answers from the sequences shown in a, b, or c below.
    1. _____ echo
    2. _____ direct sound
    3. _____ on-air studio
    4. _____ reverberation
    5. _____ absorbed sound
    6. _____ egg cartons
    7. _____ reinforced sound
    8. _____ cubic construction

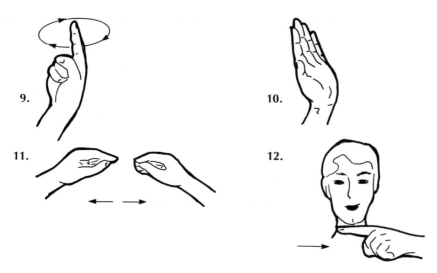

w. sound that goes into the walls of a studio
l. used for live broadcasting
m. sound that goes from the announcer to the mic
o. sound bounced off one surface
t. sound bounced off two or more surfaces
v. sound that causes something in the studio to vibrate at its frequency
s. used for soundproofing
h. rooms with height, width, and length dimensions that are the same
b. stand by
n. slow down
u. speed up
c. cut

a) 1.t 2.w 3.l 4.o 5.v 6.s 7.m 8.h 9.u 10.b 11.n 12.c
b) 1.o 2.m 3.l 4.t 5.w 6.s 7.v 8.h 9.u 10.b 11.n 12.c
c) 1.o 2.m 3.l 4.t 5.w 6.s 7.v 8.h 9.c 10.n 11.b 12.u

■ ANSWERS

If you answered A:
1a. No, this is not working combo. Reread 1.1 and try again.
2a. No, this needs one for sending the mixed signal out. Reread 1.1 and 1.2 and try again.
3a. No. If anything, absorbed sound would be diminished. Reread 1.5 and try again.
4a. Yes. Echo is sound that has reflected off a single surface.
5a. No. This is close to (but not exactly) describing reverb route.
6a. No. Painted walls would be less expensive. Reread 1.7 and try again.
7a. No. Just the opposite is true. Reread 1.8 and choose the other answer.
8a. Right. The operator can reach around the "horseshoe."
9a. Yes. This is exactly what it means.
10a. Wrong. Although a cut signal will come at the end of a program, it won't be right after a stand-by signal. Reread 1.10 and try again.
11a. No. Crossed index fingers indicate thirty seconds. Reread 1.10 and try again.
12a. No. You are confused about different kinds of sound. Reread 1.5 and 1.6 and try again.

If you answered B:
1b. Correct. The announcer is also equipment operator when working combo.
2b. No, this needs one for mixing. Reread 1.1 and 1.2 and try again.
3b. Wrong. Reread 1.5 and 1.6 and then try again.

4b. No. Reverb is sound that has reflected off two or more surfaces. Reread 1.6 and try again.

5b. Yes. This is what we call reverb ring.

6b. Correct. Carpeting walls helps soundproof, as would use of acoustic tiles designed for the production studio.

7b. Yes. This is the correct response.

8b. No. Lights have no relevance. Reread 1.3 and 1.9 and try again.

9b. No. A hand signal that resembles pulling taffy signifies this. Reread 1.10 and try again.

10b. Wrong. This signal would usually occur in the middle of a production. Reread 1.10 and try again.

11b. Yes. This is the correct hand signal.

12b. Right. You have now finished this chapter.

If you answered C:

1c. No, this is not working combo. Reread 1.1 and try again.

2c. Correct. It usually only has mics.

3c. Right. This is the correct response.

4c. No. Direct sound does not bounce off any surface before reaching the mic. Reread 1.6 and try again.

5c. No. Echo and reverb are both reflected sound, but distinctly different. Reread 1.6 and try again.

6c. No. Just the opposite would happen. Soundproofing with carpeting would help produce a dead sound in the studio. Reread 1.7 and try again.

8c. No. In a cost-minded facility, this could be a negative. Reread 1.3 and 1.4 and try again.

9c. No. This hand signal involves rolling your hands in front of you. Reread 1.10 and try again.

10c. Correct. Stand-by and cue talent hand signals are always given one after the other.

11c. No. There is another hand signal to move the announcer closer to the mic, and exact steps are never indicated. Reread 1.10 and try again.

12c. No. You are confused about hand signals. Reread 1.10 and try again.

Projects

■ PROJECT 1

Tour a radio station and write a report describing its production facilities.

Purpose

To enable you to see a commercial radio production facility firsthand.

Advice, Cautions, and Background

1. Don't push a station that seems reluctant to have you come. Some stations (especially smaller ones) are happy to have you. Others are pestered to death with would-be visitors or aren't equipped to handle visitors.
2. Make sure that before you go you have some ideas about what you want to find out so that you can make the most of your tour.
3. Keep your appointment. Once you make it, don't change it, for this will breed ill will for you and your school.

How To Do the Project

1. Read the Information section and complete the Self-Study Questions on the production studio.
2. Select a station you would like to tour. (If the instructor has arranged a station tour for the whole class, skip to step 5.)
3. Call the station, tell them you would like to see that station so you can write a report for a radio production class, and ask if you may come.
4. If so, set a date; if not, call a different station.
5. Think of some things you want to find out for your report. For example:
   a. How many production studios do they have?
   b. What types of equipment (CD player, reel-to-reel recorder, etc.) do they have?

c. What manufacturers (brand names) have they bought equipment from?
d. How is the production studio soundproofed?
e. Is the on-air studio different from the production studio(s)?
f. Do the announcers ever use hand signals during a production?
g. Are their studios designed for stand-up operation?
h. What is the physical layout of the studios and station?
6. Go to the station. Tour to the extent they will let you and ask as many questions as you can.
7. Immediately after leaving the station, jot down notes so you will remember main points.
8. Write your report in an organized fashion, including a complete description of the production studio and the other points you consider most pertinent. It should be two or three pages, preferably typed. Write your name and ''Radio Facility Tour'' on a title page.
9. Give the report to your instructor for credit for this project.

■ PROJECT 2

Get a restricted radiotelephone operator permit.

Purpose

To enable you to obtain this license, which is required to perform some technical duties at a radio station.

Advice, Cautions, and Background

1. A radio station that is on the air must be under the direct control of a licensed operator. Anyone may announce or operate broadcast equipment in the production studio, but the Restricted Radiotelephone Operator Permit is the ticket to actual radio broadcasting.
2. There is no longer an examination required to obtain this license.
3. To be eligible for this license you must be at least fourteen years of age and legally employable in the U.S.

How To Do the Project

1. Obtain an FCC Form 753 from your instructor or by writing directly to the FCC (Federal Communications Commission), at 1919 M Street N.W., Washington, DC 20554 (202-632-7260).
2. Certify on the application form that:
   a. you have a need for the permit
   b. you can keep a log
   c. you are familiar with the rules and regulations of radio broadcasting
   d. you will keep up-to-date with the rules and regulations
   e. you will preserve the secrecy of radio communications not intended for public broadcast
3. Your instructor may hold a brief training session with you before you complete the application so that you can honestly certify the above.
4. Your instructor may want to review your completed application before you send it to the FCC, as they will return applications that are incorrectly filled out.
5. Send your application directly to the FCC.
6. Give your temporary license (a portion of the application form) to your instructor to get credit for this project. When you receive your license back from the FCC it will have their official stamp on it. If you are broadcasting at a station, you will need to post the license or keep it in a book at that station. If you are not broadcasting at a station now, keep your license in a safe place until you need it. It is a lifetime license.

■ PROJECT 3

Demonstrate various hand signals.

Purpose

To make sure you are familiar with the hand signals that are sometimes used in radio.

Advice, Cautions, and Background

1. For this assignment, you will need a video camera, tripod, microphone, and videotape recorder. A consumer camcorder will work fine. If you don't have a tripod, you can have a friend hold the camera. If you do have a tripod, you can set the camera up on a shot of yourself and do the whole project single-handed. A mic is necessary to pick up your voice, but it can be the mic that is built into the camera. If you have access to a TV studio, you can use that.
2. Ask your instructor what formats of videotape—one-half-inch VHS or Beta, three-fourths-inch U-matic, etc.— can be used and select one.
3. If you are sure your facility uses hand signals that are different from those described in the chapter, use the ones common to your facility for this project.
4. You will not be demonstrating all the hand signals discussed in this chapter, just the ones listed below.
5. You may be asked to complete this project live in front of your instructor instead of videotaping it.

How To Do the Project

1. Read the Information section of this chapter, particularly concentrating on 1.10.
2. Complete the Self-Study Questions on the production studio.
3. Set up the video equipment (camera on tripod, videotape recorder, mic, videotape) and aim the camera so that it has a shot of you from the knees up.
4. Say each of the following hand signals loudly enough that it will record on the videotape. After you have named each signal, demonstrate it.
   a. stand by
   b. cue talent
   c. move closer to the mic
   d. move further away from the mic
   e. two minutes left
   f. speed up
   g. slow down
   h. thirty seconds left
   i. wrap it up
   j. cut
5. Label the videotape with your name and a description of the project.
6. If you have used a TV production studio, make sure you put everything back where it was.
7. Turn in your videotape to the instructor to receive credit for this project.

Microphones

Information

2.1 INTRODUCTION

In the radio production room, the **microphone** takes on an important role. It is the one piece of equipment that changes the announcer's voice into an electrical signal that can then be mixed with other sound sources and sent to a recorder or broadcast over the air. Because the purpose of the microphone is to change sound energy into electrical energy, it is called a **transducer** (a device that converts one form of energy into another).

2.2 MICROPHONE CATEGORIES

There is no one correct mic to use in radio production work, but certain types of microphones will work better than others in certain situations. Microphone types are usually determined by three factors: the sound-generating element of the mic, the microphone pickup pattern, and the impedance of the mic.

Categorized by their sound-generating element, there are two types of microphones commonly used in radio—the dynamic mic, and the condenser mic.

2.3 THE DYNAMIC MICROPHONE

The **dynamic mic** is sometimes known as the **pressure mic** or the **moving-coil microphone.** This microphone's sound-generating element is constructed of a diaphragm, a permanent magnet, and some coils of wire wrapped around the magnet. The diaphragm is positioned within the field of the magnet and responds to the pressure of the sound. Movements of the diaphragm caused by sound waves result in a disturbance of the magnetic field, and this induces a small electric current into the coils of wire (see Figure 2.1). In a later chapter, you'll see that the basic loudspeaker consists of similar elements and works just like a dynamic microphone in reverse by changing electrical energy into sound energy.

The dynamic mic is very commonly used in radio and has many advantages that make it such a popular microphone. It is a small, fairly inexpensive mic, and yet it has excellent **frequency response** so that both highs and lows reproduce accurately. The reason it has seen such acceptance by broadcasters is its sturdy design. The dynamic mic can withstand a moderate amount of abuse (which often occurs in the broadcast setting). It is also fairly insensitive to wind and this, along with its ruggedness, makes it an excellent remote mic. The dynamic mic can be used in most broadcast situations—as a stand mic, a hand-held mic, or a lavalier (a small mic hung around the neck or clipped to clothing below the neck). The main disadvantage of the dynamic mic is that it does not satisfactorily reproduce the voices of certain individuals. With some announcers, the mic exaggerates plosives (popping on p's) and sibilance (hissing on s's).

2.4 THE CONDENSER MICROPHONE

The other type of microphone is the **condenser mic.** Also known as a **capacitor mic,** it uses an electronic component, the capacitor, to respond to the sound. The sound-generating element consists of a charged conductive diaphragm and metallic backplate. The diaphragm responds to sound waves changing the distance between the diaphragm and the backplate; this alteration changes the capacitance and generates a small electrical signal (see Figure 2.2).

The condenser mic requires a power supply to charge the backplate and diaphragm. Because of this, early condenser mics were both inconvenient and expensive. Today's condenser mics utilize small internal power supplies or phantom power supplies in the mic cable line. The condenser microphone is an excellent radio mic because it is fairly rugged and produces excellent sound quality and wide frequency response. While the dynamic mic is the most-used radio production mic, the condenser mic is also frequently found in the modern radio production studio. In addition, the built-in microphone on mod-

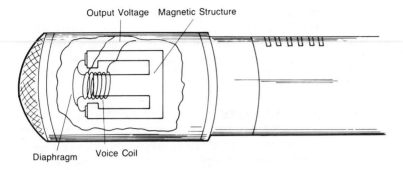

FIGURE 2.1 Internal structure of a dynamic microphone.

ern portable cassette recorders is usually a condenser mic that provides fairly good quality on both consumer and professional models.

2.5 OTHER MICROPHONES

There are other types of microphones. One is the **carbon mic,** which was once used in broadcasting, but it does not offer good sound quality so its use is now limited to telephones and communications equipment. There are also **crystal** and **ceramic microphones** that were used widely for cheap home tape recorders but not in broadcasting. They are inexpensive but have limited frequency response.

For many years the **ribbon mic** was common in radio. Its sound-generating element consisted of a thin metallic ribbon stretched in the field of a magnet. Sound waves vibrating the ribbon generated an electrical signal. It had an excellent warm, smooth sound, but it was bulky and fragile and has been largely replaced by the condenser mic, which has a similar high-quality sound.

All microphones are fragile to some extent and should be handled with care like any other piece of audio production equipment. Beginning announcers often misuse a

mic by blowing into it to see if it is live cr to set a level. This is the worst way to test a mic and can result in serious damage to the microphone. In fact, the higher the quality of the microphone the more likely that it will be damaged in this manner.

2.6 MICROPHONE PICKUP PATTERNS

Another way of classifying microphones is by their pickup patterns. Microphones can be constructed so they have different directional characteristics. In other words, they pick up sound from varying directions. The four basic sound patterns are omnidirectional, bidirectional, unidirectional, and cardioid.

2.7 THE OMNIDIRECTIONAL PICKUP PATTERN

The **omnidirectional** mic is also known as a **nondirectional** mic. These two terms may seem to contradict each other—"omni" (all) and "non" (no)—both terms, however, are correct. The mic picks up sound in all directions, but it also has no particular pickup pattern. Omnidirectional mics pick up sound equally well in just about any

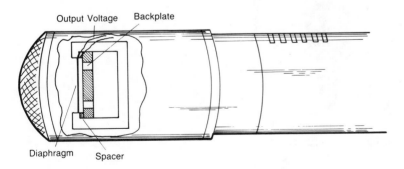

FIGURE 2.2 Internal structure of a condenser microphone.

direction. Think of an orange with a microphone right in the middle. No matter where the sound (the orange) comes from, the mic responds to it equally well. Figure 2.3 illustrates the pickup pattern for typical omnidirectional mics and cardioid microphones (which will be discussed later).

Omnidirectional mics are used whenever it is desirable to pick up sound evenly from all sides of the mic, including above and below it. The omnidirectional mic is commonly used in broadcast situations outside the studio when the ambience of the location needs to be picked up along with the announcer's voice.

2.8 THE BIDIRECTIONAL PICKUP PATTERN

The **bidirectional** mic picks up sound mainly from two directions—the front and the rear of the mic. Its pickup pattern can be visualized as a figure 8 with the microphone located at the intersection of the two circles. It was often used for radio dramas so actors could face each other, but it is not a common pickup pattern for today's broadcast mics. Although you may not utilize it in radio production situations, it is a good mic for the basic two-person interview.

2.9 THE UNIDIRECTIONAL PICKUP PATTERN

The **unidirectional** mic picks up sound mainly from one direction, the front of the microphone. Since the mic does not pick up sound well from the rear or sides, this mic can be particularly useful when it is desirable to cut down background noise. It is often employed in sports remote

broadcasts when the sportscaster talks into the live side of the mic and the crowd and action sounds arriving from the rear and sides are limited. In modern production work, most unidirectional microphones are merely cardioid mics with an extremely narrow pickup pattern.

2.10 THE CARDIOID PICKUP PATTERN

A variation of the unidirectional mic is the **cardioid** microphone. Commonly used in radio and television studio applications, the cardioid mic has a heart-shaped pickup pattern (refer to Figure 2.3 again). Another way to visualize this is to think of an upside-down apple of which the stem represents the mic and the rest of the apple approximates the cardioid pickup pattern. This mic picks up sound from the front and from the sides but doesn't pick up sound well from the rear.

2.11 POLAR RESPONSE PATTERNS

The diagrams shown in Figure 2.3 indicate pickup patterns. One of the concepts that you need to understand is the difference between **pickup pattern** and **polar pattern.** A microphone's pickup pattern we have already described as the area around the microphone in which the mic best "hears" or picks up the sound. This is a three-dimensional shape, as demonstrated by the apple and orange analogies. The diagrams shown, however, are two dimensional. When a microphone's pickup pattern is shown by a two-dimensional drawing, we call that drawing the mic's polar pattern or polar response pattern. Compare the cardioid pickup pattern shown in Figure 2.4

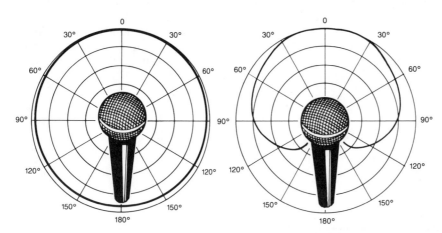

Polar pattern diagrams for typical omnidirectional and unidirectional (cardioid) microphones

FIGURE 2.3 Omnidirectional and cardioid microphone pickup patterns. (Courtesy of Shure Brothers, Inc.)

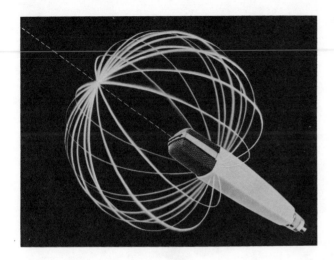

FIGURE 2.4 Three-dimensional view of cardioid pickup pattern. (Courtesy of Sennheiser Electronics Corporation)

with the cardioid polar response pattern shown in Figure 2.3.

2.12 IMPEDANCE OF MICROPHONES

The third factor we use to categorize microphones is **impedance,** a characteristic that is similar to resistance. Mics can be either high- or low-impedance. A high-impedance mic has a higher output level than a low-impedance mic. In spite of this, most broadcast mics are low-impedance since this type of mic provides the best frequency response and most broadcast equipment is designed to accept this type of mic. High-impedance mics are also quite limited in the length of mic cable that can be used with them before hum and severe signal loss occur. High-impedance mics should not be plugged into tape recorders or other equipment designed for low impedance; similarly, low-impedance mics should not be used with high-impedance equipment. If impedance is mismatched, sound will be distorted. There are impedance converters that can convert one type of impedance to the other.

2.13 MICROPHONE SENSITIVITY

Sensitivity refers to a microphone's efficiency. For the same sound source (say one particular announcer's voice), a highly sensitive mic produces a better output signal than a less sensitive mic. To compensate for this, the gain control (volume) must be increased for the less sensitive mic; this increased gain produces more noise. Although different sensitivity-rating systems can be employed, generally condenser mics have high-sensitivity

specifications, and dynamic mics have medium sensitivity.

2.14 THE PROXIMITY EFFECT AND BASS ROLLOFF

Announcer use of microphones sometimes produces a sound phenomenon known as the **proximity effect.** The proximity effect is an exaggerated bass boost that occurs as the sound source gets closer to the microphone. This should be noticeable as the announcer gets about two or three inches from the mic and is especially noticeable with mics that have a cardioid pickup pattern. Although it could help deepen a normally high voice, the proximity effect is usually defeated by a **bass roll-off switch** on the mic. This switch, when turned on, will electronically ''roll off'' or turn down the bass frequencies that would be boosted by the proximity effect, thus leaving the desired flat response.

2.15 MICROPHONE FEEDBACK

Feedback is a ''howling'' signal produced when a sound picked up by a microphone is amplified, produced through a speaker, picked up again, amplified again, and so on endlessly. Reducing the volume or turning off the mic ends the feedback. Feedback is a common mic problem in public address situations, but not usually in radio production since the speaker is muted when the mic is switched on. Occasionally, announcers can produce feedback in the production studio by operating their headphones at an excessive volume or accidentally picking up a stray speaker signal from an outside source, such as another studio speaker.

2.16 MULTIPLE MICROPHONE INTERFERENCE

Sometimes when two or more microphones receiving the same sound signal are fed into the same mixer, the combined signal becomes **out of phase.** What happens is that the sound reaches each mic at a slightly different time so that while the sound wave is up on one mic, it is down on the other. Under these circumstances, the sound is diminished or cancelled out altogether.

This situation is known as multiple microphone interference and can be avoided by remembering a three-to-one ratio. That is, if the mics are about one foot from the announcer (sound source), they should be at least three feet apart from each other. In this way the signals will not overlap (see Figure 2.5A). Another solution to this problem is to place microphones that must be close together head-to-head. Then they will get the signal at the same time (see Figure 2.5B). Although multiple microphone in-

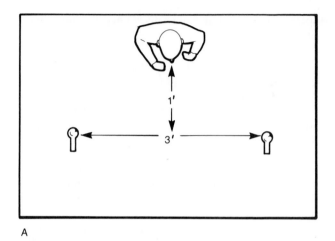

A

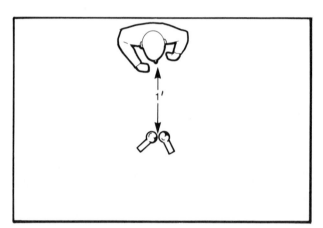

B

FIGURE 2.5 Methods of avoiding multiple microphone interference.

FIGURE 2.6 Microphone with pop filter. (Courtesy of Shure Brothers, Inc.)

terference isn't usually a problem in the studio, it can occur in some radio remote situations.

In addition to the basic microphones, the radio production person will find one or more of the following accessories necessary for proper audio production work: pop filters, shock mounts, and stands or booms.

2.17 POP FILTERS

Pop filters (sometimes referred to as **blast filters** or **windscreens**) are ball-shaped accessories that can be placed over the head or front of the microphone to help reduce the chance of a plosive sound. Often they are built into the grill of the microphone as shown in Figure 2.6. Announcing words that emphasize the *p, b,* or *t* sound naturally produces a sharp puff of air and can produce a pop

or thump when hitting the mic (especially when a dynamic mic is closely worked). The pop filter, however, eliminates or reduces this problem.

2.18 SHOCK MOUNTS

A **shock mount** is often employed to isolate the microphone from any mechanical vibrations or shocks that may be transmitted to the mic through its stand. The mic is physically suspended (usually by an arrangement of elastic bands) and isolated from the stand or boom to which it is attached (see Figure 2.7). If the mic stand is accidently bumped, the sound of this thud will not be passed on and amplified by the mic.

2.19 MIC STANDS AND BOOMS

Mic stands consist of two chrome-plated pipes, one of which fits inside the other. A rotating clutch at one end of the larger diameter pipe allows the smaller pipe to be adjusted at any height desired. At the other end of the larger pipe is a heavy metal base (usually circular) that supports the pipes in a vertical position. The mic is attached to the top of the smaller pipe by a standard thread and mic stand adapter (see Figure 2.8A). **Floor stands** adjust for the announcer in a standing position and **desk stands** are used for the seated announcer. A **boom stand** is a long horizontal pipe that attaches to a floor stand (see Figure 2.8B). One end of the boom is fitted with the standard thread (for the mic), and the other end is weighted to balance the mic. The horizontal pipe allows the boom

FIGURE 2.7 Microphone shock mount. (Courtesy of Sennheiser Electronics Corporation)

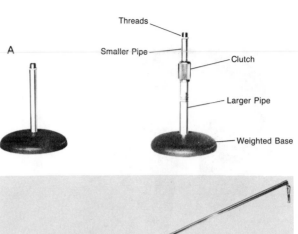

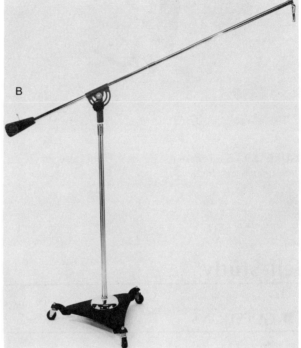

FIGURE 2.8 Microphone stands: (A) desk stands; (B) boom stand. (Courtesy of Atlas/Soundolier)

stand to be away from the announcer and positions the mic in a workable relationship to the announcer.

2.20 MICROPHONE USAGE

An understanding of the microphone types, pickup patterns and other mic characteristics is only useful if you can apply this knowledge to everyday radio production use. It seems reasonable to assume the microphone in a broadcast studio will be a dynamic mic because that is the most commonly used mic in broadcasting, but it could also be a condenser mic. Perhaps the more important consideration is its pickup pattern. In the studio, we mainly want to pick up the announcer's voice and some ambience of the studio. A cardioid pickup pattern, with its pickup of front and side sounds, works best to accomplish this and not pick up unwanted sounds from the rear, such as the announcer moving papers or turning on and off various switches.

When using a microphone in the standard studio setup, keep in mind two basic rules concerning distance from the microphone and position of the microphone. The announcer's mouth should be about six inches away from the mic. That's about the length of a dollar bill—a good way to remember mouth-to-mic distance. This is a good starting point for using a mic. You may find that you need to be closer or farther away because of the strength of your voice or the vocal effect that you are trying to achieve. Position the microphone so that you are not talking directly into it. Put the mic below your mouth with

the front of the microphone tilted up toward your mouth, allowing you to talk across the top of the mic.

In radio production work, it is not uncommon to leave the studio to record an interview. Certainly the radio news person does this frequently. In a remote location interview, the dynamic microphone would probably be used because of its ruggedness and good quality. In most cases, at a remote site we do want to pick up the ambience of the location and various voices (particularly the announcer and the interviewee). The omnidirectional pickup pattern with its ability to pick up sound equally well in all directions provides a solution for this situation. If there is likely to be a great deal of background noise, a cardioid mic might be better, but it will have to be carefully placed so it picks up both voices well.

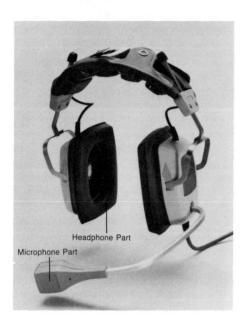

Headphone Part

Microphone Part

FIGURE 2.9 Sportscaster's headset. (Courtesy of Telex Communications, Inc.)

Sportscasters are commonly out of the studio to broadcast games and other sports events. The sportscaster headset provides both earphones and a microphone in a single unit, leaving the announcer's hands free (see Figure 2.9). The mic is usually a dynamic mic with either a unidirectional or omnidirectional pickup pattern. If a unidirectional mic is employed, the sportscaster may want to have an additional mic for picking up crowd and sports action noise.

2.21 CONCLUSIONS

We said earlier that there is no one correct microphone to use in radio production. When using mics in any production, don't be afraid to experiment in each particular situation. The final judge in any production should be how it sounds. It's good to be flexible in radio production because often you will not have a wide variety of microphones available. If you use what you've learned in this chapter, you should be able to obtain clear appropriate sound under various circumstances.

Self-Study

■ QUESTIONS

1. Another name for the dynamic microphone is _____.
   a) carbon
   b) pressure
   c) capacitor

2. The dynamic mic's sound-generating element is constructed of a diaphragm, a permanent magnet, and some coils of wire wrapped around the magnet. Into which of these is a small electrical current induced during use?
   a) diaphragm
   b) magnet
   c) coil

3. The condenser mic differs from the dynamic mic in that _____.
   a) the dynamic mic has a diaphragm and the condenser mic doesn't
   b) the condenser mic needs a power supply and the dynamic mic doesn't
   c) the dynamic mic has better sound quality than the condenser mic

4. Which kind of mic is most likely to be found in a consumer-quality audio cassette recorder?
   a) condenser
   b) ribbon
   c) carbon

5. The mic that picks up sound on all but one side is _____.
  a) unidirectional
  b) cardioid
  c) nondirectional

6. Which mic would be most appropriate for picking up crowd noises at a baseball game?
  a) unidirectional
  b) bidirectional
  c) omnidirectional

7. Which mic would be most appropriate for picking up a sportscaster announcing at a baseball game?
  a) unidirectional
  b) nondirectional
  c) bidirectional

8. Most broadcast quality-microphones are _____.
  a) low-impedance
  b) high-impedance
  c) low-sensitivity

9. Which of the following is most likely to exaggerate the bass sounds of a person's voice?
  a) feedback
  b) proximity effect
  c) multiple microphone interference

10. The purpose of a shock mount is _____.
  a) to reduce plosive sounds
  b) to keep the announcer's head at least twelve inches away from the microphone
  c) to isolate the microphone from mechanical vibrations

11. Which type of mic stand can be furthest away from a person and still allow the person to be close to the microphone?
  a) desk stand
  b) floor stand
  c) boom stand

12. As a final test on microphones, match the items in the top list (1, 2, 3 . . .) with the choices in the bottom list (o, a, c . . .) and then select the correct set of answers from the sequences shown in a, b, or c on page 20.

  1. _____ cardioid
  2. _____ dynamic
  3. _____ high impedance
  4. _____ feedback
  5. _____ sensitivity
  6. _____ capacitor
  7. _____ omnidirectional
  8. _____ pop filter

  o. a mic that picks up from all directions
  a. a mic that picks up from all but one direction
  c. another name for a condenser mic
  d. a microphone with a diaphragm, magnet, and coil
  w. another name for a windscreen
  s. a howling sound
  h. a mic that can not have a very long cable without developing hum
  e. a microphone's efficiency

a) 1.a   2.d   3.h   4.s   5.e   6.c   7.o   8.w
b) 1.o   2.c   3.h   4.s   5.e   6.d   7.a   8.w
c) 1.a   2.d   3.s   4.h   5.w   6.c   7.o   8.e

■ ANSWERS

If you answered A:

1a. No, this is a mic from the very early days of radio. Reread 2.3 and 2.5 and try again.

2a. Wrong. The diaphragm feels the pressure. Reread 2.3 and try again.

3a. No. Both mics have a diaphragm. Reread 2.3 and 2.4 and try again.

4a. Yes, most consumer audio cassette recorders have a built-in condenser mic.

5a. No, unidirectional picks up on only one side, not all but one side. Reread 2.7–2.10 and try again.

6a. Wrong. It only picks up in one direction, so it would not pick up much of the crowd. Reread 2.7–2.10 and try again.

7a. Yes, it would pick up the sportscaster without much of the background noise.

8a. Right. Low-impedance is what most broadcast equipment is.

9a. No. Feedback is a howling noise caused by having open mics near speakers. Reread 2.14 and 2.15 and try again.

10a. No, a pop filter is used to reduce plosive sounds. Reread 2.17 and 2.18 and try again.

11a. No. A desk stand has to be right in front of the person. Reread 2.19 and try again.

12a. Correct. You have now finished the section on microphones.

If you answered B:

1b. Correct. The dynamic mic is also called the pressure mic.

2b. Wrong. The magnet sets up the field. Reread 2.3 and try again.

3b. Right. The condenser mic power supply is needed to charge the backplate and diaphragm.

4b. No. This is a professional-quality mic that is not used much anymore. Reread 2.5 and try again.

5b. Right. The cardioid picks up sound on all but one side—usually the one right behind the mic.

6b. Wrong. It would not pick up from all sides. Reread 2.7–2.10 and try again.

7b. No. The crowd noise would tend to drown out the announcer. Reread 2.7–2.10 and try again.

8b. No. Consumer-quality mics are usually high-impedance, but not broadcast quality. Reread 2.12 and try again.

9b. Right. When an announcer gets too close to the mic, the bass may be exaggerated.

10b. No. For one thing, the announcer's head should be about six inches away, not twelve inches away. Reread 2.18 and try again.

11b. No, a person must stand right beside a floor stand. Reread 2.19 and try again.

12b. No. You are confused regarding the sound-generating elements and the pickup patterns. Reread 2.1–2.11 and try again.

If you answered C:

1c. No. This is another name for the condenser mic. Reread 2.3 and 2.4 and try again.

2c. Correct. The current is in the coil.

3c. No. The condenser mic has slightly better quality than the dynamic mic. Reread 2.3 and 2.4 and try again.

4c. No. The carbon mic was used in the very early days of radio. Reread 2.5 and try again.

5c. No. A nondirectional (also known as an omnidirectional) mic picks up on all sides. Reread 2.7–2.10 and try again.

6c. Correct. It would pick up from all sides.

7c. No. A bidirectional mic picks up on two sides and the sportscaster would only be on one side. Reread 2.7–2.10 and try again.

8c. No. Condenser mics are high-sensitivity and dynamic mics are medium-sensitivity. Neither are low-sensitivity. Reread 2.12 and 2.13 and try again.

9c. No. This will create a distorted signal. Reread 2.14 and 2.16 and try again.

10c. Yes. This is a special type of stand that suspends the mic.

11c. Right. This is the best selection.

12c. Wrong. You are confused about many of the elements of microphones. Reread from 2.12 to the end of the chapter and try again.

Projects

■ PROJECT 1

Inventory the microphones in your facility.

Purpose

To make you more aware of the sound-generating elements, pickup patterns, and impedance of microphones.

Advice, Cautions, and Background

1. If possible, examine every mic in your facility. If, however, you have many of the same type or some that are semipermanently mounted, do not bother doing all of them.
2. In some instances the mics will have their characteristics written on them somewhere. In other instances they will not, so you may need to test the microphone or use logical deduction. For example, if a mic has an external power supply, you can be fairly sure it is a condenser mic. If the pickup pattern of the mic is not indicated, you will have to connect it to a piece of equipment and talk into it from all sides, recording as you do. Then you can listen to the recording and determine which are the live pickup sides.
3. Do *not* take the microphones apart to see the internal construction. This can permanently ruin a mic.
4. If you can not determine characteristics of the mics, try to find a specifications sheet. (Your engineer may have one.)

How To Do the Project

1. Read the Information section on microphones.
2. Complete the Self-Study Questions on microphones.
3. Collect all of the microphones your facility has. Don't forget mics that go with portable cassette recorders as well as mics used in the studio.
4. Make a chart that contains the following information for each mic:
   a. brand name and model number
   b. sound-generating construction
   c. pickup pattern
   d. impedance
5. Your chart might look something like this:
   1. Electro-Voice 623
      dynamic omnidirectional
      low-impedance
   2. Teac ME-120
      condenser cardioid
      low-impedance
6. When you have completed your chart, turn it in to your instructor to get credit for this project.

■ PROJECT 2

Position microphones various ways to create different effects.

Purpose

To enable you to experience proximity effect, feedback, multiple mic interference, and the sound quality that occurs when a microphone is placed at different distances and angles from an announcer.

Advice, Cautions, and Background

1. You have not read the chapters on audio console operation or tape recorders yet, so you may need some help from your instructor or the engineer in setting up the equipment.
2. For the proximity effect, try to find a mic that does not have a bass roll-off switch.
3. Don't allow feedback to occur for too long. It can be damaging to all the electronic equipment—and your ears. You may have to plug the mic into something other than the audio board if the board automatically shuts off the speakers when the mic is turned on.
4. For the multiple mic interference, make sure the mics are closer than three feet. Omnidirectional mics will demonstrate the effect the best.
5. Use a unidirectional mic for the distance and angle experiments because it will demonstrate the points better. The second-best mic to use is a cardioid.

How To Do the Project

1. Read the Information section on microphones.
2. Complete the Self-Study Questions on microphones.
3. Set up an audio board so that two microphones are going into it and the sound of those two mics can be recorded on a tape recorder.
4. Put the tape recorder in record and activate one of the microphones. Start talking about two feet away from the mic and keep talking as you move closer until you are about two inches from it. As you talk say how close you are to the mic and mention that you are experimenting with the proximity effect. Stop the tape recorder.
5. Position a microphone so that it is close to an activated speaker. Turn on the tape recorder and talk into the mic. Record a short amount of the feedback and turn off the tape recorder.
6. Position two mics in front of you that are less than three feet apart. Put the tape recorder in record and talk into the microphones saying that you are testing for multiple microphone interference. Turn off the tape recorder.
7. Position one mic in front of you. Put the tape recorder in record. Position yourself twelve inches from the mic and talk into it. Then position yourself six inches from the mic and talk directly into it. Then talk across the top of the mic. Move six inches to the side of the mic and talk into it with your head positioned to talk across the top of it. Get behind the mic, either by moving behind it or by turning it around, and talk from about six inches away. Describe each action as you do it.
8. Listen to the tape to hear the various effects and see that you have, indeed, recorded all the assignments. If some of them did not turn out as well as you would have liked, redo them.
9. Turn the tape in to your instructor for credit for the project. Make sure you put your name on the tape and the tape box and indicate that this is ''Microphone Project 2.''

CHAPTER THREE

Turntables

Information

3.1 INTRODUCTION

In an audio production facility, the **turntable** that spins records is one of the main sources of sound. Because records are often aired one right after the other, there are usually two turntables in each production room or on-air studio. In this way, one can be cued while the other is playing on the air.

3.2 BROADCAST VERSUS CONSUMER TURNTABLES

Unlike some home phonographs, a turntable is not a record player. A **record player** is a self-contained unit that not only spins the record and picks up the signal, but also amplifies the signal through a speaker. A turntable designed for professional use requires some other means of amplification. Usually the signal is sent into a preamplifier and then into the audio console for further amplification.

Professional-grade turntables are different from consumer-grade turntables in that the former have the following qualities:

a. heavy-duty (designed for long hours of continuous use)
b. extremely accurate (maintain precise speeds)
c. capable of quick speed buildup
d. housed in a sturdy base or cabinet
e. capable of being cued (record or platter can be turned backwards)

3.3 BASIC TURNTABLE PARTS

The basic parts of the broadcast-quality turntable include a platter (a heavy metal plate covered by a felt or rubber top), a tone arm, a cartridge/stylus, and a preamplifier (see Figure 3.1). Additionally, most production turntables have an on/off switch and speed selector switch that work in conjunction with the motor. Some broadcast turntables offer the option of an equalizer/filter switch or a pitch control.

3.4 TURNTABLE FUNCTIONS

In a radio production facility, the turntable has two functions—to spin a record at the precise speed at which it was recorded and to convert the variations in the grooves of the record to electrical energy (utilizing the tone arm).

3.5 TURNTABLE SPEEDS

The **on/off switch** and the **speed selector switch** work with the motor to rotate the platter at a precise speed. The on/off switch controls power to the motor. In most broadcast facilities, this motor is designed to run for long periods of time. This switch may be left in the on position as long as the control board is in use. Most broadcast turntables use only the 45 RPM and 33 1/3 RPM speeds, though some include a 78 RPM selection. **RPM** stands for revolutions per minute and is just that—the number of times the record goes around in a minute. In addition to these speed selections, the speed selector switch usually has a neutral position. Turntables should be left in neutral when not in use. The neutral position also allows the operator to move the turntable in either direction by hand for cueing.

3.6 TURNTABLE DRIVE SYSTEMS

The basic types of turntable drive systems used in professional turntables are idler-wheel drive, belt drive and direct drive. In a **direct drive turntable,** the platter sits on top of the motor (see Figure 3.2). In fact, the shaft of the motor is the spindle of the turntable. Precise speeds are controlled electronically rather than mechanically as they are in the idler-wheel and belt drive systems. More and more broadcast turntables are using a direct drive system. In a **belt drive turntable,** the motor is coupled to the platter (usually a subplatter) by a thin rubber belt. Turntable, platter and tone arm can be isolated from the motor to prevent unwanted vibrations and noise. Belt drive systems work on friction only, so start-up time is not as quick

FIGURE 3.1   Basic turntable parts. (Courtesy of Panasonic/Technics)

as direct drive. In an **idler-wheel turntable,** the motor shaft drives a rubber disc (pressure roller), which in turn drives the platter. The diameter of the motor shaft varies to change speeds depending on what part of the shaft contacts the pressure roller. If the motor shaft is left in contact with the pressure roller (meaning the turntable is left in gear), it can cause a dip in the rubber that causes improper platter rotation. Many older broadcast turntables found in the production studio employ the idler-wheel drive system and should be kept in neutral when not being used.

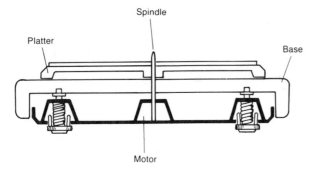

FIGURE 3.2   Direct drive turntable drive system.

3.7 TONE ARM/CARTRIDGE/STYLUS ASSEMBLY

The function of the **tone arm** is to house the cartridge and stylus and allow them to move freely across the record as it is played. This is a very sensitive piece of equipment and should be handled carefully. Some tone arms have small handles next to the cartridge that should be used to pick up the arm and place it on the record. This should be done carefully to avoid damage to the cartridge/stylus and to avoid changing the weight and angle of the tone arm. The weight of a tone arm is called **tracking force.** It is usually under two grams and it can be adjusted by counterbalancing weights at the rear end of the tone arm. This adjustment requires a tracking force gauge and is best left to the station engineer. Improper weight results in damage to the record or poor tracking ability. Never place additional weight (such as a dime or paper clip) on the tone arm to increase its tracking force.

The cartridge/stylus assembly is the working end of the tone arm that actually picks up the signal from the record (see Figure 3.3). The **cartridge** receives the minute vibrations from the **stylus** and converts them into variations in voltage. It acts similarly to the sound-generating element in a microphone (another transducer), and sends the signals to the control board. The stylus is a very small, highly compliant strip of metal. The end that touches the record groove is made of a hard material, usually diamond. The other end is connected to a coil of wire suspended in a magnetic field in the cartridge. As the record grooves vi-

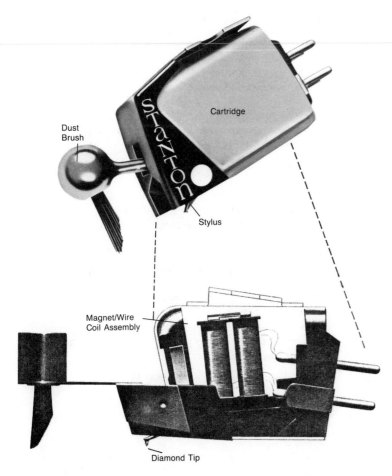

FIGURE 3.3 Cartridge/stylus assembly. (Courtesy of Audio-Technica
U.S., Inc.)

brate the stylus, a small voltage is generated in the cartridge. This electrical signal is then sent to the preamplifier.

Styli are either spherical or elliptical; spherical styli are
preferred for broadcast use (for cueing up records). The
stylus should not be touched with fingers. If it is necessary to remove dust from the stylus, do this by blowing
lightly on it, or use a special fine-hair stylus brush. Brush
lightly from back to front on the stylus only. The cartridge
normally found in broadcast quality tone arms is designed
to play 33 1/3 RPM and 45 RPM records. If it is necessary
to play 78 RPM records, a different stylus and cartridge
must be inserted in most tone arms. The modern stylus is
very tiny so that it may ride in the microgrooves of today's
records. The 78 RPM stylus is larger because these records
have wider grooves. Playing a 33 1/3 RPM record with a
78 RPM stylus will seriously damage the grooves of the
record by cutting away the smaller grooves. Playing a 78
RPM record with a 33 1/3 RPM stylus will damage the
stylus.

3.8 DUST PROBLEMS

Dust is probably the biggest problem for turntables. Dust
in record grooves causes undue record and stylus wear.
Ultimately dust develops permanent pops and scratches
on the record. The static electricity produced by playing a
record compounds the problem by attracting more dust.
Use a good quality record cleaner before playing records
to help minimize the dust problem.

3.9 TURNTABLE EQUALIZERS AND FILTERS

Some professional-quality turntables include an **equal-
izer/filter switch.** Originally, this switch was used to compensate for frequency differences between American and
European recordings. Filters and equalizer switches can
also compensate for poor recordings or records that have
been scratched. These scratches usually appear in the
high frequencies of the sound. Using the equalizer on a

setting for poor records will chop off the high frequencies of the record, eliminating some of the scratch. Not all scratches can be eliminated easily. For example, some appear not only in the higher frequencies, but also the upper midrange. Filtering or equalizing so much of the audio signal can greatly change how the record sounds, perhaps to the point of making it unusable.

3.10 "WOW"

"**Wow**" is a distortion in record reproduction that sounds like an off-speed record (slight pitch variation). It is commonly caused by

a. not backtracking far enough when cueing a record (the record wows as it builds up to speed)
b. record defect (warp or off-center hole)
c. turntable defect (worn motor bearings or idler-wheel dip)

Wow should be avoided in radio production and broadcast work.

3.11 THE TURNTABLE PREAMPLIFIER

The function of the preamplifier is to increase the level of the signal produced by the cartridge/stylus before sending it to the audio console for further amplification. Figure 3.4 shows a typical broadcast turntable preamplifier.

3.12 CUEING RECORDS

In most broadcast and production situations, you will want the sound to begin immediately when playing a record. Broadcasters **cue** the record to avoid any silence (**dead air**) between the start of the record and the first sound heard. To cue a record,

a. gently place stylus in outer groove of record
b. put gear selector switch in neutral
c. rotate turntable platter clockwise until first sound is heard
d. backtrack the turntable platter enough to avoid wowing the record (this will vary depending upon the turntable drive system, age of turntable, etc.)—usually 1/8 turn for 33 1/3 RPM records and 1/4 turn for 45 RPM records
e. put the speed selector switch in the proper speed
f. turn on/off switch to on just before you want actual sound to begin

Another way to cue a record is known as **slip cueing:**

a. cue as above in steps a through e
b. hold edge of record with finger with enough force to

FIGURE 3.4 Turntable preamplifier. (Courtesy of Radio Systems, Inc.)

keep it from spinning when on/off switch is turned to on (turntable platter will be spinning below record)

c. release record when you want actual sound to begin

You can only attempt to slip cue if the turntable has a felt-type mat. The typical rubber mat on most home turntables and some professional ones does not allow the platter to continue to spin as you hold the record edge.

Slip cueing allows tighter cueing than conventional cueing, but it takes some practice to become proficient at it. The slip cue technique is often used in production to lift a specific phrase or portion of music off a disc so that it starts cleanly (no wow) and at a precise time.

Both methods for cueing records, but especially slip cueing, cause some deterioration of the outer grooves of the record as the stylus moves back and forth. After a period of time, most broadcast records develop **cue burns**—the name broadcasters give to the damaged outer grooves of the record.

3.13 SOUND TRANSITIONS

Sound transition is the merging of one sound into another. The basic transition is the **fade** (which means to gradually increase or decrease volume), where we mix one sound with silence. For example, to **fade-in** a record means to slowly increase the volume from silence to the desired level. A **fade-out** accomplishes just the opposite as the record goes from normal full volume to silence. Most records are recorded so that they fade out at the end naturally, but in production work it is sometimes necessary to end a song early and the production person can do so with a manual fade-out.

The other common transitions are the cross-fade and the segue. As the name implies, a **cross-fade** occurs when one sound is faded down as another sound is faded up. There is a point as the two sounds cross when both sounds are heard. Because of this, care should be taken in choosing records to cross-fade. Some combinations of songs can sound extremely awkward. The speed of a cross-fade is determined by the board operator and depends on the type of effect desired; most cross-fades, however, are at a medium speed to give a natural, brief blending of the two sounds. A **segue** is quite different: it is the transition from one sound to the next with no overlap or gap. A segue can best be accomplished when the first record ends cold, or does not fade out. Unlike fades of any kind, the segue is accomplished with both sounds at full volume. Most disc jockey work is a mixture of cross-fades and segues and all the sound transitions are used frequently in radio production work.

3.14 DEAD ROLLING

In production work it is frequently important to end a piece of music at an exact time. For example, at the end of a program you might want the music and closing narration to end at the same time or a radio show's musical theme to end right at the top of the hour so that a newscast can begin. In any case, you will not often find music that fits exactly the time that you have to fill. One method of dealing with this is the **dead roll**. To dead roll a record means to begin playing the record with the volume turned down. If you had a record 4:30 minutes long, but needed to fill 3:00 before the top of the hour, you would dead roll the record at 55:30 and fade in the music at 57:00. In other words, the first 1:30 of the music would not be heard, but the music would end exactly as desired at the top of the hour. Obviously, you usually dead roll music that is instrumental so that it is not noticeable that you have cut out part of the song.

3.15 CONCLUSIONS

Becoming comfortable while working with the broadcast turntable should come fairly easily, as most radio production people have already had experience with their home stereo systems. Remember the differences between home stereo systems and broadcast-quality turntables and observe good production techniques to improve turntable operation.

Turntables have been a primary workhorse in most radio stations for years. But with the advent of compact discs and the quality and convenience they offer, the turntable's days are surely numbered.

Self-Study

■ QUESTIONS

1. Which of the following is *not* a function of a turntable?
   a) spinning a record at the proper speed
   b) converting variations in the grooves to electrical energy
   c) amplifying the signal

2. Which of the following picks up a signal from a record?
   a) equalizer
   b) cartridge/stylus
   c) speed selector switch

3. The part of the turntable that changes vibrations into variations in voltage is the _____.
   a) cartridge
   b) stylus
   c) diamond

4. If you play 78 RPM records with a 33 1/3 RPM stylus, you will damage the _____.
   a) stylus
   b) cartridge
   c) record

5. When you are between records, the motor power switch of the turntable should be _____.
   a) off
   b) on
   c) in neutral

6. On the speed selector switch, the neutral position is used for _____.
   a) 45 RPM records
   b) 78 RPM records
   c) cueing

7. The tone arm is used to _____.
   a) pick up sound
   b) contain the instruments that pick up sound
   c) act as a weight

8. A purpose of a turntable equalizer is to _____.
   a) get rid of scratchy noises
   b) compensate for room noises
   c) pick up vibrations

9. Which turntable drive system maintains precise speeds electronically, rather than mechanically?
   a) idler-wheel drive
   b) belt drive
   c) direct drive

10. As a final test on turntables, match the items in the top list (1, 2, 3 . . .) with the choices in the bottom list (m, g, t . . .) and then select the correct set of answers from the sequences shown in a, b, or c below.

   1. _____ vibrates in record groove
   2. _____ selects speed
   3. _____ converts vibrations into variations in voltage
   4. _____ makes the turntable rotate
   5. _____ gets rid of scratchy noises
   6. _____ allows for free movement across a record
   7. _____ often has a diamond point

   m. motor
   g. speed selector switch
   t. tone arm
   c. cartridge
   s. stylus
   e. turntable equalizer

   a) 1.s   2.g   3.c   4.m   5.e   6.t   7.s
   b) 1.c   2.g   3.s   4.m   5.e   6.c   7.c
   c) 1.s   2.m   3.c   4.m   5.s   6.c   7.s

■ ANSWERS

If you answered A:

1a. Wrong. This is one of the functions. Reread 3.4 and try again.
2a. No. Reread 3.9 and try again.
3a. Right. The cartridge converts vibrations into voltage.
4a. Right. The stylus would be damaged in the 78 RPM record grooves.
5a. No. Leave it on until completely finished. Reread 3.5 and try again.
6a. No. There is a separate position for this. Reread 3.5 and try again.
7a. No. It isn't actually responsible for making sound. Reread 3.7 and try again.
8a. Yes. The equalizer/filter gets rid of scratchy noises.
9a. No. The idler-wheel motor-pressure roller-platter drive system is mechanical. Reread 3.6 and try again.
10a. Very good. You have now completed the self-study section on turntables.

If you answered B:

1b. Wrong. This is one of the functions. Reread 3.4 and try again.
2b. Right. The cartridge and stylus are the working end of the turntable tone arm.
3b. Wrong. The stylus picks up vibrations. Reread 3.7 and try again.
4b. No. A cartridge isn't damaged by this. Reread 3.7 and try again.
5b. Right. The motor can be on for long periods.
6b. No. There is a separate position for this. Reread 3.5 and try again.
7b. Right. It houses the stylus and cartridge, which pick up sound.
8b. No. Reread 3.9 and try again.
9b. No. The belt drive system of motor-belt-subplatter is mechanical. Reread 3.6 and try again.
10b. No. One obvious mistake is 1. The cartridge does not vibrate. It receives vibrations. Reread 3.7 and try again. If you had a great deal of difficulty, review this chapter on turntables again.

If you answered C:

1c. Right. A turntable itself does not amplify. Amplification is done through the preamplifier and the audio console or control board.
2c. No. Reread 3.5 and try again.
3c. Wrong. This is part of the stylus. Reread 3.7 and try again.
4c. No. This would be the case if a 33 1/3 RPM record were played with a 78 RPM stylus. Reread 3.7 and try again.
5c. There is no such thing. Reread 3.5 and try again.
6c. Right. In the neutral position, the turntable moves freely.
7c. No. That is not its function. Reread 3.7 and try again.
8c. No. That's the cartridge. Reread 3.9 and try again.
9c. Yes. The direct drive system's precise speeds are controlled electronically.
10c. No. One obvious mistake is 2. The motor does not select speeds. Reread 3.5 and try again. If you had a great deal of difficulty, review this chapter on turntables again.

Projects

■ PROJECT 1

Diagram and label the turntable setup in your production room.

Purpose

To familiarize yourself with the basic parts of the broadcast-quality turntable.

Advice, Cautions, and Background

1. You will be judged on the completeness, accuracy, and clearness of your drawing, not on artistic ability.

How To Do the Project

1. Read the Information section on turntables.
2. Complete the Self-Study Questions on turntables.
3. Sketch the turntable setup in your production studio.
4. Label all the basic parts—platter, tone arm, stylus/cartridge, on/off switch, speed selector switch, and preamp. (The preamp may be located in the cabinet housing the turntable; ask the instructor or engineer if it's not readily accessible.)
5. Also label any optional equipment on your turntable, such as pitch control or equalizer/filter.
6. Show brand names of equipment.
7. Give your completed drawing to the instructor for credit for this project.

■ PROJECT 2

Cue several records using the regular cueing method.

Purpose

To enable you to feel comfortable working with turntables.

Advice, Cautions, and Background

1. If you're not sure of what you are doing, ask the instructor for assistance. Don't take the chance of ruining the equipment, especially the cartridge/stylus assembly.
2. Remember to record your work on reel or cassette tape.
3. You will be judged on proper tightness of record cueing (avoid dead air and wows).

How To Do the Project

1. Read the Information section on turntables.
2. Complete the Self-Study Questions on turntables.
3. Familiarize yourself with the operation of the turntables in your production studio. If you have questions, ask the instructor.
4. Cue a record using the standard cueing techniques:
    a. After putting record on turntable platter, gently place stylus in outer groove of record.
    b. Put speed selector switch in neutral.
    c. Rotate turntable platter clockwise until first sound is heard.
    d. Backtrack turntable platter (rotate counterclockwise) about 1/8 to 1/4 of a turn.
    e. Put speed selector switch in the proper speed.
5. Make sure your audio tape is recording.
6. Announce record title and artist in an ad-lib manner.
7. Turn on/off switch to on just before you want actual sound to begin.
8. Fade out record after twenty to thirty seconds.
9. Repeat the above steps for at least two more records.
10. Have the instructor listen to your tape so that you receive credit for the project.

■ PROJECT 3

Cue several records using the slip cue method.

Purpose

To enable you to feel comfortable working with turntables.

Advice, Cautions, and Background

1. If you're not sure of what you are doing, ask the instructor for assistance.
2. Remember to record your work on reel or cassette tape.
3. You will be judged on proper tightness of record cueing (avoid dead air and wows).

How To Do the Project

1. Read the Information section on turntables.
2. Complete the Self-Study Questions on turntables.
3. Familiarize yourself with the operation of the turntables in your production studio. If you have questions, ask the instructor.
4. Cue a record using the slip cue method:
    a. After putting record on the turntable platter, gently place stylus in outer groove of record.
    b. Put speed selector switch in proper speed.
    c. Turn on/off switch to on.
    d. When first sound is heard, hold edge of record with your finger with enough force to keep it from spinning (the platter will continue to rotate).
    e. Backtrack the record about 1/8 to 1/4 of a turn and continue to hold the edge of the record.
5. Make sure your audio tape is recording.
6. Announce record title and artist in an ad-lib manner.
7. Gently release edge of record just before you want actual sound to begin.
8. Fade out record after twenty to thirty seconds.
9. Repeat the above steps for at least two more records.
10. Have the instructor listen to your tape so that you receive credit for this project.

The Audio Console

Information

4.1 INTRODUCTION

The **audio console** or **control board** is the primary piece of equipment in any production facility. It can be more difficult to understand than other pieces of equipment in the radio production studio, but most other pieces of equipment operate through the audio console, so that without being able to operate the audio console you can't really utilize other studio equipment such as a turntable or audio tape recorder. An audio console is very much like the receiver or amplifier that your home stereo system employs. To use your record player or CD, you must have it plugged into that receiver.

All control boards have basic similarities. Even though you will run across many different brands of audio consoles in your radio production work, a thorough knowledge of any one control board will enable you to use any control board after a brief orientation.

Look at the audio console shown in Figure 4.1 and locate these basic controls: individual channel volume controls, VU meters, audition/program switches (output selectors), and A/B source switches (input selectors). The board may look intimidating because of all the buttons, knobs, and levers, but most of them are repeats of each other because the board has many different inputs and outputs. These will be explained in detail as we begin to explore the operation of the audio console.

4.2 AUDIO CONSOLE FUNCTIONS

The control board has three primary functions: to mix, to amplify, and to route. First, the audio console enables the operator to select any one or combination of various inputs (microphones, CDs, turntables, tape cartridge players, for example). Audio consoles are sometimes referred to as mixing boards because of their ability to select and have several inputs operational at the same time. Much production work will be a mix of voice, music, and sound effects.

The second function of the control board is to amplify the incoming audio signal to an appropriate level. Most sound sources (such as a microphone or turntable) produce a small electrical current that must be amplified to be used.

A third function of the audio console is to enable the operator to route these inputs to a number of outputs such as monitor speakers, the transmitter, or an audio tape recorder.

4.3 BASIC AUDIO CONSOLE PARTS

All control boards operate in basically the same way. For purposes of simplicity, let's assume a very small monaural audio console with two inputs (one for a microphone and one for a turntable) and one output, which goes to the radio station transmitter. Look at Figure 4.2. This is considered a two-channel board with the microphone assigned to channel one and the turntable assigned to channel two. In general terms, a channel refers to the path an audio signal follows. On an audio console, a **channel** refers to a group of switches, faders, and knobs that are usually associated with one sound source. On this board, note the individual input selectors, output selectors, and input volume controls associated with channel one and channel two. The output volume control, VU meter, and monitor volume control are associated with both channels.

4.4 INPUT SELECTORS

The **input selectors** on this particular model of audio console are toggle switches that can either be put in mic or line position. The reason for the two positions is that different pieces of equipment are amplified differing amounts. Microphones generally do not have amplifiers built into them, whereas turntables, CDs, and audio tape recorders have already put their signals through a small amount of amplification. When the input switch is in the mic position, it sends the signal coming into it through a stage of preamplification that is not present for signals coming into the line position. In other words, the mic po-

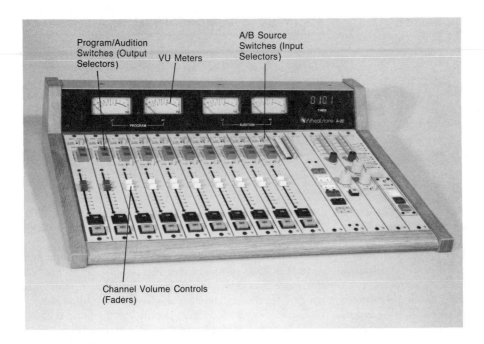

FIGURE 4.1   The audio console. (Courtesy of Wheatstone Corporation)

sition allows a signal to catch up to a signal coming into the line position in terms of amplification. Then they both often go through additional preamplification.

The way the input selector switches in Figure 4.2 are arranged, the microphone comes into the first (left) input and the turntable comes into the second input. This means the mic has to be patched into the first input and

the turntable into the second input. This patching involves running a cable from the mic and turntable to the back (or bottom) of the audio console. Such wiring is usually done in a semipermanent way by the engineer (see Figure 4.3).

The way this console is designed, the microphone could be coming into the second input and the turntable

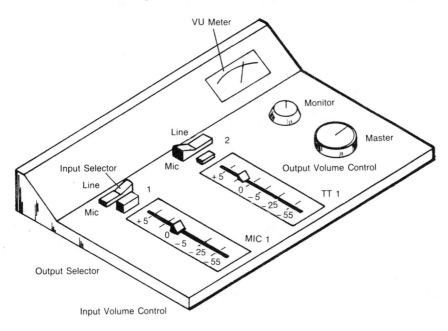

FIGURE 4.2   Simplified audio console.

into the first. The patching would need to be changed (as shown by the dotted lines in Figure 4.3). The toggle input selector switches on the front of the audio console would also need to be reversed.

The mic and the turntable could also both be patched into the first input. Then when the toggle input selector switch is in the mic position, the mic would be activated, and when it is in the line position the turntable would be activated. Under this configuration, however, the mic and turntable could not be used at the same time.

Not all audio boards have input selector switches. Some radio production boards have certain inputs that must be at the mic level and other inputs that can only accommodate equipment that has been preamplified and is ready for a line level. On boards of this type, usually only microphones can be patched into the first two inputs, and only turntables, CDs, tape recorders and other line level equipment can be patched into the remaining inputs.

On the other hand, some boards have input selector switches that have three or more positions for one input. For these boards, it is possible to patch a turntable at position A, a CD at position B, and a cartridge tape player at position C, all into the same input. The use that the facility was going to make of the various equipment would have to be carefully studied because, of course, no two pieces of equipment could be used at the same time on a single channel.

Regardless of the configuration of an audio board, the first two channels (from the left) are almost always utilized as mic level channels. Channel one is normally the main studio mic, and channel two is often an auxiliary microphone.

4.5 INPUT VOLUME CONTROL

The input **volume controls** shown in Figure 4.2 are called **sliders** or **faders.** They are merely **variable resistors.** Although they are called volume controls or **gain controls,** they do not really vary the amount of amplification of the signal. The amplifier is always on at a constant volume. Raising the fader (moving it from a ''south'' to a ''north'' position) decreases the amount of resistance to this signal. When the fader is raised and the resistance is low, a great deal of the signal gets through. The dynamic is like that of a water faucet. The water volume reaching the faucet is always the same, even when the faucet is closed. When you open the faucet (decrease the resistance), you allow the water to flow and you can vary that flow from a trickle to a steady flow.

Some boards have rotary knobs called **potentiometers** or **pots** instead of faders (see Figure 4.4). These provide the same function. As the knob is turned to the right (clockwise) the resistance is decreased and the volume is increased. Some production people feel the fader is easier to work with. For one thing, the fader gives a quick, visual indication of which channels are on and at what level. This is harder to see with a rotary knob.

The numbers on both rotary knobs and faders may be in reverse order on some audio consoles to show their relationship to resistance. For example, if a knob is completely counterclockwise or off, it may read 40; at a twelve o'clock position it may read 25; and completely clockwise it may read 0. These figures represent decreasing amounts of resistance and thus higher volume as the knob is turned clockwise. Modern boards with fader volume controls often use a range of numbers from −55 to 0 to +10

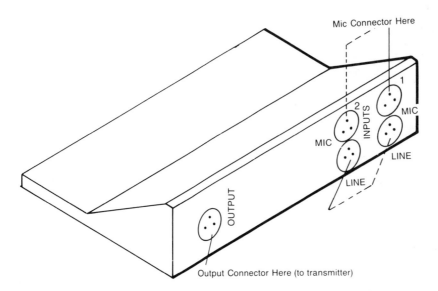

FIGURE 4.3 Rear of simplified audio console.

or +15. While the same relationship to resistance is true (the more the fader is raised the less resistance), these numbers actually relate to decibels and the VU meter. If the board has been set up properly, a 0 setting of the fader will produce a 0 reading on the VU meter. Some boards avoid using any numbers at all and merely use equally spaced indicator lines to provide some kind of reference for various knob and fader settings.

Of course, most boards have more than the two inputs of our example board. In most radio production studios, boards have ten to twelve channels. In professional audio production facilities, sixteen or twenty inputs is not uncommon. Each input has its own volume control.

4.6 MONITORING

Once the signal is through the input volume controls, it is amplified in a program amplifier and then sent several places (see Figure 4.5). One of these is a **monitor amplifier.** This amplifies the signal so that it can be sent into a **monitor speaker** to enable the operator to hear the signal that is going out. Boards usually contain a simple potentiometer to control the volume of the monitor speaker. This control in no way affects the volume of the sound being sent out to the transmitter (or audio tape recorder, etc.). It only controls the volume for the person listening to it in the control room. A common mistake of beginning broadcasters is to run the studio monitors quite loud and think all is well, while in reality they have the signal going through the audio board (and therefore on the air) at a very low level. It's important for the operator to be aware of the level of sound going out the line.

4.7 VU METERS

Another place the signal is sent after program amplification is the **volume unit indicator (VU meter)** (see Figure 4.6). This is a metering device to enable the operator to determine what level of sound is going out the line.

The most common VU meter is a moving needle on a graduated scale. Usually the top position of the scale is calibrated in **decibels,** and the lower portion of the scale is calibrated in percentage. In audio engineering, a reading of 0 decibels (dB) is 100% volume, or the loudest you want the signal to go. The VU meter is important for consistent audio production work. How loud something sounds is very subjective. What is loud to one announcer may not be deemed loud by another, especially if they set the monitor speaker volume differently. The meter gives an electronic reading of volume that is not subjective.

The accuracy of VU meters is sometimes questioned in two areas. First, VU meters have trouble indicating transients, or sudden, sharp, short increases in volume of the sound signal. Most VU meters are designed to indicate an average volume level and ignore these occasional sound bursts. Secondly, VU meters tend to overreact to the bass portion of the sound. In other words, if a sound signal is heavy in the bass frequencies, it will probably indicate a higher VU reading than the total sound signal is actually providing. In spite of these concerns, the VU meter re-

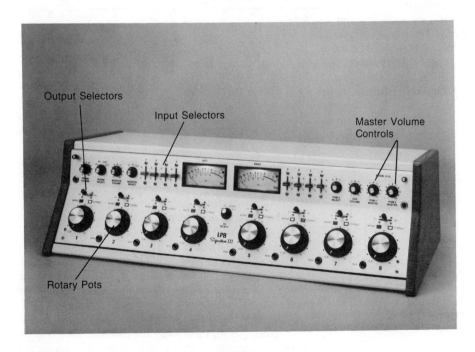

FIGURE 4.4 Audio console with rotary pots. (Courtesy of LPB, Inc.)

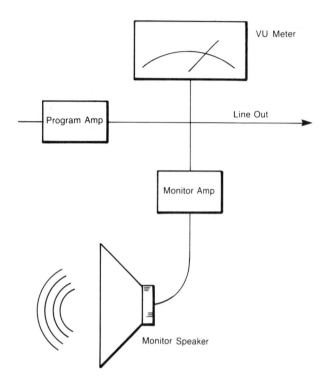

FIGURE 4.5 Monitor amp section of audio console.

mains the best indicator of volume levels in broadcast production.

Generally, an operator should control the signal so that it stays approximately between 80% and 100%. When the needle swings above 100%, we say the signal is **peaking in the red** because that portion of the VU meter usually has a red line. This is an indication to the operator to lower the volume (increase the resistance) of the fader or pot. Occasional dips into the red portion of the scale are likely, but having the needle consistently above 0 dB should be avoided.

Often at the end of the needle's movement is a metal peg to prevent the needle from going off the dial. Allow-

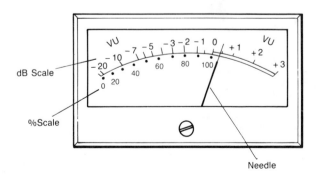

FIGURE 4.6 Standard VU meter.

ing the gain to become so high that the needle reaches the upper peg is called **pegging the meter** or **pinning the needle** and should be avoided to prevent damage to the meter as well as distortion of the signal.

When the signal falls below 20% consistently, we say the signal is **riding in the mud** and the operator should increase the volume. If it is necessary to adjust the level during the program, we say that the operator is **riding the gain.** Gain is an audio engineer's term for loudness or volume. This is why a radio operator is often called a disc jockey. He plays record *discs* and *rides* the gain.

Our simple audio board has only one VU meter that indicates the volume of the sound going out (review Figure 4.2). Many boards have multiple VU meters. For example, they might have separate meters for each input. On our simple board, if the meter is peaking in the red, we would not know just by looking at the VU meter if the mic or the turntable is the culprit. But separate meters for the mic and turntable would show which had the high volume. Boards also have multiple meters if they have multiple outputs. For example, a board that is stereo will have one meter for the right channel and one for the left.

On some boards, the VU meter is not a mechanical meter as has been described so far, but a succession of digital lights (LEDs or light-emitting diodes) that indicate how high the volume is. Another electronic meter replaces the LEDs with fluorescent indicators, and the advantage of both these meters over mechanical meters is that they can indicate volume changes more quickly and accurately.

4.8 OUTPUT SELECTORS

Another place that sound goes after program amplification is to the radio station transmitter. On the board in Figure 4.2, the output selectors are just on/off buttons because the only place that the signal is intended to go is the transmitter. The configuration of **output selector** buttons, however, varies from board to board. If there are a large number of outputs, six for example, then there may be six output buttons for each input. The input signal will be sent to whichever buttons are down or selected. For example, the microphone could be sent to the transmitter, the turntable to a reel-to-reel recorder, and the CD to a cassette recorder. Sometimes there are no output selectors; every input either goes out or it doesn't depending on the master volume control. Other boards have buttons labeled "send" that determine where the signal goes.

Many radio production boards have as an output selector a three-position switch called the **program/audition switch.** When the switch is in the off position (usually the middle), the output is stopped at this point. When the switch is in the program position (usually to the right), the signal goes to the transmitter or to a tape recorder. The program position would be the normal operating position when using an audio console. If the switch is in the audition position, the signal is sent to an audition amplifier and then out to monitor speakers, tape recorder, and so on. The signal will *not* be sent to the transmitter. The purpose of the audition switch is to allow off-air recording and previewing of the sound quality of a particular signal. For example, you could be playing a record on one turntable through channel three of the audio console (in the program position) and at the same time be previewing another record on the other turntable through channel four in the audition position. Each channel of the audio console can be used either in the program or audition position. Some boards just use two push buttons (one for program and one for audition) in place of a single switch. The functions are exactly the same depending on which push button is depressed; if neither is pushed, the signal stops at that point (just like the off position of the single switch).

4.9 OUTPUT VOLUME CONTROL

The only output volume control on our simple board in Figure 4.2 is called the **master fader** because the signal is intended to go only one place. If both output select buttons are in the down (on) position and the master fader is up, the signal will go to the transmitter. It is, of course, possible to send the microphone but not the turntable signal or vice versa. Also, if both buttons are on but the master fader is all the way down, the signal will not be transmitted.

Many boards have more than one output volume control. Again, a stereo board requires two masters, one for the right and one for the left channel. Often board operators want to record what they are sending to the transmitter, so they need additional outputs to go to an audio tape recorder. If there are a large number of output volume controls, then there is usually a master volume control that overrides all the other output volume controls. In other words, if the master is down, the signal will not go anywhere even though one or more of the output volume controls are up.

Boards are often referred to by their number of inputs and outputs. A six-in/four-out board has six inputs and four outputs.

4.10 REVIEW

Most boards, from the simplest to the most complex, include some method for input selection (mic/line switch, input selectors) and input volume control (faders and pots) and some method for output selection (program/ audition switch, output selectors) and volume control (master volume control). They should also have some method of indicating to the operator the strength of the signal (VU meter) and some way of allowing the operator to hear the mix of sources (monitor speakers). Boards also have amplifiers at various stages so that the signal is loud enough when it eventually goes to the transmitter. These amplifiers are buried inside the board and are not something the board operator can control.

In addition, audio consoles can have many other special features to help the board operator work more efficiently and creatively.

4.11 EQUALIZERS AND PAN POTS

Many boards have simple **equalizers (EQ).** These increase or attenuate certain frequencies, thus altering the sound of the voice or music. In some instances, they eliminate unwanted sound. For example, scratches in records are heard mainly on high frequencies. By filtering out these frequencies, the record will sound scratch-free. Likewise, a low rumble can be removed by eliminating or turning down low frequencies. It's important to note that when you equalize a sound, you affect both the unwanted and wanted sound: equalization is usually a compromise between eliminating a problem and keeping a high-quality, usable audio signal.

Equalizers can also be used for special effects, such as making a voice sound like it is coming over a telephone line. Usually the equalizers are knobs or switches that increase or attenuate a certain range of frequencies. They are placed somewhere above each input volume control (see Figure 4.7). Equalizers are discussed in further detail in chapter 10.

If a board is stereo, each input may have a **pan pot** or **pan knob.** By turning (panning) this knob to the left or right you can control how much of the sound from that input goes to the right channel and how much goes to the left channel (review Figure 4.7).

4.12 HEADPHONE USE

Most audio consoles also have provision for listening to the output of the board through **headphones.** Since live microphones are often used in production work, the monitor speakers are muted when the mic is on so that feedback does not occur. To be able to hear an additional sound source such as a record, headphones are necessary. Audio consoles allow you to monitor by headphones any of the outputs by selecting an appropriate switch. There is usually a volume control to adjust the signal level going to the headphones.

4.13 CUE

Another function found on most boards is called **cue** and allows you to preview an input. Both rotary pots and fader controls go into a cue position, which is below the off position for that control. If you turn the rotary pot all the way counterclockwise to off, it will reach a detent or

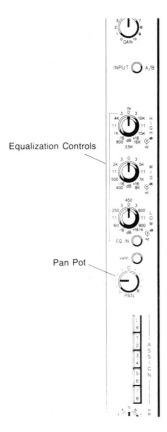

Equalization Controls

Pan Pot

FIGURE 4.7 Portion of a single channel of an audio console. (Courtesy of Wheatstone Corporation)

stop. Keep turning the knob (with a little extra pressure) until it clicks into the cue position. Faders are brought down or "south" until they click into cue. This position is usually marked on the face of the audio console.

In the cue position the audio signal is routed to a cue amplifier and then to a small speaker built into the control board. Since the quality of this small internal speaker is usually marginal at best, the cue signal is often sent to a small, but better quality, external speaker located near the audio console.

As the name implies, this position is designed to allow the operator to cue up the sound source. For example, a record can be cued to the exact beginning so that the sound will start immediately when the turntable is turned on. If an input is in cue, the signal does not go to the transmitter or to any other output source such as a tape recorder. Its only purpose is to allow off-air cueing.

Many beginning announcers and production people forget to move the volume control out of the cue position after cueing up the sound source. If something is left in cue, it will not go out on the air or be routed to an audio tape recorder. It will only play through the cue speaker.

4.14 TONE GENERATORS

Some boards have a built-in **tone generator.** This reference tone is usually placed on a tape before the program material. The tone generator sends out a tone through the board that can be set at 100% using the board VU meter. The VU meter on the source to which the signal is being sent (e.g., an audio tape recorder) is simultaneously set at 100%. After the two are set, any other volume sent through the board will be the exact same volume when it reaches the tape recorder. Having a tone generator allows for this consistency. Otherwise, sounds that register at 100% coming through the board might peak in the red and be distorted on the tape recorder.

The tone on the tape is also used when the tape is played back. The audio engineer or board operator listens to the tone and sets that tape recorder VU meter to 100%. That way the tape will play back exactly as it is recorded.

4.15 REMOTE STARTS, CLOCKS, TIMERS, AND OTHER FEATURES

Other "bells and whistles" appear on audio boards. Some have **remote start switches.** These are usually located below each individual channel volume control, and if the equipment patched into that channel (such as a tape cartridge player or turntable) has the right interface, it can be turned on or started by depressing the remote start. This makes it easier for the announcer to start a record while talking into the microphone without having to reach off to the side and possibly be pulled off mic.

Many control boards now include built-in **clocks** and **timers.** Digital clocks conveniently show the announcer the current time (hours, minutes, and seconds), and timers can be reset at the start of a record or tape to count the elapsed time.

Some audio boards have a **solo switch** above each input. When this switch is on, only the sound of that particular input will be heard over the monitor. Other boards have a **trim knob** that fine-tunes the volume of each input. Boards also have provisions for echo, reverberation, and some interface with computers. To see if you understand the various functions of an audio console, look at Figure 4.8 and see if you can tell what each control does.

4.16 CONCLUSIONS

If you have followed the descriptions and explanations offered in this chapter, the audio console should be a less frightening assemblage of switches, knobs, and meters than it was when you began. You should begin to have a good idea of how to operate each board and feel comfortable working with the controls of your own board.

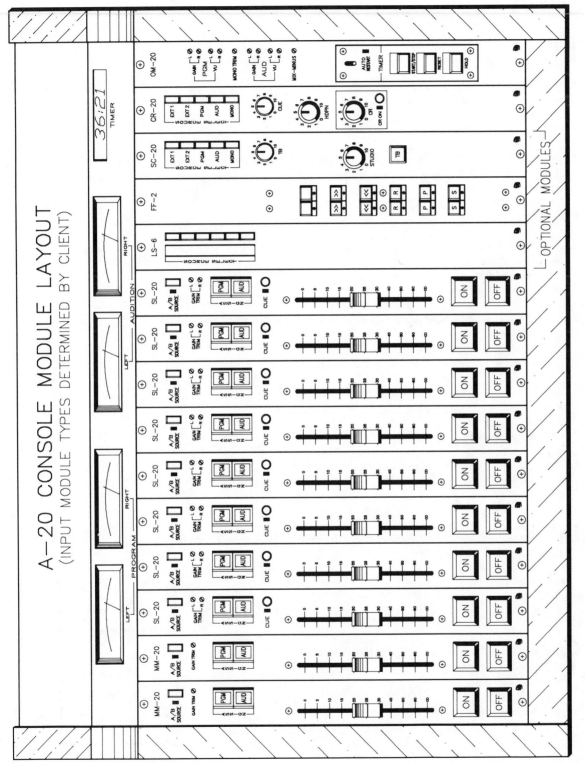

FIGURE 4.8 Audio console with numerous features. (Courtesy of Wheatstone Corporation)

39

Self-Study

■ QUESTIONS

1. It is possible to have music from an audio tape recorder go into a control board and then come out and be recorded on another tape recorder.
   a) true
   b) false

2. In Figure 4.7, according to the pan pot indicator, the sound signal going to the left channel would be _____ the signal going to the right channel.
   a) less than
   b) the same as
   c) greater than

3. In Figure 4.2, if the fader were at −5 and you changed it to −25, you would have _____.
   a) amplified the signal
   b) decreased the volume
   c) decreased the resistance

4. In Figure 4.2, sound would not get to line out on channel one because _____.
   a) the fader is at 0
   b) the output selector switch is off
   c) the program amplifier is off

5. In Figure 4.5, audible sound comes from the _____.
   a) VU meter
   b) monitor amplifier
   c) monitor speaker

6. In Figure 4.6, 50% on the scale is roughly equivalent to _____.
   a) −6 dB
   b) −4 dB
   c) 50 dB

7. The relative position of the needle of the VU meter below is an example of _____.
   a) peaking in the red
   b) turning up the pot
   c) riding in the mud

8. The relative position of the needle of the VU meter below is an example of _____.
   a) pegging the meter
   b) broadcasting in stereo
   c) peaking in the red

9. The line position on an input selector would be used to bring in _____.
   a) CDs and audio tape recorders
   b) microphones and turntables
   c) microphones and tape recorders

10. The monitor/speaker is an example of _____.
   a) an input
   b) a mix
   c) an output

11. If the program/audition switch is in the audition position _____.
   a) sound will not reach the mic/line switch
   b) sound can be going to a tape recorder
   c) sound can be going to the transmitter

12. The master volume control _____.
   a) must be up in order for sound to leave the board
   b) is required only if the board is stereo
   c) controls only the volume of the line inputs

13. Which control could be used to help eliminate scratches on records?
   a) the pan knob
   b) the equalizer
   c) the solo button

14. The cue position on a fader _____.
   a) allows sound to go to the transmitter
   b) sometimes substitutes for the trim control
   c) sends sound to a small speaker in the audio board

15. Which of the following can help assure that the level that is being recorded on a tape recorder is the same as that coming from the audio board?
   a) tone generator
   b) remote switch
   c) digital timer

16. In Figure 4.8, if channels one and six were in audition position, channels two, three, four, and five were in program position, and channel three were in cue, then sound would get to the transmitter from _____.
   a) inputs one, two, and three
   b) inputs two, four, and five
   c) inputs four, five, and six

17. As a review of audio boards, match the items in the list below (1, 2, 3 . . .) with the choices in the list at the top of page 42 (a, d, p . . .) and then select the correct set of answers from the sequences shown in a, b, or c below.

   1. _____ mic/line switch

   2. _____ fader

   3. _____ VU meter

   4. _____ program/audition switch

   5. _____ preamp

   6. _____ monitor amp

   7. _____ program amp

a. amplifies sound before it goes to the pot
d. determines how much preamplification a signal will receive
p. pegging the meter
t. determines whether sound goes to the transmitter or stays within the control room
s. amplifies sound before it goes to a monitor
l. amplifies sound before it goes to line out
v. varies resistance
r. peaking in the red

a) 1.d 2.v 3.r 4.t 5.a 6.s 7.1
b) 1.t 2.v 3.p 4.d 5.s 6.1 7.a
c) 1.d 2.v 3.r 4.t 5.s 6.1 7.a

■ ANSWERS

If you answered A:

1a. Right. A tape recorder can be both input and output.
2a. No. Check the setting of the pan pot. Reread 4.11 and try again.
3a. No. The fader never amplifies the signal. This is done at the preamp. Reread 4.5 and try again.
4a. Wrong. When a pot is at 0, it is on. Reread 4.5 and 4.8 and try again.
5a. No. This indicates level, but you hear nothing from it. Reread 4.6 and 4.7 and try again.
6a. Right. You read the scale correctly.
7a. No. The needle would be at the other end for this. Reread 4.7 and try again.
8a. Right. Pegging the meter is correct. We could also have used the term ''pinning the needle.''
9a. You are correct. Both of these are inputs that are already amplified.
10a. No, you are at the wrong end. Reread 4.2 and try again.
11a. No, the mic/line switch is long before the program/audition switch and really has nothing to do with it. Reread 4.4 and 4.8 and try again.
12a. Right. The purpose of the master volume is to allow all appropriate sounds to leave the audio console.
13a. No, this controls how much sound is going to the left and right channels of a stereo board. Reread 4.11 and try again.
14a. No, it specifically prohibits it from going to the transmitter. Reread 4.13 and try again.
15a. Right, if the board VU meter and the tape recorder VU meter are both set at 100% tone, the levels should be the same.
16a. No, it wouldn't get there from either input one or input three. For input one, the program/audition switch is in the audition position. For input three, the fader is in the cue position. Reread at least 4.8 and 4.13, but if you had a great deal of difficulty figuring this out, reread the whole chapter and then try again.
17a. Right. You chose the correct sequence.

If you answered B:

1b. Wrong. A tape recorder can be fed in and another tape recorder can be placed at the output. Reread 4.2 carefully and then choose the other answer.
2b. No. Check the setting of the pan pot. Reread 4.11 and try again.
3b. Right. This is an increase in resistance to the signal; not as much of the signal gets through and it is softer.
4b. Right. The output selector switch is in the off position, so sound would stop there.
5b. No. This amplifies so the sound can come out, but you don't hear the sound from it. Reread 4.6 and try again.
6b. No. You went the wrong direction. Reread 4.7 and try again.
7b. No. If anything, the pot is being turned down. Reread 4.7 and try again.
8b. No. Reread 4.7 and try again.
9b. No, a microphone should come in a mic input because it needs to be amplified to reach the level of amplification of a turntable. The turntable would be plugged into the line in position. Reread 4.4 and try again.
10b. No, this is way off. Reread 4.2 and try again.
11b. Yes, the purpose of the audition position is to send the sound to someplace other than the transmitter. Sound would not necessarily need to go to a tape recorder, though it could.
12b. No, a master volume control functions the same for both mono and stereo. Stereo boards, however, usually have two master volume controls, one for each channel. Reread 4.9 and try again.

13b. Right, this can eliminate high frequencies where scratches reside.

14b. No, the two have nothing to do with each other. Reread 4.13 and 4.15 and try again.

15b. No, this will turn on the recorder remotely but will do nothing about levels. Reread 4.14 and try again.

16b. Right, for all of these channels the volume is up, the switch is in program, and the master volume controls are up.

17b. No. You made many errors. Reread the chapter and redo all the self-study questions before you try again.

If you answered C:

2c. Right. The pan pot is set so that more of the sound from the input goes to the left channel.

3c. You are warm but not right. Changing the level from −5 to −25 would increase resistance. Reread 4.5 and try again.

4c. Wrong. The program amp, like the preamp, is always on. Reread 4.5 and 4.8 and try again.

5c. Right. You hear sound from the monitor speaker.

6c. There is no such thing on a VU meter. Reread 4.7 again and look carefully at Figure 4.6. Try again.

7c. Right. "Riding in the mud" is the term for a low reading.

8c. No. It is worse than that. Reread 4.7 and try again.

9c. No, a microphone should come in a mic input because it needs to be amplified to reach the level of amplification of a tape recorder. The tape recorder would be plugged into the line in position. Reread 4.4 and try again.

10c. Right, sound comes out to the monitor/speaker.

11c. No, the purpose of the audition position is to keep the sound from going to the transmitter. Reread 4.8 and try again.

12c. No, it controls all the sound that is set to leave the board. Line and mic positions have no bearing on it. Reread sections 4.4 and 4.9 and try again.

13c. No, this allows you to hear one input by itself. Reread 4.11 and try again.

14c. Right, cueing is just for the person operating the board.

15c. No, this is simply a clock. It has nothing to do with levels. Reread 4.14 and try again.

16c. No, the sound wouldn't get there from input six, because the program/audition switch is in audition. Reread 4.8 and try again.

17c. No. You are confused about the various types of amplification. Reread 4.4 and 4.6–4.8 and then try again.

Projects

■ PROJECT 1

Diagram and label the audio console in your production room.

Purpose

To familiarize you with the positioning of the various switches and controls so that you can access them quickly.

Advice, Cautions, and Background

1. Some boards are very complicated and have more functions than discussed in this chapter. Usually this is because they are intended to be used for sound recording of music. If you have such a board, you only need to label the parts that you will be using frequently.

2. If you can not find controls for all of the functions given in this chapter, ask for help. Because there are so many different brands and types of boards, sometimes functions are combined or located in places where you can not identify them easily.

3. You do not need to label each switch and knob. If your board has ten inputs, it will obviously have ten channel volume controls. You can circle them all and label them together or make one label that says "input volume controls" and draw arrows to all ten.

4. You will be judged on completeness and accuracy of your drawing. You will not be graded on artistic ability, but be as clear as possible.

How To Do the Project

1. Read the Information section on the audio console.
2. Complete the Self-Study Questions on the audio console.
3. Sketch the audio console in your production studio.
4. Label all the basic parts—input selectors, channel volume controls, VU meters, output selectors (program/ audition switches), and master volume controls.
5. Also label any other parts of the board that you will be using frequently, such as equalizers, cue positions, and headphone connections.
6. If possible, give the brand name and model number of the board.
7. Give your completed drawing to the instructor for credit for this project.

■ PROJECT 2

Learn to operate an audio board.

Purpose

To acquaint you with the operation of a basic audio console and to make you somewhat proficient at some of its functions.

Advice, Cautions, and Background

1. Audio boards are generally the most complicated pieces of equipment in a radio station. It may take you a while to master a board, but don't despair. Take it slowly and don't be afraid to ask for help.
2. Audio boards all have the same general purpose. Sounds come into the board, are mixed together, and are sent out to somewhere else.
3. The actual exercise is to be done as quickly as possible. You will not be judged on aesthetics. In other words, when you are fading from one record to another, do it as fast as you can. Don't wait for the proper musical beat, phrase, or pause.

How To Do the Project

1. Read the Information section on the audio console.
2. Complete the Self-Study Questions on the audio console.
3. Familiarize yourself with the operation of the audio console in your production studio. Learn the inputs, the outputs, the method for changing volume, and other special features of the board.
4. As soon as you feel you understand the board, do the following exercise as rapidly as possible while recording it on a tape recorder. Practice as much as you like first.
   a. Play part of a record and fade it out.
   b. Announce your name and the time using the studio mic.
   c. Begin a second record.
   d. Cross-fade to a third record and then fade it out.
   e. Bring in an auxiliary microphone and ad-lib with another announcer; then fade it out.
   f. Announce something clever on the studio mic.
5. Make sure your audio tape is recording.
6. Play your tape for the instructor for credit for the project.

■ PROJECT 3

Do a fifteen-minute disc jockey show.

Purpose

To enable you to develop disc jockey skills.

Advice, Cautions, and Background

1. Make sure your voice intonations fit the style of music you choose.
2. Listen to several disc jockeys and pick up whatever ideas you feel will be helpful.
3. Vary your pitch, volume, and tone so that your voice doesn't become monotonous.
4. Make your program exactly fifteen minutes. One way to insure proper timing is to have some material near the end of the program that you can easily shorten or lengthen as needed, e.g., facts about the career of a particular artist or a weather report.

How To Do the Project

1. Read the Information section on the audio console.
2. Complete the Self-Study Questions on the audio console.
3. Select the music you wish to play and time it. You may choose any style of music you wish. You will be playing each piece in its entirety. Try not to have selections over five minutes.
4. Plan and write the commercials, station breaks, or other commentary you wish to include.
5. Think through how to introduce the various selections.
6. Make sure you have approximately fifteen minutes' worth of material including music and talk.
7. Do the program and tape it, ending at fifteen minutes. Use your own creativity and style. If it is good enough, give the tape to the instructor to receive credit for the project. If not, do it again until it is acceptable.

Digital Broadcast Equipment

Information

5.1 INTRODUCTION

If there is one buzzword in broadcasting today, especially in the area of radio production, it is **digital.** Digital technology has ushered in tremendous improvements in sound quality—better **frequency response range,** improved **signal-to-noise ratio,** increased **dynamic range,** and lower **noise** and **distortion,** to name a few. (If these sound quality terms are unfamiliar to you, then read Appendix A before continuing with this chapter.)

From the advent in the early 1980s of the compact disc player to the development in the late 1980s of the digital audio tape recorder to the projected total digital production studio, radio has embraced this technology and eagerly awaits its maturation. This chapter introduces the concept of digital technology, some of the digital audio equipment used in the radio production studio, and some thoughts about what the future may hold in this unfolding area.

5.2 DIGITAL VERSUS ANALOG RECORDING

Most radio production people would agree that eventually digital technology will replace analog technology. By digital technology we mean the process of converting audio information into an electrical signal composed of a series of on and off pulses. In other words, the digital process is a conversion into **binary** numbers. Computers handle information in this manner by associating a binary number with each letter of the alphabet and number and then manipulating this binary data.

Before digital technology was developed, audio recording relied on an **analog** process. An analog signal (for example, the audio signal produced by a microphone or record) is a continuously variable electrical signal whose shape is defined by the shape of the sound wave produced (see Figure 5.1). In the analog recording process, a duplicate or electromagnetic representation of the sound wave of the original sound source is stored on magnetic tape. Each time the analog signal is recorded or processed in some fashion, it is subject to degradation because the signal

changes shape slightly. Analog encoding is similar to creating a line graph to show a statistical analysis. All measurements are on a continuous line that curves up and down with no discrete points. The recording process is like trying to retrace a curve on a graph; the reproduction is always slightly different than the original.

On the other hand, digital encoding is accomplished in a discrete fashion, like looking at individual numbers in a statistical analysis and writing them down in a set order. The audio signal (from a microphone or record) starts out as analog, but can be converted to digital for recording or processing. To convert to digital, the original sound source must be analyzed by **sampling** (see Figure 5.2). These samples are merely a series of voltage levels that indicate the loudness and timbre information of the sound at that particular moment. By taking enough samples and converting the samples to binary data, an exact reproduction of the original sound signal can be recorded onto tape. Basic digital equipment utilizes a sampling rate of just over forty-four thousand times per second; many pieces of digital equipment, however, are designed to oversample at a rate up to four times that for even better sound quality and accurate reproduction.

Remember, it is the binary data that is actually recorded on the tape, *not* an analog representation of the signal. With digital technology, we can copy from tape to tape with no measurable loss of quality. Along with the improved frequency response, wide dynamic range, and unmeasurable noise and distortion, this ability to rerecord with no decrease in quality has been a big part of digital's acceptance in radio production.

5.3 ADVANTAGES OF THE CD PLAYER

The **compact disc** player has been the first piece of digital equipment to be embraced in radio production and broadcast work. The CD player offers all the advantages of any piece of digital equipment—greater frequency response, better signal-to-noise ratio, improved dynamic range, and almost no distortion. In addition, there is no physical contact between the player and the actual CD. Unlike the sty-

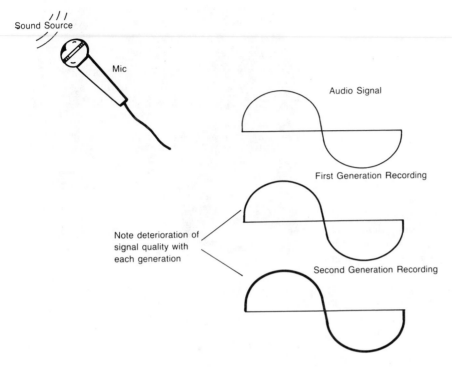

FIGURE 5.1 Analog recording.

lus, which rides the grooves of a record, the CD is read by a **laser** light, and there is no wear or degradation of the CD. Many sound effect and production music libraries that used to be available on record are now produced on compact disc. The ease of cueing and the consistently high quality obtained makes the use of CDs and the CD player an important part of the production process in the modern studio.

Many radio stations and production facilities just use consumer CD players, but these often require special in-

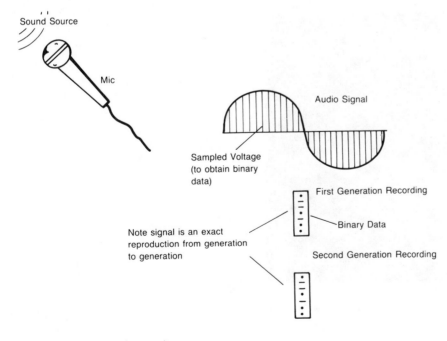

FIGURE 5.2 Digital recording.

terfaces to be compatible with other broadcast equipment and are not designed for daily use. There are broadcast-quality CD players available, and good production practice dictates the use of these units rather than consumer models.

5.4 COMPACT DISCS

Unless some other technology develops, the CD will probably replace the vinyl record, and the CD player will replace the turntable in the radio studio. The CD is a small plastic disc 4.7 inches in diameter (see Figure 5.3). On one side of the disc, the music is stored as a spiral of microscopic pits that contain the encoded information about the sound. A thin aluminum reflective coating (less than seventy-millionths of a millimeter) makes it possible for the laser light to read the encoded data, and a lacquer coating protects the entire disc. CDs were designed to hold sixty minutes of recorded material; some, however, have been released with close to seventy-five minutes of music. CD singles (three-inch CDs) have also been developed and are capable of holding about twenty minutes of music.

The compact disc was originally promoted as indestructible, but practical use in the radio studio has shown that they do require some care. Some CD players can be mistracked by dust or finger prints on the CD surface, and serious scratches can also render the CD unplayable.

FIGURE 5.3 Compact disc (in CD player tray).

5.5 THE CD PLAYER

The CD player shown in Figure 5.4 is typical of a unit designed specifically for broadcast use. Its main feature, and main difference from a consumer unit, is a large **cue wheel** that allows the operator to ''rock'' the CD back and

FIGURE 5.4 Professional CD player. (Courtesy of Studer Revox America, Inc.)

forth much like cueing a record. In this manner, the exact start point of the music can be found, and then the player can be paused at that spot ready for play. Similar systems use a single microprocessor control unit that allows cueing of two separate playback units. Other normal CD controls include a play button to start the CD, several controls to select specific tracks (or songs) on the CD, and an open/close control to load the CD into the machine. Regardless of the exact design, the CD ends up in a **tray** or **well** where it spins so the laser can read it.

The internal structure of the CD player centers around the laser beam system that reads the encoded data on the surface of the CD. Figure 5.5 shows a simplified drawing of this optical pickup. A **laser diode** generates the laser light beam and a **prism system** directs it toward the disc surface. Different types of lenses focus the laser beam exactly on the pits of data. Reflected light is directed back through the lens and prism to a wedge lens and a **photodiode** that provides the data signal that will be converted to an audio signal.

A different design approach to CD players has been to build them so that the CD must be put into a plastic housing before it can be played in the unit (see Figure 5.6). As you'll see in the next chapter, this is more similar to the audio tape cartridge than to the turntable design previously used. Special broadcast features include the ability to select one track while another is playing (so two songs can be played back-to-back from the same CD), a countdown timer (so the operator knows exactly how much time remains on the song currently playing), and a cue wheel (for precise cueing). While the plastic cartridge increases the cost of this system, it also affords the CD extra protection from dirt and damage.

As the radio station CD library continues to grow, some use has developed for a professional **multiplay** CD player. With an ability to hold up to one hundred CDs and with interfacing capability, this unit has been used as a music source in automation systems. Not only does the operator have random access to over a thousand individual songs, but also all the CDs are secured under lock and key.

As of this writing, the newest development in the compact disc area is Tandy Corporation's (and others) work on a CD recorder. CD players are merely "turntables" for

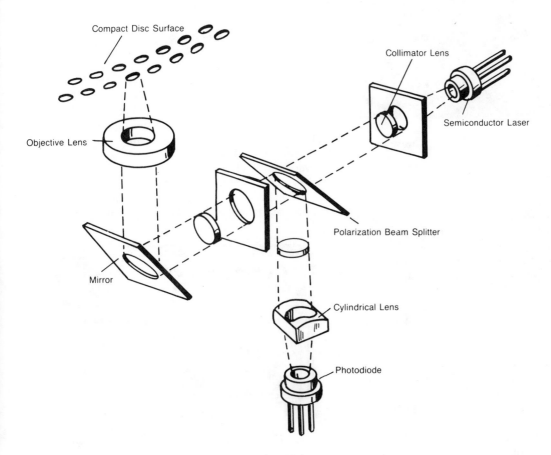

FIGURE 5.5   Simplified internal structure of a CD laser.

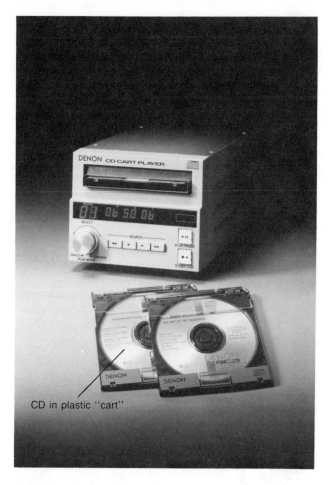

FIGURE 5.6 Cartridge style CD player. (Courtesy of Denon America, Inc.)

prerecorded CDs at this point, but Tandy could change that with its THOR-CD system. THOR-CD (Tandy High-Intensity Optical Recording) would allow a blank CD disc to be recorded over and over. The THOR-CD would use an erasable optical material that could change its physical and optical characteristics when heated by a recording laser. This recordable CD is fully compatible with current CDs and initial pricing estimates should make it attractive to both consumers and broadcast production people.

5.6 ADVANTAGES OF THE DAT RECORDER

Another entry in the digital arena is the **digital audio tape** recorder (DAT), also known as R-DAT (**rotary head digital audio tape**). If the CD replaces the turntable, it is highly likely that the DAT will replace the audio tape cartridge in broadcast production and probably the reel-to-reel and cassette machines as well. The DAT recorders have the

same superior sound quality associated with CDs—exceptional frequency response and signal-to-noise ratio, wider dynamic range, and virtually no wow, flutter, hiss, hum or distortion. In addition, the DAT has been developed with recording capability and the material recorded can be dubbed almost endlessly without degradation of quality. Even if a recordable CD is developed, the DAT will have the advantage of a longer recording time—two hours, or about twice as long as the CD. Perhaps DAT's biggest advantages are its convenience of handling (similar to working with a cassette) and the relative compactness of its portable units.

5.7 DAT CASSETTES

The actual R-DAT cassette tape is similar to a small VCR tape and consists of two small reels encased in a plastic housing about the size of a deck of playing cards (see Figure 5.7). The audio tape is permanently attached to the two reels, and the longest DAT tapes are capable of recording two hours. While cueing time for the CD player is only one to two seconds, cueing time from one end of the DAT tape to the other is about forty seconds. This slower access time is of some concern to broadcasters and would probably necessitate more DAT sources available than CD sources in practical use. On the other hand, cueing a DAT deck within a twenty minute window (ten minutes either side of the current position) can be done in ten seconds or less, which compares with the normal run-out time on the audio tape cartridge, making the DAT a possible replacement for the cart machine. Tape speed for the DAT recorder is not a factor in the quality of the recording, since only binary data is recorded on the tape; tape speed will vary, however, depending on the mode the DAT machine is in. For example, standard DAT recording speed is 8.15 millimeters per second, but prerecorded DAT tapes play back at a tape speed of 12.225 millimeters per second.

FIGURE 5.7 Digital audio tape cassette. (Courtesy of TDK Electronics Corporation)

5.8 THE DAT RECORDER

The DAT recorder is technically part VCR, part traditional cassette recorder, and part CD player (see Figure 5.8). Although it has the normal tape recorder controls (play, record, pause, etc.), the tape cassette goes into a slide-out drawer (operated with an open/close control) like many CD players. The DAT unit, like the CD, has several controls for selecting specific songs on the tape. An AMS (**Automatic Music Sensor**) button allows the operator to skip forward or backward to the start of the next song. Subcodes can be recorded along with the music on a DAT tape so that the operator can select any individual song by entering in that song's "start ID" or "program number." A DAT system records with rotating heads, putting the digital encoded data (music or program material and subcodes) on the tape in a diagonal manner like the VCR. This is unlike the analog system that usually records with a stationary head that puts data on the tape in a straight line (linear) fashion.

5.9 DAT COPYRIGHT AND PIRACY

DAT, like the CD, was developed with the consumer market in mind, but met resistance from those concerned about copyright and piracy. Because DAT recorders have the same general operational characteristics as regular analog reel-to-reel, cassette, and cartridge recorders, theoretically they can be recorded from and on by anyone. People in the business of selling prerecorded tapes are worried that, because tapes can be reproduced infinitely, people will make copies from friends and not buy tapes. Likewise, if in the future DAT signals were ever broadcast

FIGURE 5.8 Digital audio tape recorder. (Courtesy of Sony Corporation of America)

from a radio station, they would be a prime target for taping because of their superior quality. Attempts have been made to prevent the sale of consumer DAT recorders in the United States, and this has slowed somewhat the adoption of DAT by radio stations although broadcast models are readily available. A recordable/erasable CD is likely to meet the same resistance, but DAT (and CD) recorders will probably eventually become the primary recorders in radio on-air and production studios.

5.10 DIGITAL REEL-TO-REEL

While CD and DAT are the better known and accepted digital formats in radio production, there are digital systems in the reel-to-reel format too. For example, the **DASH (Digital Audio Stationary Head)** system is available for two-track and multitrack reel-to-reel recorders. The two-track systems use standard quarter-inch audio tape (although specially formulated) and standard digital technology (although the stationary head approach is different from the rotary heads of DAT recorders). The multitrack systems have found frequent use in the recording studio, but a very high price tag (even the audio tape for the DASH format is far more expensive than a DAT cassette) has kept almost all broadcast stations away from the multitrack system and even the less expensive (still around twenty thousand dollars) two-track DASH machines.

5.11 THE DIGITAL AUDIO WORKSTATION

While the CD, DAT, and DASH systems are digital improvements over older analog equipment, a further extension of digital technology in the radio production studio has been the development of the DAW or **digital audio workstation** (see Figure 5.9). These are hard disc systems that incorporate computer keyboards, touch screens or mouses to manipulate music, dialogue, and sound effects. The original sound signal is converted to digital form and can then be stored, manipulated, and recalled using the workstation.

5.12 ADVANTAGES AND DISADVANTAGES OF THE DAW

One of the main advantages of the DAW is the ability to edit without using razor blades to physically cut the audio tape. Not only does it provide a safer work environment in the production studio, but also it allows you to preview the editing, and most DAWs have an undo button to put the sound back into its original form if you don't like the way the edit came out. Another advantage of the DAW includes a fast random access or the ability to immediately

FIGURE 5.9 Digital audio workstation. (Courtesy of Waveframe Corporation)

cue up at any point all of the material stored in the system. Other advantages include a potentially large storage capacity for audio material and the ability of the digital medium to reproduce copy after copy with no loss of quality.

The disadvantages of the DAW technology are tied more to its newness than to inherent problems in the system. For example, learning to operate a DAW can take several months, so they've been labeled as not very user friendly, and, at this time, there are very few people in the radio production area skilled in their use. The high cost of setting up a DAW has also been considered a drawback, but like most new technologies, the cost factor should decrease with continued development. Other concerns include reliability of operation, maintenance costs, and the transportability of digital material.

5.13 THE FUTURE OF THE DAW

The future of the DAW can not be determined yet, but those who embrace the concept are looking at more than a very high-tech production studio. Most proponents of the DAW see it as the center of the all-digital radio station (see Figure 5.10). Not only can the DAW produce a radio commercial, but it can store the commercial or several variations of it (all the time maintaining digital quality),

play the commercial on-air by sending the signal to a digitized transmitter, and even send logging and bookkeeping information about the airing of the commercial to the appropriate station personnel. These systems are not common in radio stations yet, but they are being used in music recording studios, and radio is starting to experiment with them.

5.14 DIGITAL EDITING

Without investing in a full-blown DAW, radio production rooms can, for an investment of about seven thousand dollars, become involved in digital audio tape editing with the development of computer editing programs. The software works with almost any audio source and an IBM or compatible computer. One such program is SpeakEasy. With it, up to six different audio sources can be dumped into the computer (totaling thirty minutes of audio), and then edited as desired. The systems being developed use familiar editing terms in their operation, such as forward, play, mark in (starting point of the edit), and mark out (end of the edit) and can usually be learned in a couple of days of training sessions. Most systems are mainly designed for newsroom work, as the audio is mono, but they will have several applications in the music area as they are further developed.

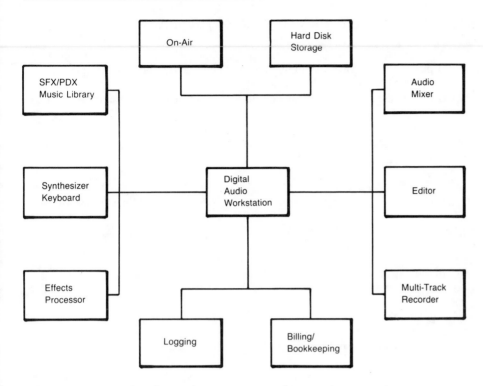

FIGURE 5.10 Digital audio workstation integrated into station operations.

5.15 CONCLUSIONS

There seems to be little doubt that radio production will benefit from the various developments of the digital technology. It is no longer a question of if this will happen, but rather when it will all come together. Some industry experts feel that within five years, digital technology will have replaced analog. Others feel it will take longer. In any case, a basic understanding of digital technology and the operation of digital-based equipment will be more and more important in the future and may soon be a prerequisite for success for the radio production person.

Self-Study

■ QUESTIONS

1. In the digital recording process, an electromagnetic representation of the sound wave of the original sound source is stored on magnetic tape.
   a) true
   b) false

2. Digital recordings can be copied over and over with no measurable loss of sound quality because _____.
   a) the sound signal is a continuously variable electrical signal, the shape of which is defined by the shape of the sound wave produced
   b) the original sound source is sampled over forty-four thousand times per second
   c) it is binary data that is recorded on the tape and this can be accurately copied from tape to tape

3. One reason for using a professional-quality CD player rather than a consumer model in the radio production studio is _____.
   a) the professional-quality CD player uses a higher-powered laser to read the CD than a consumer model
   b) the professional-quality CD player is built for heavy-duty, continuous operation and the consumer model isn't
   c) the professional-quality CD player offers a greater frequency response and better dynamic range than the consumer model

4. The lacquer coating on the compact disc makes it virtually indestructible in normal broadcast use.
   a) true
   b) false

5. Currently, the main advantage of the digital audio tape recorder over the CD is the fact that the DAT has _____.
   a) recording capability
   b) better signal-to-noise ratio
   c) virtually no distortion

6. One of the main advantages of the digital audio workstation in radio production is _____.
   a) it's an inexpensive system to put together and maintain
   b) it's easy to operate
   c) it's capable of editing without cutting

7. The audio tape format used in DAT machines is most similar to the format of _____.
   a) VCR tapes
   b) cassette tapes
   c) reel-to-reel tapes

8. The CD/CD player format is an improvement over the record/turntable format because _____.
   a) CDs are less expensive than records
   b) CD players are more durable than turntables
   c) CD players don't wear out discs as turntables wear out records

9. A multiplay CD player can _____.
   a) record
   b) hold up to one hundred CDs
   c) use a digital audio stationary head

10. Copyright has been more of a concern for CD technology than for DAT technology.
   a) true
   b) false

11. As a review of digital broadcast equipment, match the items in the top list (1, 2, 3 . . .) with the choices in the bottom list (l, c, r . . .) and then select the correct set of answers from the sequences shown in a, b, or c below.
   1. _____ analog
   2. _____ CD
   3. _____ DASH
   4. _____ DAT
   5. _____ DAW
   6. _____ SpeakEasy

   l. a disc that is read by a laser
   c. a format that uses a cassette tape that is recorded on diagonally
   r. a digital recording system for reel-to-reel recorders
   i. an editing program that can be used on an IBM computer
   s. a computer-based system that can store and manipulate sound in a variety of ways
   v. a continuously variable signal that represents the shape of a sound wave

a) 1.i   2.c   3.v   4.s   5.l   6.r
b) 1.v   2.l   3.c   4.s   5.r   6.i
c) 1.v   2.l   3.r   4.c   5.s   6.i

■ ANSWERS

If you answered A:

1a. No. This statement describes analog recording, not digital recording. Reread 5.2 and select the other response.

2a. Wrong. This refers to an analog signal. Reread 5.2 and try again.

3a. No. Both professional and consumer model CD players use a similar laser system. Reread 5.3 and try again.

4a. No. Although the lacquer coating helps protect the CD, it is far from indestructible—fingerprints, dust, and scratches have damaged CDs. Reread 5.4 and select the other answer.

5a. Correct. While recordable CDs are being developed, they are not available yet, but DATs were developed with recording capability initially.

6a. No. DAWs are quite expensive. Reread 5.12 and try again.

7a. Correct. A DAT cassette is like a small videotape cassette.

8a. Wrong. CDs are more expensive than records. Reread 5.3–5.5 and then try again.

9a. Wrong. No CD player can record yet. Reread 5.5 and try again.

10a. No. Because CDs can not presently record, problems associated with copyright have not really arisen. Reread 5.9 and select the other answer.

11a. You made many mistakes. Reread the entire chapter and try again.

If you answered B:

1b. Correct. This is not digital recording, but rather analog recording.

2b. No. But you're heading in the right direction. Sampling rate is important for exact reproduction of the original sound, but it isn't really the reason why digital recordings can be copied over and over. Reread 5.2 and try again.

3b. Yes. Most consumer model CD players can not stand up to the daily use of the broadcast facility.

4b. Yes. CDs require careful handling even though the lacquer coating helps prevent problems.

5b. No. Both DAT and CD (in fact, all digital equipment) have similar signal-to-noise ratios. Reread 5.6 and try again.

6b. No. DAWs are complicated and take some time to learn to operate. Reread 5.12 and try again.

7b. Wrong. While it is called a cassette tape, it is different from the standard audio cassette. Reread 5.7 and 5.8 and then try again.

8b. Wrong. Both professional-quality CD players and turntables are durable. Reread 5.3–5.5 and then try again.

9b. Right. A multiplay CD player holds many CDs, enabling a station to be automated.

10b. Right. The recording capability and digital quality of DAT causes copyright concerns.

11b. No. You are confusing DAT, DASH, and DAW. Reread sections 5.6–5.13 and then try again.

If you answered C:

2c. Yes. Binary data can be accurately recorded over and over, making digital copies sound exactly like the original.

3c. No. All CD players have similar frequency response and dynamic range characteristics. Reread 5.3 and try again.

5c. No. All digital equipment has virtually no distortion. Reread 5.6 and try again.

6c. Yes. DAWs offer digital editing ability without cutting and splicing the tape.

7c. Wrong. Although there are tiny reels inside the DAT cassette, it is far from being like an open reel audio tape. Reread 5.7 and 5.8 and then try again.

8c. Right. Since there is no physical contact between CD and CD player, the CD doesn't wear out as a record's grooves will.

9c. Wrong. This deals with DASH, not CDs. Reread 5.5 and 5.10 and try again.

11c. You are correct. You have now finished this chapter.

Projects

■ PROJECT 1

Play and record several compact disc selections.

Purpose

To familiarize you with the operation of CD players.

Advice, Cautions, and Background

1. You will be able to do this project only if your facility has at least one CD player.
2. You will need to do this in conjunction with a microphone, audio board, and tape recorder, so you may need help from your instructor to operate the pieces of equipment you have not yet learned.
3. Different brands of CD players have slightly different features, so you will need to learn the particular characteristics of your player.
4. You can play several selections from one CD or use several CDs, whichever you prefer.

How To Do the Project

1. Read the Information section on digital broadcast equipment.
2. Complete the Self-Study Questions on digital broadcast equipment.
3. Make sure your CD is connected so that it can be faded out and will record onto either a reel-to-reel or cassette recorder.
4. Make sure a microphone is available so you can announce the title of the selections you choose.
5. Examine the CD player and practice with it so that you can cue, play, and pause it.
6. When you feel familiar with the player and have decided on three selections to play, start the tape recorder.
7. Complete the project by doing the following:
   a. Announce the name of the first musical selection, bring it in, and then fade it out after about thirty seconds.
   b. Announce the name of the second selection, bring it in and fade it out after about thirty seconds. (If you have two CD players, you can cue the second one while the first is playing. If not, you will need to cue a second selection while you are introducing it. This is not particularly difficult because most CDs enable you to cue easily.)
   c. In the same manner, announce the name of the third selection, bring it in, and then fade it out.
8. Have your instructor listen to your tape so that you receive credit for the project.

■ PROJECT 2

Record several generations of an audio signal using analog and digital recording processes.

Purpose

To enable you to hear the loss of signal quality inherent in the analog recording process, but not in digital.

Advice, Cautions, and Background

1. This project assumes that you have DATs in your production facility.
2. As you make the analog recordings, watch levels and other elements that might introduce a poor quality recording due to operator error.

How To Do the Project

1. Read the Information section on digital broadcast equipment.
2. Complete the Self-Study Questions on digital broadcast equipment.
3. Use a phonograph record as your original sound source, preferably a brand-new record without scratches or excessive wear.
4. Make a dub of the record onto an analog audio tape recorder. This will be the first generation recording. If you have not studied the use of the audio tape recorder, you may need assistance from your instructor or station engineer.
5. Now, using the tape that you just made as the sound source, make another analog tape recording. This will be the second generation recording.
6. Now, using the second generation recording as the sound source, make another dub, or the third generation recording.
7. Listen to and compare the three recordings you just made with the original sound source (phonograph record). You should notice a loss of sound quality and increased noise and distortion among other things.
8. Repeat steps 3 through 6 using your digital audio tape recorders.
9. Listen to and compare the digital recordings with the original sound source.
10. Write a one-page report that summarizes what you feel are the differences between the analog and digital recordings.
11. Turn in your report and both the analog and digital recordings to your instructor for credit for completing this project.

■ PROJECT 3

Write a report about the digital audio workstation.

Purpose

To allow you to investigate an emerging technology in the area of digital electronics.

Advice, Cautions, and Background

1. It is unlikely that any radio facility near you will have a DAW in operation, but if one does, try to use it as an information source.
2. Prepare questions that you want answered before you begin your research.
3. This project requires material from various manufacturers, so give yourself plenty of time to complete the project.

How To Do the Project

1. Read the Information section on digital broadcast equipment, paying particular attention to the parts on the digital audio workstation.
2. Complete the Self-Study Questions on digital broadcast equipment.
3. Develop some questions that you want answered about the digital audio workstation; for example:
   a. What components make up the DAW?
   b. What exactly can a DAW do in the area of radio production?
   c. How much does it cost?
   d. What problems are associated with this technology?
   e. When will DAWs be common in the radio field?
4. Gather information about DAWs through research at your library or by writing directly to some of the manufacturers. (Some equipment manufacturers in this area are listed on page 58.)
5. Organize your material into an informative report on DAWs. It should be several pages long. Write your name and ''Digital Audio Workstation Report'' on a title page.
6. Turn the report in to your instructor for credit for this project.

New England Digital
49 North Main Street
White River Junction, VT 05001

Fairlight Instruments
2945 Westwood Boulevard
Los Angeles, CA 90064

Compusonics
2345 Yale Street
Palo Alto, CA 94306

Waveframe Corporation
4725 Walnut Street
Boulder, CO 80301

CHAPTER SIX

Audio Tape Recorders

Information

6.1 INTRODUCTION

Audio tape recorders enjoy a prominent position in the radio production room because they are involved in all radio production work. There are three kinds of recorders found in the radio production facility: reel-to-reel recorders, cartridge recorders, and cassette recorders. They are all similar in that they store electrical impulses that can be changed back into sound, but their construction and mode of operation differ. Although both the audio cartridge and cassette machines were introduced almost thirty years after the reel-to-reel, they have seen greater technological advancement and more than hold their own with reel machines in modern radio production work.

6.2 REEL-TO-REEL RECORDERS

The early parts of this chapter deal with the reel-to-reel recorder, although many of the general concepts are equally true for the cartridge and cassette recorders as well. Often the term *recorder* is used even though, as we will see, some of the machines can only play back. Developed in the mid-1930s, the reel-to-reel audio tape recorder has been the real workhorse of the production room. Most radio production starts with a vocal track being recorded on reel-to-reel, then edited and mixed with music and sound effects to produce the final product.

6.3 HEAD ARRANGEMENT

Tape recorders are devices that rearrange particles on magnetic tape so that sound impulses can be stored on the tape and played back later. This rearranging of particles is done by **heads.** You'll learn more about audio tape in the next chapter, but for now it is useful to understand that the magnetic layer of tape consists of metallic particles. When a tape is unrecorded, the magnetic particles are not aligned and are on the tape in a random pattern (see Figure 6.1).

Usually, professional-quality recorders have three heads—one to erase, one to record, and one to play. The erase head is always before the record head so that old material can be erased and new material recorded at the same time. It is erased an instant before the new material is recorded on the audio tape. With the play head behind the record head, it is possible to monitor what you've just recorded. When the machine is just in play, the erase and record heads are disengaged. The easiest way to remember the arrangement of heads in an audio tape recorder is to remember "every recorder plays" or "ERP"!

If the recorder appears to have a single head, it may be because the erase head has been combined into the same case with a record/play head. However, some playback-only machines, cartridge players, for instance, truly have just a single play head. Less expensive recorders (and many home recorders) have only two heads—one for erase and another for both play and record. Regardless of the possible head arrangements, ERP is the most common one for audio tape recorders found in the radio production room.

6.4 SEL SYNC

One feature often found on audio tape recorders is **sel sync,** or selective synchronization. Because of the ERP head arrangement, you can not record one track in synchronization with a previously recorded track. If, for example, you record one voice and want to record another voice on the same tape, you run into this problem: as the previously recorded voice is playing, the sound signal is coming from the play head, but the second voice is recording at the record head and because of the distance between these two heads, you hear the previously recorded material a split second before you can record the second voice. To overcome this problem and allow this type of recording, the sel sync feature makes the record head also act as the play head. Now you are hearing the previously recorded material at the same time as you are recording the new material, so there is no time difference between them, and you can easily synchronize the two recordings (see Figure 6.2). This can be an important pro-

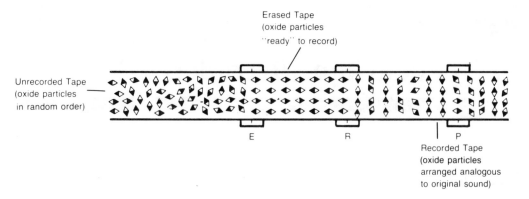

FIGURE 6.1   Head arrangement and tape recording. (Reprinted from Local Radio, by Barry Redfern)

duction tool, especially when you are doing multivoice spots.

6.5 TAPE RECORDER FUNCTIONS—ERASE, RECORD, AND PLAY

The erase, record, and play heads are very similar. The head consists of a laminated metal core that is wound with an extremely fine wire coil at one end. At the other end of the core is a gap between the two magnet poles of the head (see Figure 6.3). Tape recorder heads are merely small electromagnets; an electrical current through the coil creates a magnetic field at the head gap. Since there is a change from one form of energy to another (electrical energy to magnetic energy), we consider tape recorder heads to be **transducers.**

When recording, the audio tape is pulled across the head gap at a right angle. The sound signal is delivered to the record head from the record amplifier in the tape recorder and is transformed from an electrical signal to a magnetic signal. This magnetic signal jumps the head gap and magnetizes the iron oxide layer of the audio tape (remember, the tape was just erased) passing by in a pattern analogous to the original sound signal (refer to Figure 6.1).

During play, the process is reversed. A recorded (magnetized) tape is drawn across the gap of the play head. The magnetic field of the tape (at the gap) passes into the core and then into the coil, creating an electrical current. This current is sent to a play amplifier in the recorder and is an exact reproduction of the original sound signal.

The erase head is on during the recording process. A magnetic field is produced at the erase head gap that is so powerful that it demagnetizes the audio tape as it passes by. During the erase process, the random pattern

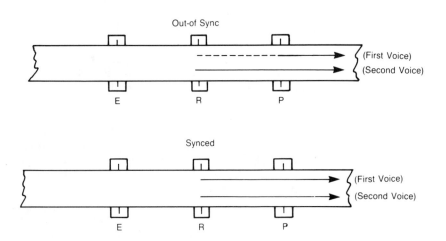

FIGURE 6.2   Sel sync recording.

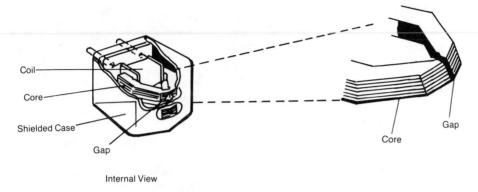

Internal View

FIGURE 6.3   Audio tape recorder head.

of metallic particles on the unrecorded audio tape are arranged in a pattern that makes them ready to be recorded (refer to Figure 6.1).

6.6 BIAS AND EQUALIZATION

To further understand the complexity of the audio tape recorder's operation, you need to become familiar with the concepts of biasing and equalizing. **Bias** is a high-frequency signal (inaudible) that is added to the audio signal during the recording process. The addition of this bias tone improves the frequency response of the recording and provides a distortion-free signal. If the recording sounds too bright and fuzzy, there may be too little bias used; too much bias can result in the loss of the audio recording's high frequencies. Proper bias settings are accomplished by the engineer and are usually set for one particular brand of audio tape. As a radio production person, avoid using a hodgepodge of different audio tapes and stick to the brand that your tape recorders have been set to for best recording results.

Equalization is an adjustment that affects the amount of amplification that is given to the highs and lows of the sound signal. Audio tape reproduces low and high frequencies at differing levels; equalization is used to compensate for this. Generally, the highs are boosted during recording and the low frequencies are increased during playback. The ultimate goal is a flat signal response. Again, equalization adjustments are often handled by the engineer, although some tape machines do have controls that can be adjusted by the radio production person.

6.7 TAPE RECORDER SPEEDS

Most tape recorders found in the production studio can record at different speeds, ranging from 15/16 IPS (inches per second) to 15 IPS. The most common are 3 3/4 IPS, 7

1/2 IPS, and 15 IPS. A tape machine operating at 7 1/2 IPS means 7 1/2 inches of recording tape go past the head each second. The more tape that goes past the head, the better the recording, because greater frequency response can be put on the tape with a better signal-to-noise ratio. Most radio production work is done at 7 1/2 IPS or 15 IPS. You'll find that if you are editing audio tape, the faster the tape recorder speed, the easier it is to edit. (Obviously, the pauses between words, etc., will be longer at the faster speed.) A tape recorder speed of 3 3/4 IPS is usually acceptable for recorded material that is voice only. To get high-quality music recordings, avoid the slower speeds (most recording studios use tape recorders that record at 30 IPS and higher). The advantage of the slower speed is that you can get more material on the tape. Most modern tape recorders can be set to operate at any of the three most common speeds.

6.8 TAPE COUNTERS/TIMERS

Most audio tape recorders have a built-in timer, or tape counter. Modern machines have a digital timer that gives an accurate minutes and seconds count. Some machines have a mechanical counter that counts up from "0000," but the numbers have no relationship to time and are merely a gauge as to where you are on the tape. Most timers and counters also have a "zero set" that allows you to rewind to an exact location. For example, at the beginning of a voice track you are recording, you set the timer (or counter) to "00:00" and enable the zero set button. When you complete the recording, just push the rewind button on the recorder and it will rewind to the point where you set the "00:00." Timers are also useful to get a timing of a longer radio program. You don't have to listen to the program in real time, since most timers work in the fast forward mode of the recorder. An accurate timing of a half-hour radio show may only take a few minutes in fast forward: just reset the timer to "00:00" at the first sound at the beginning of the tape, fast forward to the last sound at the end of the tape, and look at the timer reading!

6.9 TAPE RECORDER TRANSPORT

Figure 6.4 shows the face of a typical reel-to-reel recorder that is found in the production studio. The labeled parts in this diagram are referred to as parts of the **tape transport.** As the name suggests, the tape transport is that part of the recorder that is involved with the actual motion of the audio tape as it passes the tape recorder heads. Starting with the tape reels, since the audio tape threads on a recorder from the left to the right, the left reel is the **supply reel** or the **feed reel** (the reel that has audio tape on it as you begin to use the recorder). The right reel is the **take-up reel,** which starts out empty. Behind each reel (inside the tape recorder) are motors that drive the tape from one reel to the other.

The three standard reel sizes used in radio production facilities—5 inch, 7 inch, and 10 1/2 inch—are shown in Figure 6.5. Although there are reels smaller than 5 inches, these should be avoided for radio production work. The 10 1/2-inch reel shown in the diagram has an NAB hub (center) that requires an adaptor when used with most recorders. It is important that both the feed reel and the take-up reel be the same size for keeping the audio tape at the proper tension. There is often a reel size switch on the recorder that the operator should set properly. The

FIGURE 6.5   Reel-to-reel reel sizes.

small reel setting generally refers to 7-inch or smaller reels and the large reel setting is for the 10 1/2-inch reels.

The audio tape is kept in line with the tape heads by various tape guides and tension arms. The **tape guides** are usually just stationary pins that provide a track or groove the width of the audio tape. The **tension arms** are generally movable. As the audio tape threads through them, they provide some spring or tension against the tape. There is usually a tension arm on each side of the tape heads. One of the tension arms is often an **idler arm.** In addition to providing proper tension on the audio tape, if the tape breaks, this arm drops down into an off position and the reel-to-reel recorder stops running, so the tape doesn't spill off the feed reel and all over the studio floor. The idler arm also keeps the recorder transport in neutral even though it is on, which helps prolong the life span of the machine.

The heart of the tape transport is the capstan and pinch roller. Normally located just to the right of the tape heads, the **capstan** is a metal shaft, and the **pinch roller** is a rubber wheel. The audio tape passes between these two components. When the recorder is running, the pinch roller holds the tape against the revolving capstan. The capstan controls the speed of the tape as it passes the heads.

The final components of the tape transport are the actual controls of the audio tape recorder. Most recorders have an on/off button, rewind and fast forward buttons, a play button, a stop button, a pause button, a cue button, and a record button. Most of these functions are obvious and merely control the direction and speed of the audio

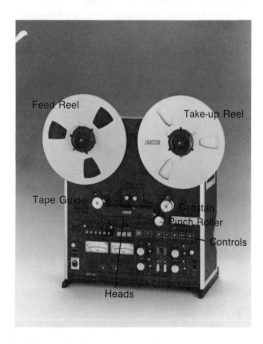

FIGURE 6.4   Audio tape recorder transport. (Courtesy of Otari Corporation)

tape through the transport. Rewind moves the audio tape from the take-up reel to the feed reel, and fast forward moves it in the other direction. The cue button allows the tape to stay in contact with the tape heads during rewind and fast forward, so you can audibly find a certain spot on the tape. Usually, the tape is lifted away from the heads in the rewind or fast forward position to save wear and tear on the heads. Some tape recorders require the operator to depress both play and record to put the machine into the record mode, but some will go into record when just the record button is pressed.

6.10 TAPE RECORDER ELECTRONICS

The other half of the face of the audio tape recorder involves the electronics of the recorder (see Figure 6.6). These controls include a record level and a play level pot, VU meter, and source/tape switch. The **record level pot** (pots if stereo) adjusts the volume or level of the incoming sound signal. If the signal is being fed from an audio console, there is a pot or channel on the console that also controls the incoming volume. The best recording procedure is to make sure the level indicated on the audio board VU is near 100% and then fine-tune the volume with the record level pot on the audio tape recorder. The **play level pot** controls the volume of the sound signal as it is being played from the audio tape. Again, there is also a volume control that adjusts the output volume of the

recorder as it plays through the audio console. These pots should adjust closely together so that you don't have the tape recorder pot turned way down and then have to turn the audio console pot for the tape recorder way up to get a good signal level.

The **VU meter** indicates the signal level just like those on the audio console that were presented in an earlier chapter. What signal you see on the audio tape recorder VU meter is dependent on where the **source/tape switch** is set. The source position is sometimes labeled ''record'' or ''input'' and the tape position is sometimes labeled ''play,'' ''reproduce,'' or ''output.'' In the source position, the VU meter shows the volume of the incoming signal at the record amplifier, usually just before the bias current is added. If this switch is set at the tape position, the VU meter shows the output level of the reproduced signal at the playback head. You can use the source/tape switch to make comparisons between the two levels.

If the tape recorder is properly calibrated, there should be very little level change as you switch between the source and tape positions. Some machines, however, have an output level control that is not calibrated with the input level control, or dirty record or playback heads, so that you should not always expect the two levels to be equal.

Also associated with the electronics of the audio tape recorder are the inputs found on the back of the recorder. Most tape recorders have provisions for plugging other electronic equipment such as mics and phonographs into

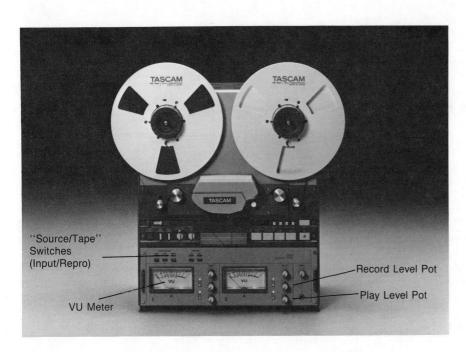

FIGURE 6.6 Audio tape recorder electronics. (Courtesy of Teac Corporation of America)

them. The main concept to understand for this is the concept of **preamplification.** Some electronic devices, such as phonographs and tape recorders, have provisions within them for amplifying their electrical impulses. Others, mainly microphones, do not. If a phonograph is plugged into a tape recorder, it should be plugged into the **line level** input because it has already been preamplified in the phonograph. In this way the tape recorder will not amplify the sound again, causing distortion. A microphone, on the other hand, should be plugged into **mic level** input that allows the tape recorder to amplify the signal.

Most recorders also have a line out connector so the sound from the recorder can be fed to other electronic equipment such as an audio console. Some recorders also have a speaker out position so that the sound can be transferred to speakers located away from the recorder. Normally, in the radio production facility, the audio tape recorders are patched or wired to the other equipment through the audio console and the operator does not have to worry about the various inputs and outputs.

6.11 TRACK CONFIGURATION

Another thing to understand about tape recorders is the recording patterns (tracks) on tape. Various audio tape recorders record differently by using different portions of the tape. Reel-to-reel recorders and cartridge tape recorders use audio tape that is one-quarter inch wide, while most cassette recorders use one-eighth-inch wide tape. There are four different track configurations reel-to-reel recorders use. They differ in the number of signals put on the tape and the placement of the signals. All of the recording patterns have **guard bands**—small portions of blank tape between each track and at the edges to prevent **crosstalk.** Crosstalk occurs when the signal from one track is picked up simultaneously with the signal from an adjacent track.

Some recorders are **full-track,** that is, they essentially use the whole one-quarter-inch space to record one signal. This was the first tape recording method developed and since it is one signal on the whole width of the tape, it is a monophonic recording. Also, full-track recording can occur in only one direction (see Figure 6.7A). In general, the more tape that is used in the recording process, the higher quality the recording will be, so full-track is a high-quality recording method.

There is also **half-track** recording on quarter-inch tape. In this instance, the tape is recorded on twice. The top is recorded on as the tape moves from left to right. Then the tape is flipped over and what was the bottom half becomes the top half, and it is recorded on. The two signals go in opposite directions because the tape has been flipped (see Figure 6.7B). In no instance is the back of the audio tape recorded on. The half-track recording method just described is also a mono recording method.

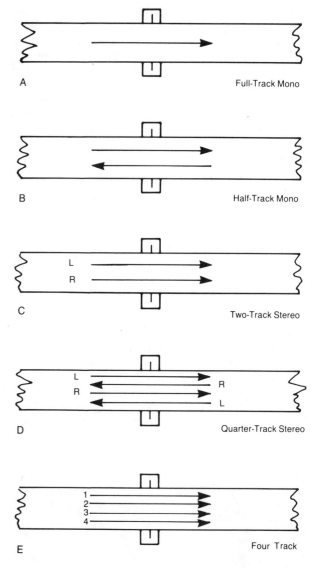

FIGURE 6.7 Reel track configurations.

To understand recording in both directions (as mentioned above), take a piece of paper and place it on a table or desk between your two hands. Imagine your left hand is the feed reel, the paper is the tape recorder heads, and your right hand is the take-up reel. Draw a line that divides the paper in half and draw an arrow going from left to right in the upper half. Now imagine the paper moving from your left hand to your right hand. This would be recording in one direction and when you had completed the tape you would exchange reels. If you turn the paper top-to-bottom you will simulate what happens to the audio tape. The top half is now blank and you can draw another arrow (again going from left to right) to indicate you are recording on the other half of the tape. You'll note the arrows are going in opposite directions and if you turn the tape top-to-bottom again to put it in its original position, the alignment of the arrows is the same as shown in Figure 6.7B.

Most recorders used in radio production today are stereo or multitrack. Although quarter-inch audio tape is still used, stereo requires two tracks for each recording—one for the right channel and one for the left channel. When recording in **two-track stereo** (sometimes called **half-track stereo**), each of the two tracks uses half the tape and both go in the same direction. One track is for the right channel and one track is for the left channel (see Figure 6.7C). Recording can only be done in one direction on this tape because the two tracks use the entire width of the audio tape. This is probably the most common recording method found in the radio production facility.

Many home recorders (and some professional ones) use a **quarter-track stereo** recording method. Tracks one and three (the top one and the next-to-bottom one) are used for the first side going from left to right. Then the tape is flipped and tracks two and four become one and three and are recorded. The two recordings go in opposite directions (see Figure 6.7D). The track widths naturally have to be narrower, since four actual tracks have to fit on the quarter-inch audio tape.

Multitrack recording is becoming more and more common in the radio production facility. For example, a **four-track recorder** uses four separate tracks all going in one direction (see Figure 6.7E). Although a few machines use quarter-inch tape for the four tracks, most multitrack recorders use half-inch-wide audio tape. Multitrack recorders used in radio are normally four or eight track, and the recording studio may employ recorders with sixteen, twenty-four, thirty-two and more tracks. Obviously, at some point in the production process the multitracked signal is mixed down to stereo or mono for broadcast. Four-track recording should not be confused with quarter-track recording. Both use four tracks, but a review of each description will show they are quite different.

An important consideration is compatibility. Since all the tapes we've mentioned so far are quarter-inch, it is possible to play a tape recorded on one machine on a different machine. In other words, a tape recorded on a quarter-track stereo machine can be played on a full-track mono recorder. All the tracks will be heard, however, so there will be recorded material going both frontward and backward, and the resulting sound will be a garble. If the stereo tape were recorded only on one side, then playback on the mono full track would be intelligible, but, of course, it would not be stereo and probably would have some hiss noises from nonrecorded sections. Half-track mono tapes can be played on two-track stereo machines, but will be heard only through the left channel. Many two-track stereo recorders found in the production studio have an extra playback head that is quarter-track stereo. A switch allows the operator to select which one will be active at any particular time. Certainly the best production practice would be not to mix track configurations even though some are compatible.

6.12 CASSETTE TAPE RECORDERS

The **cassette recorder** has found its way into the broadcast facility mainly because of its portability and ease of use, but also because the modern cassette recorder offers recording whose quality often exceeds that of reel-to-reel recorders. Tape machines like the one shown in Figure 6.8 are commonly found in the radio studio. Portable units are also used, mainly in the news area, to record events or conduct interviews. From time to time, however, a cassette recorder is also handy for production work. For example, you might not have a sound effect that you need on record or CD, but you can easily record your own on a portable cassette.

The cassette tape is a small reel-to-reel tape housed in a plastic case (see Figure 6.9). A short **leader tape** is attached at each end, and both ends of the tape are permanently attached to the reels. When recording onto cassettes it's important to remember the leader tape, because if you are at the very beginning of the cassette, the actual recording will not begin for a few seconds until you are past the leader tape. Another feature of the cassette is the knock-out tabs on the back edge of the cassette shell. These two little plastic tabs (one for each side of the cassette) allow the recorder to go into the record mode. If you wish to save an important cassette and be sure no one records over the tape, you can knock out the tab. If, at a later date, you want to record on this cassette, you can put a small piece of cellophane tape over the hole where the tab was and it will work just as if the tab were there. The audio tape in a cassette is about one-eighth-inch wide and often quite thin so that thirty, sixty, and ninety minutes of recording time (both sides) can be fit into the plastic shell.

One of the reasons the cassette tape became popular is that it doesn't have to be threaded on the machine as the reel-to-reel does. Just pop the audio tape cassette in the machine and you're ready to record. As mentioned before, cassette tape is one-eighth-inch wide so it can never be played back on a quarter-inch reel-to-reel recorder. There are two basic cassette tape recording methods. One is **half-track mono,** which is like half-track mono on a quarter-inch tape except it records the bottom of the tape first (see Figure 6.10A). The other recording method of cassettes is **quarter-track stereo.** This is not the same as quarter-inch quarter-track stereo (review Figure 6.10); rather the bottom two tracks are used for one side going in a left-to-right direction. When the tape is turned over, the top two tracks are the bottom two, so they are recorded going in the opposite direction (see Figure 6.10B). Cassettes were designed this way so that mono and stereo cassettes would be compatible.

There is a wide variety of cassette recorders available.

FIGURE 6.8 Cassette recorder. (Courtesy of Teac Corporation of America)

Many are only suitable for home use and not the broadcast studio. Most cassette recorders have a built-in microphone. Avoid using this mic for broadcast work, as it often picks up as much internal noise (tape recorder motor, etc.) as the sound you want. Use a good quality mic like those mentioned earlier in the chapter on microphones. Some other features that should be on a professional-quality cassette machine are a VU meter, three heads (rather than two), standard mic inputs, and durable construction. Review Figure 6.8 for additional items that make a good broadcast quality cassette recorder.

One of the reasons that cassette recorders did not gain complete acceptance in radio production was that their sound quality was poor. Cassettes operate at 1 7/8 IPS and use one-eighth-inch wide tape—a combination that kept the sound quality quite poor when cassettes first came on the scene. Although broadcast-quality cassette recorders today boast excellent frequency response and sound characteristics and enjoy widespread use in radio, broadcasters still have not embraced them as they have reel-to-reels and cart machines. Perhaps another reason is the fact that you can not splice cassettes. Cassette recordings are commonly dubbed to reel-to-reel first and then edited for radio production purposes.

6.13 CARTRIDGE TAPE RECORDERS

Another type of tape recorder is the **cartridge recorder** (see Figure 6.11). The cart machine is favored in broadcast

FIGURE 6.9 Audio cassette.

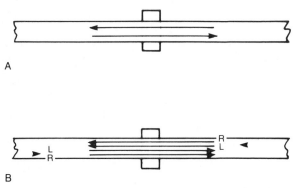

FIGURE 6.10 Cassette track configurations. (A) Mono; (B) stereo.

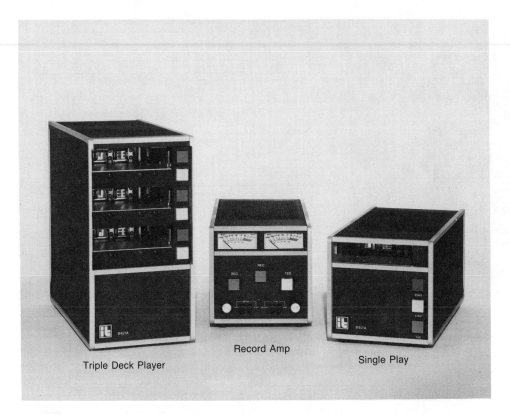

Triple Deck Player

Record Amp

Single Play

FIGURE 6.11   Cartridge recorder and players. (Courtesy of ITC)

use because it cues up automatically. Most commercials and public service announcements that you hear on the radio are being played from tape cartridge recorders. For some radio stations, even the music they play has been transferred from record to cart.

A tape cartridge recorder is similar to a cassette recorder in that you simply slip the audio tape cartridge into a machine with no threading necessary. But the cartridge is constructed differently in that it is a plastic container with an endless loop of tape. The tape is wound onto the center spool with the end next to the spool sticking up so that when the tape is cut from the master reel it can be spliced to that end, thus making a continuous loop (see Figure 6.12). The tape pulls from the inside and winds on the outside of the spool. There are tape guides that the tape goes past and pressure pads that control tension and alignment. The recording tape used in a cartridge machine is one-quarter-inch wide, but it is a special type that has a lubricant on both sides rather than just the oxide side. The tape is wound on the spool so that the oxide side is facing out away from the spool. To see if the tape on the cartridge is good, simply look at the oxide side of the tape through the holes on the front side of the cartridge. If the tape is shiny, the tape is worn (little oxide on it), but if the tape is dull, it probably has quite a bit of

oxide left. Often, before the tape gives out, the **pressure pads** will. To check the pressure pads on a tape cartridge, just press in on them (go under the tape so that oil from your fingertips does not get on the tape); if they tend to stay down and don't spring back, the tape cartridge is not going to play the tape properly, as the pressure pads keep the tape pressed against the tape heads.

Cartridge tape is driven by a **pinch roller** that swings up from the cart recorder through a drive wheel hole in the plastic cartridge. This happens when the cart is inserted into the machine. The pinch roller presses the tape between itself and the **capstan,** which is turning. The tape is pulled through in a clockwise motion (the tape travels left to right across the heads). Cart machines operate at 7 1/2 IPS.

The track configuration of the cartridge recorder is similar to some that you are now familiar with; when cartridge tape is recorded, however, a cart tape head can put a **cue tone** on the tape that can not be heard. This primary cue tone is just in front of the recorded information so that when the machine is running (in play), the special tone signals the machine to stop before it repeats itself. This also allows for putting several different spots on one cartridge and playing one without fear of playing another before stopping the machine. This self-cueing feature is

Pressure Pads

FIGURE 6.12 Audio cartridge. (Courtesy of Fidelipac Corporation)

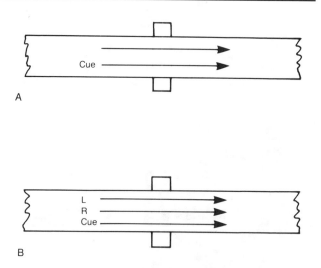

A

Cue

B

L
R
Cue

FIGURE 6.13 Cartridge track configurations. (A) Mono; (B) stereo.

extremely important for radio broadcasting and radio production work. Most cart machines can also put secondary and tertiary cue tones on the cartridge that can be used to indicate the end of a spot, to start another cart machine, and to activate other programming features often found in automated situations.

A mono tape cartridge recorder has two tracks—one for the recorded material and one for the cue tones (see Figure 6.13A). A stereo tape cartridge has three tracks—one for the left and right channel and one for the cue tones (see Figure 6.13B). Mono and stereo tape cartridges are not compatible. Although you may be able to play a cartridge recorded in stereo on a mono machine or vice versa, it is likely that the tracks will be misaligned and you will not hear all of the audio signal, or there will be problems in picking up the cue tone. Good production practice dictates that mono and stereo cartridges are clearly labeled and not mixed between various tape decks.

Tape carts only record in one direction. Tape cartridge machines can be either record/play or play only. The play-only machines still have two heads in them, but one is a dummy that merely keeps the tape tension correct as the audio tape passes the heads.

It is also very important to notice that cartridge tape recorders do not have erase heads in them. Tape carts must be erased using a bulk eraser or **degausser.** This is merely a strong electromagnet that radiates a magnetic field that erases any audio tape brought near it when it is

turned on. More will be said about the degausser in chapter 9.

6.14 DAT

As was mentioned in an earlier chapter, the newest entry into the audio tape recorder field is the **digital audio tape** recorder, or DAT. Many radio stations are now converting to DAT recorders and they may someday replace reel-to-reel, cartridge, and cassette machines. You might want to review the previous material on DAT again to put this technology in perspective with the older tape recorder technology.

6.15 TAPE RECORDER PROBLEMS

Most problems of audio tape recorders are related to the heads themselves. One common problem is simply dirty heads. Tape heads can become dirty just from day-to-day use and, as you'll see in the next chapter, editing audio tape can put unwanted grease pencil marks on the heads. It's good production practice to clean the tape heads before you begin any production work. The production studio usually has a supply of cotton swabs and head cleaner or denatured alcohol to gently clean any residue off the tape recorder heads. If in doubt about what you're doing, ask for help.

A more difficult problem concerning tape heads is **alignment.** Basically, alignment is the relationship between the tape as it passes the head and the head itself. There are five adjustments that can go awry and cause a poor alignment between the tape and head and thus poor frequency response and possible incompatibility with tapes recorded on other machines (see Figure 6.14).

AZIMUTH
IS THE HEAD LEANING TO ONE SIDE OR THE OTHER?

HEIGHT
IS THE HEAD TOO HIGH OR TOO LOW?

PENETRATION
IS THE HEAD MOVED TOO FAR FORWARD OR BACK?

ROTATION
IS THE HEAD POINTED STRAIGHT AHEAD?

ZENITH
IS THE HEAD TILTED FORWARD OR BACK?

FIGURE 6.14 Head alignment problems. (Courtesy of Lauderdale Electronics)

Azimuth refers to the head leaning to one side or the other. **Height** refers to the head being too high or too low. **Penetration** (sometimes called **wrap** or **contact**) refers to the head being too far forward or backward. **Tangency** (also called **rotation**) refers to the head being pointed straight ahead, and **zenith** (or **tilt**) refers to the head being tilted forward or backward. Alignment problems are definitely best left for the engineer, but it's not a bad idea to be familiar with the basic kinds.

Both wow and flutter are tape recorder problems that are related to changes in the speed of the tape as it passes through the tape transport. **Wow** refers to slow variations in tape speed and **flutter** refers to rapid variations. Both problems result in off-pitch sounds that are reflected in their names.

A final tape recorder problem is a buildup of magnetism on the tape recorder heads. After extended use, the tape heads will tend to become magnetized permanently. This could result in the heads actually erasing part of the signal that you don't want erased. Usually it will affect the high-frequency signals first. To prevent this, a **demagnetizer** is used to get rid of any built-up magnetism. Usually this is part of the general maintenance done by the engineer, but in some production facilities this type of maintenance along with cleaning of the heads is left to the operators. A demagnetizer is brought near to (but not in contact with) the heads. Since it operates like a bulk eraser, you must be sure to turn it on and off away from the heads (refer to chapter 9).

6.16 CONCLUSIONS

The amount of information contained in this chapter should be an indication to you of the importance of the material covered. You will only become a good production person through practice and use of the equipment described, but if you've absorbed the basic information in this chapter, you have a good solid background for working with the audio tape recorders you'll find in any production facility.

Self-Study

■ QUESTIONS

1. Which of the following could be a proper head arrangement for an audio tape recorder, assuming the tape goes from left to right?

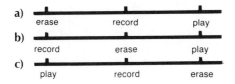

a) erase   record   play

b) record   erase   play

c) play   record   erase

2. If you put a 5-inch reel of tape on a recorder at 7 1/2 IPS, another 5-inch reel on a recorder at 15 IPS, and a third 5-inch reel on a recorder at 3 3/4 IPS and start all recorders at once, which one will run out of tape first?
   a) the reel at 3 3/4 IPS
   b) the reel at 7 1/2 IPS
   c) the reel at 15 IPS

3. If you have finished a recording and wish to get back to the beginning of it, you push _____.
   a) rewind
   b) fast forward
   c) zero set

4. A sel sync feature in an audio tape recorder _____.
   a) makes the record head act as a play head
   b) places the erase head after the play head
   c) converts a two-head recorder to a three-head recorder

5. If sound is to go from a tape recorder to an audio console, a connection should be made in the tape recorder at _____.
   a) line in
   b) line out
   c) speaker out

6. Of the tapes in the diagram below, tape B would probably be used on a _____.
   a) cassette recorder
   b) reel-to-reel recorder
   c) cartridge recorder

7. The erase head _____.
   a) rearranges the iron particles so they are in a random pattern
   b) is on during the recording process
   c) closes the gap on the metal core so that the signal jumps to magnetic energy

8. Which of the following represents half-track mono recording?

9. Which of the following is an adjustment that changes the amount of amplification given to highs and lows of the sound signal?
   a) digital
   b) bias
   c) equalization

10. Which of the following represents reel-to-reel quarter-track stereo recording?

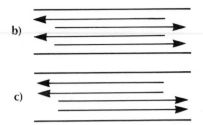

b)

c)

11. Referring to Figure 6.4, which of the following controls the speed of the tape as it passes the head?
    a) feed reel
    b) tape guide
    c) capstan

12. What would happen if a two-track stereo tape were played back on a half-track mono recorder?
    a) both stereo tracks would be heard, but one would be going backwards
    b) the tape would be intelligible, but the lower tracks' material would be missing
    c) four sounds would be heard—two going forward and two going backward

13. If the source/tape switch on a tape recorder is in the source position, the VU meter shows _____.
    a) the incoming signal that is being recorded
    b) the outgoing signal that has been recorded
    c) the signal that was erased

14. Which of the following represents half-track mono cassette recording?

    a)

    b)

    c)

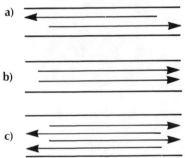

15. What would happen if a stereo cassette recorded on both sides were played on a mono cassette recorder?
    a) two sounds would be heard, one going forward and one going backward
    b) the stereo tape would be intelligible but would not be stereo
    c) there would be a garbled sound

16. One difference between a cassette recorder and a cartridge recorder is _____.
    a) a cartridge recorder needs to be threaded
    b) only cassette recorders are used in radio stations
    c) the cartridge tape has no actual beginning or end

17. Worn cartridge tape will look _____.
    a) shiny
    b) dull
    c) oily

18. Which type of tape must be erased with a degausser?
    a) reel-to-reel
    b) cassette
    c) cartridge

19. If a tape has a cue tone on it, it will _____.

    a) start automatically

    b) stop automatically

    c) repeat itself

20. As a review of audio tape recorders, match the drawings below (1, 2, 3 . . .) to the descriptions (x, e, q . . .) and then select the correct set of answers from the sequences shown in a, b, or c below.

    x. a tape that has a recording on it

    e. tape that is erased and ready to play

    q. quarter-track stereo reel-to-reel

    f. full-track mono reel-to-reel

    s. cassette stereo configuration

    t. cartridge stereo configuration

    h. a tape recorder head

    r. a reel for a reel-to-reel recorder

    c. a cassette

    a. a cartridge

    a) 1.a 2.h 3.e 4.q 5.x 6.c 7.f 8.s 9.r 10.t

    b) 1.c 2.h 3.e 4.f 5.x 6.a 7.q 8.t 9.r 10.s

    c) 1.c 2.h 3.x 4.f 5.e 6.a 7.q 8.t 9.r 10.s

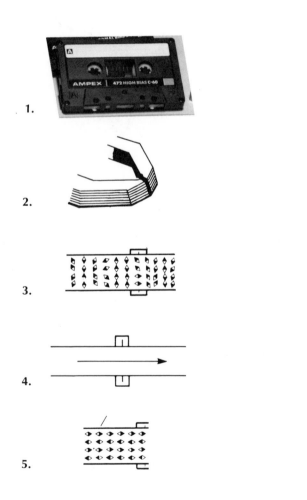

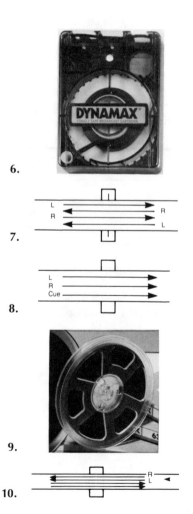

■ ANSWERS

If you answered A:

1a. Right. And this is the most common head arrangement.
2a. No. Reread 6.7 and try again.
3a. Right. You would push rewind.
4a. Right. This feature allows you to hear previously recorded material that matches with what you are recording.
5a. No. You want an output, not an input. Reread 6.10 and try again.
6a. Yes, it is one-eighth-inch wide, so it would be used on a cassette.
7a. No, it rearranges them into an orderly pattern. Reread 6.5 and try again.
8a. No. The signals must go in opposite directions. Reread 6.11 and try again.
9a. No. This is a recording technique using binary technology. Reread 6.6 and 6.14 and try again.
10a. Right. You figured the tracks correctly.
11a. Wrong. This is the reel that the tape is placed on, but it has nothing to do with speed. Reread 6.9 and try again.
12a. No. At first glance, this looks logical, but it's not. A half-track mono only plays back half a tape at a time. If it played back the full track, it would play back both sounds of its own tapes. All that is played back is the top half of the tape. Now you should be able to try again and answer correctly.
13a. Correct. "Source" shows the source.
14a. Correct. This is a similar configuration to quarter-inch half-track mono.
15a. No. Review Figure 6.10. Reread 6.12 and try again.
16a. No. Neither need to be threaded. Reread 6.12 and 6.13 and try again.
17a. Right. A worn cartridge tape looks shiny.
18a. No, a reel-to-reel recorder has an erase head that can erase right before new material is recorded. Reread 6.13 and try again.
19a. No. It must be started by hand. Reread 6.13 and try again.
20a. You made a lot of mistakes. Reread the whole chapter and redo all the Self-Study Questions.

If you answered B:

1b. No. Erase must be before record. Reread 6.3 and try again.
2b. No. Reread 6.7 and try again.
3b. No. Fast forward will get you to the wrong end of the tape. Reread 6.9 and try again.
4b. No. You can't move the heads and you wouldn't want that configuration. Reread 6.3 and 6.4 and try again.
5b. Right. Line out would go to the audio console.
6b. No. Reread 6.11 and try again.
7b. Right. It is on so that the tape can be erased before it is recorded on again.
8b. No. This is, if anything, backwards full-track. Reread 6.11 and try again.
9b. No, bias improves frequency response and provides a distortion-free signal. Reread 6.6 and try again.
10b. No. Reread 6.11 and try again. Pay particular attention to which tracks are used in which direction.
11b. No, this guides the tape through the recorder mechanism but not at any particular speed. Reread 6.9 and try again.
12b. Your answer is correct, for half-track mono only plays back the top half of the tape.
13b. No, the tape position would do that. Reread 6.10 and try again.
14b. No. This is like two-track stereo on quarter-inch tape. Reread 6.12 and try again.
15b. Right. Cassette mono tape and stereo tape each can be played on the other recorder and be understood.
16b. No. In fact, cart machines are more common in radio stations than cassettes. Reread 6.13 and try again.
17b. No. Reread 6.13 and try again.
18b. No, a cassette recorder has an erase head that can erase right before new material is recorded. Reread 6.13 and try again.
19b. Right. Because of the cue tone, it will stop automatically before whatever is next can play.
20b. The only mistake you made dealt with erased and recorded tape. Reread 6.3 and try again.

If you answered C:

1c. No. Erase must be before record. Reread 6.3 and try again.

2c. That's right. It goes through the recorder the fastest and so would finish first.

3c. You're partly correct, but merely pushing the zero set would not move the tape in any direction. Depressing zero set before you began recording would allow you to get back to the beginning by pressing rewind after you'd finished. Reread 6.8 and 6.9 and try again.

4c. Wrong. Adding a head is a much more complex process. Reread 6.3 and 6.4 and try again.

5c. No. This could go to an external speaker, but not an audio console. Reread 6.10 and try again.

6c. No. Reread 6.11 and try again.

7c. Wrong. This answer really doesn't make sense. You are probably confused about many of the terms in this chapter, so reread the entire chapter and try again.

8c. Good. Your answer is correct.

9c. You are correct.

10c. No. Reread 6.11 and try again. Pay particular attention to which tracks are used in which direction.

11c. Right. This, in conjunction with the pinch roller, pulls the tape through at a uniform speed.

12c. No. There are only two tracks on two-track stereo, so it couldn't play back four. Review Figure 6.7 and try again.

13c. No, nothing shows the signal erased. Reread 6.10 very carefully and try again.

14c. No. You are way off; this has four tracks. Reread 6.12 and try again.

15c. No. Review Figure 6.10. Reread 6.12 and try again.

16c. Right. The cartridge tape is a continuous loop.

17c. No. The tape has a lubricant, but it doesn't look oily. Reread 6.13 and try again.

18c. Right. A cartridge machine has no erase head.

19c. No. The purpose of the cue tone is to prevent the tape from repeating itself. Reread 6.13 and try again.

20c. Very good. You got them all right. This chapter covered a great deal of material, so you should be proud you mastered it.

Projects

■ PROJECT 1

Label diagrams of reel-to-reel, cassette, and cartridge tape recorders.

Purpose

To familiarize you with the various functions of your production room tape recorders.

Advice, Cautions, and Background

1. No two brands of recorders are exactly alike, so you may find buttons or switches not specifically discussed in this chapter. Ask your instructor for help if you can not decide how to label something.
2. If there are repetitive switches and knobs, you do not need to label all of them, but make sure that you understand and have indicated all the main functions.
3. Use a separate piece of paper for each recorder so that you have plenty of room to write.
4. You will be judged on completeness and accuracy of your drawings. You will not be graded on artistic ability, but be as clear as possible.

How To Do the Project

1. Read the Information section on audio tape recorders.
2. Complete the Self-Study Questions on audio tape recorders.
3. Sketch a reel-to-reel recorder, a cassette recorder, and a cartridge recorder as found in your production room. If necessary draw several sides of the recorders so that you have included all the important function switches.
4. Label the basic parts—heads, speed controls, counters, reels, tape guides, capstan, pinch roller, idler arm, play, record, fast forward, pause, VU meters, pots, source/tape switches, etc.
5. Make sure that you know what each of these does.
6. If possible, give the brand name and model number of each tape recorder.
7. Give your completed drawings to the instructor for credit for this project.

■ PROJECT 2

Dub taped material between cassette and reel-to-reel recorders.

Purpose

To make sure you are able to do even, clear dubbing, which is one of the most common exercises done in production work.

Advice, Cautions, and Background

1. The material you are to dub was not recorded properly in that it is not all at the same level. (A tape will be provided by your instructor.) You are to make it as much at the same level as possible. On professional equipment, there are sophisticated meters to help you. On less expensive equipment, you will have to do this by practicing a few times and getting the feel of it.
2. If you are unsure of what you are doing, get help. Don't ruin the equipment.

How To Do the Project

1. Read the Information section on audio tape recorders.
2. Complete the Self-Study Questions on audio tape recorders.
3. Make sure you know how to operate your cassette recorder. If in doubt, ask the instructor.
4. In the same way, make sure you know how to operate the reel-to-reel recorder.
5. Thread the tape to be dubbed on the reel-to-reel recorder.
6. Listen to the material, noting where the level changes are, and decide on a strategy for dubbing it so that it is all at one level.
7. Rewind the tape and connect the cable from the proper audio output on the reel-to-reel to the proper audio input on the cassette recorder. If your equipment is already connected through an audio console, just be sure the switches and knobs are set properly so that you can record from reel-to-reel to cassette.
8. Place a tape in the cassette recorder.
9. Put the reel-to-reel recorder in play and listen to the recording. At the same time, adjust the volume on one of the recorders so the level will be even.
10. Rewind the reel-to-reel recorder and set the cassette recorder so it will record and the reel-to-reel recorder so it will play. The sound will then go from the reel-to-reel to the cassette recorder.
11. Practice your dub several times, adjusting levels until you get the feel of how much you need to vary the volume. Then make the dub.
12. Now you are ready to make your dub from cassette back to the reel-to-reel recorder. Place a different tape on the reel-to-reel recorder.
13. If necessary, change cables so that one goes from the proper audio output on the cassette to the proper audio input on the reel-to-reel. (Again, you may just have to set the proper switches and knobs on your audio console.)
14. Decide on a volume for both recorders and put the cassette recorder in play and the reel-to-reel recorder in record.

15. Make your dub. This time you shouldn't have to adjust levels. Listen to the dub to make sure it recorded properly.
16. Play your second dub for the instructor to get credit for this project.

■ PROJECT 3

Make two erasures on a cassette recorder.

Purpose

To enable you to become more proficient with the operation of audio tape recorders.

Advice, Cautions, and Background

1. Don't expect this to work exactly right the first time. Your erase head is ahead of the play head, so unless you have sel sync you won't be erasing exactly what you hear. Each tape recorder is a little different, so you are going to have to get the feel of the ones in your production studio. It may not come out cleanly.
2. Since you will have to experiment until you do it correctly, you might want to do this experimenting several minutes into the tape so you don't have to worry about erasing mistakes.
3. This is the nearest thing you can do to an edit on a cassette. It is difficult to cut the tape physically because of its inaccessibility. If you needed to really edit a cassette, you would have to dub from one tape to another, leaving out words you don't want. Or you could dub to a reel-to-reel tape and edit it. (We'll explore audio tape editing in the next chapter.)

How To Do the Project

1. Read the Information section on audio tape recorders.
2. Complete the Self-Study Questions on audio tape recorders.
3. Make sure you know how to operate your cassette recorder. If in doubt, ask the instructor.
4. Record the following sentences on your recorder: ''This is one of the newest hits on the market today,'' and, ''We've run out of time so that's all for today.'' Be sure to leave a little blank space between them.
5. Make a dub of your original cassette and do the rest of the project with this dub. If you make a drastic mistake, you can always make a new dub from your original tape and start over.
6. Erase ''on the market today'' from the first sentence so that all that is left on the tape is ''This is one of the newest hits.'' The best way to erase on most recorders is to put the machine in record without having a mic plugged in or any other type of input coming into the recorder.
7. Erase ''so that's all for today'' from the other sentence so that all that is left on the tape is ''We've run out of time.''
8. Let the instructor hear your edits so that you receive credit for this project.

Audio Tape Editing

Information

7.1 INTRODUCTION

As a radio production person, one of the more important skills you need to learn is audio tape editing. From creating a music bed, to adding sound effects, to editing out vocal "fluffs" or mistakes, tape editing is a day-to-day part of radio production work. Before looking at the techniques of audio tape editing, let's examine the material you'll be working with—the audio tape itself.

7.2 PHYSICAL MAKEUP OF AUDIO TAPE

Audio tape for a radio production person is like paper to a writer. In other words, it's the storage medium on which various ideas are put down and then manipulated. Both the writer and radio person can erase unwanted segments or edit long segments into shorter workable concepts, but (for the radio person) it all starts with getting something onto tape first.

Although we see audio tape as merely a thin ribbon of tape, its physical makeup actually consists of three layers: a **plastic base** sandwiched between a **backing layer** and a **magnetic layer** (see Figure 7.1). The back coating provides traction as the audio tape moves through a tape recorder transport, and it also provides protection from tape breakage and print-through.

Print-through can occur when audio tape is stored on a reel for long periods of time. Print-through is defined as an effect of the magnetic signal on one layer of tape bleeding over to the magnetic signal on an adjacent layer of tape, either above it or below it on the reel of tape. Think of the sandwich concept again and visualize a jelly sandwich stacked on top of a peanut butter sandwich. If the jelly soaks through the bottom piece of bread and onto the top piece of bread on the peanut butter sandwich, print-through has occurred.

The plastic base (the middle of our sandwich) in modern audio tape is polyester. This produces a strong tape that rarely breaks; it will, however, stretch if pulled too hard. Early audio tape used an acetate backing that broke cleanly, but it was susceptible to temperature and humid-

ity effects. Often, polyester audio tape is **tensilized,** or prestretched, to prevent stretching problems.

The top of the audio tape sandwich is an iron oxide coating. This coating is composed of tiny slivers of magnetic oxides that are capable of storing an electromagnetic signal that is analogous to the original sound made during the recording process. Instead of an iron oxide coating, modern audio tape offers different magnetic coatings, such as chromium dioxide, for better recording characteristics.

7.3 PHYSICAL DIMENSIONS OF AUDIO TAPE

Audio tape is only about one-thousandth of an inch thick. Audio tape thickness is measured in mils, or thousandths of an inch. Most tape used in radio production work is either 1 mil or 1 1/2 mil; the latter is preferred by broadcasters. There are thinner audio tapes available. The advantage of this thinner tape is that you can get more tape on a reel, which gives you more playing time. But thin tape also stretches more easily, is more susceptible to print-through, and is very difficult to handle in splicing.

The other physical dimension of audio tape that concerns production people is its width. The standard width for reel-to-reel audio tape is one-quarter inch. Cassette tape is usually considered to be one-eighth-inch wide (actually .15 inch), and some multitrack recorders found in the radio production studio use half-inch tape. Most wider audio tape (one and two inch) is only found in the recording studio.

7.4 AUDIO TAPE DEFECTS

Although audio tape has proven to be an excellent working medium for radio production, it is not perfect. Perhaps the biggest problem with audio tape is signal loss due to **drop-out.** Drop-out is a defect in the oxide coating that prevents the signal at that point from being recorded at the same level or at all. Drop-out is a problem that occurs in the manufacturing process of audio tape, but it can

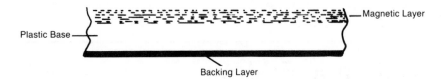

FIGURE 7.1 Cross section of audio tape.

also be caused by flaking of the oxide coating due to heavy use or abuse of the tape.

Other tape defects or problems that you are likely to encounter during production work include adhesion, scattered wind, curling, and cupping. **Adhesion** occurs when tape has been stored on reels for some time and one layer sticks to another as it is unreeled. Tape stored in humid conditions is more likely to experience adhesion problems. Occasionally tape will wind unevenly onto a reel, leaving some edges of the tape exposed above the rest of the tape on the reel. This is known as a **scattered wind,** and you must be careful not to damage the exposed tape strands. Both **curling** (tape twisting front to back)

and **cupping** (tape edges turning up) are problems due to a poor binding between the plastic base and the oxide coating. See Figure 7.2 for examples of these common tape defects. Almost every tape problem can be avoided by using high-quality tape that is 1.5 mil thick for all your radio production work.

7.5 REASONS FOR EDITING

Why edit audio tape? The answers are reasonably obvious. For example, rarely will you produce the vocal track for a commercial exactly the way you want it on the first

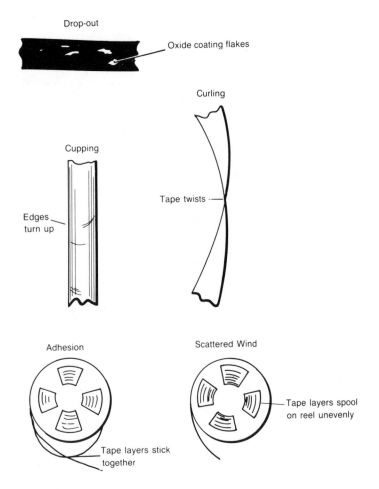

FIGURE 7.2 Audio tape problems.

try. Editing gives you the ability to eliminate mistakes. You can edit out unwanted fluffs and keep just the exact words you want. Other production work may require you to edit out excessive pauses or ''ahs'' from an interview or language not allowed by the FCC from a piece of news tape.

In addition to eliminating mistakes, editing allows you to decrease the length of production work. Radio requires exact time for commercials, news stories, etc., and editing can keep your work to the exact lengths required. Audio tape editing also allows you to record out of sequence. You might be putting together a commercial that uses the testimonial of several customers, and the one that you want to use first in your commercial may not have been recorded first. Editing allows you to easily rearrange the order or use just a portion of what you actually taped.

7.6 TYPES OF EDITING

There are two terms associated with audio tape editing: splicing and dubbing. **Splicing** normally refers to physically cutting the audio tape, taking a portion out, and splicing the remaining pieces back together. **Dubbing** is often considered electronic editing, by which portions of one tape are copied onto another tape. Although splicing has been the standard way to edit audio tape, digital technology promises to make electronic editing of audio tape as common in the future as video tape editing is today.

7.7 TOOLS OF THE TRADE

Before beginning to learn the technique of audio tape editing, let's assemble the necessary tools and supplies that we are going to need. The basic tools of the trade of audio tape editing are a grease pencil, a splicing block (see Figure 7.3), a razor blade, and splicing tape.

Editing requires physically marking on the tape the points where you are going to cut the tape. This is accomplished with a white or yellow **grease pencil** or **china marker.** Some tape recorders found in the production studio have a built-in marker and, in a pinch, you can carefully use a soft lead pencil, but most often you'll use a grease pencil. The side of the audio tape that is marked is the back or unrecorded side. When marking, make sure none of the grease pencil gets on the heads or on the front (recorded) side of the tape. The crayonlike substance in a

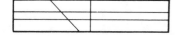

FIGURE 7.3 Splicing block. (Courtesy of Xedit Corporation)

grease pencil can clog the head, so it should not come in contact with it.

A **splicing block** is a small metal or plastic block with a channel to hold the audio tape and two grooves to guide the razor blade when cutting the tape. The channel has tiny lips at its edges so that the audio tape snaps down into it. The tape can easily be slid in the channel by the operator, but it won't move on its own. The cutting grooves are at forty-five degrees and ninety degrees to the audio tape. For almost all production work, you'll use the diagonal cut. Although broadcast supply companies offer industrial-grade razor blades, almost any standard *single-edged* razor blade will work for cutting audio tape. Be careful! Razor blades are sharp and will cut your fingers as easily as they cut audio tape.

Splicing tape is commercially available and is specially designed so that its adhesive material does not soak through the audio tape and gum up the heads of the tape recorder. Never use cellophane tape or other office tape to do editing work. Splicing tape is slightly narrower than audio tape (7/32 inch versus 1/4 inch), so that any excess adhesive material will not exceed the edge of the audio tape. In addition to rolls of splicing tape, you can get splicing tabs that are precut pieces of splicing tape on applicator strips designed to make the splicing process easier.

There are audio tape splicers that combine a splicing block, razor blade, and splicing tape dispenser into one unit. Not only do they allow you to perform normal splicing techniques, but they also allow you to slightly trim the edges of the spliced portion of the audio tape. While this insures smooth, clean edits, it also is possible to lose the edge tracks on the tape or cause misalignment when the tape passes the heads. For whatever reason, these splicers have not found universal acceptance in the radio production studio, so you may or may not run across them in your production work.

7.8 MARKING EDIT POINTS

Audio tape editing is really a two-step process: marking the edit points and then splicing. Since audio tape passes through the recorder from left to right, sounds are recorded on the tape in a like manner. For example, the phrase ''editing is really a two-step process'' would be recorded on audio tape in this manner: ''ssecorp pets-owt a yllaer si gnitide.'' The letters would appear on the tape just as they do on this page, looking at them left to right, but the rightmost word (''editing'') was recorded first. If we wanted to edit out the word ''really'' in this phrase, we would make two edit points, one on each side of the word. In tape editing, the edit point is always made in front of the word (or sound) that you wish to edit out on the one side and in front of the word (or sound) that you are leaving in on the other side. Looking at our example again, you would mark just in front of the ''r'' in ''really'' and just in front of the "a." It's important that you always mark in front of words to maintain the proper phrasing of the speech. If you had marked just before the "r" in "really" and just after the "y" to edit out the word, you would have lengthened the pause between "is" and "a" on your edited tape. Often this will be unnatural sounding and noticeable to the listener.

You already know (from the previous chapter) that the heads in an audio tape recorder and their functions are signified by "ERP" or "erase-record-play." For marking purposes, you are only concerned with the playback head because this is where you will make your mark. Look at the heads on the recorder that you will be doing your editing on (see Figure 7.4). Find the playback head and find the dead center of that head. Remember that audio tape will be covering the actual head gap so look for some kind of reference above and below this portion of the head that will allow you to consistently find this same spot. Now take "AIM." Every time you make an edit mark, make it slightly *to the right* of dead center. (Marking to the right compensates for the split second it takes to actually press the stop button when listening to the audio tape to find where to make an edit.) What you are doing is establishing an "*actual indicator mark*"! Your AIM will be exactly the same time after time and that means your edits will be the same time after time. Your goal should be to make the same edit over and over and have each one sound the same. That's uniformity in editing and that's a skill that you want. You may want to read over this section again. Make sure you understand it, because if you mismark an edit, even if your splice is perfect, it won't sound right.

7.9 STEPS IN SPLICING TECHNIQUE

If you've marked the audio tape at two points, it's time to perform the actual splice. Normal splicing technique follows these steps:

A. *Position the tape at the first edit mark in the splicing block.* (See Figure 7.5A.) Remember, the unrecorded side of the tape should be facing up in the splicing block and

the edit mark should be exactly at the forty-five-degree cutting groove. The diagonal groove is used for splicing for two reasons. One, it provides more surface for contact with the splicing tape at the point of the edit and thus a stronger bond or splice is made. More important, the diagonal cut provides a smoother sound transition. For example, if you are splicing together two pieces of music, rather than an abrupt change from one piece to another at the edit (such as a ninety-degree splice would give), you have a short blend of the music pieces at the edit. Just cut two pieces of tape—one at forty-five degrees and one at ninety degrees—and set them side by side, and you will see why the diagonal cut works best for splicing.

B. *Cut the tape at your first mark.* (See Figure 7.5B.) It is not necessary to saw away with the razor blade or apply excessive downward pressure. A simple slicing motion with the blade through the groove should cleanly cut the tape. Pressing down too hard on the blade will merely make the blade dull faster. If the tape does not seem to want to cut, the razor blade is dull and you should get a new one. You can tell that a razor blade is getting dull when it does not slice cleanly through the audio tape. A ragged cut makes it difficult to align the tape for a good splice. Frequently changing razor blades will also prevent them from becoming magnetized. Because the metal blade cuts through the magnetic layer of the audio tape, over a period of time it will become magnetized, and continued use may put a click on the audio tape or degrade the recorded signal at the point of the edit. Some production people demagnetize the razor blade on the bulk eraser prior to production work, but it's not necessary if you change blades on a regular basis.

C. *Repeat steps A and B at the second edit mark.* (See Figure 7.5C.) Remove the unwanted piece of audio tape, but don't discard it yet. It's good production practice to hang on to cut-out tape until after you're sure the splice has been accomplished as you want it. If you've erred in your AIM, it is possible (although difficult) to splice back in the cut-out piece of tape and try the splice again.

D. *Butt the remaining tape ends together.* (See Figure 7.5D.) Move both pieces of the tape slightly left or right so

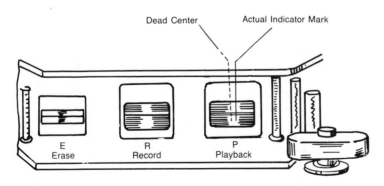

FIGURE 7.4 Tape recorder head assembly.

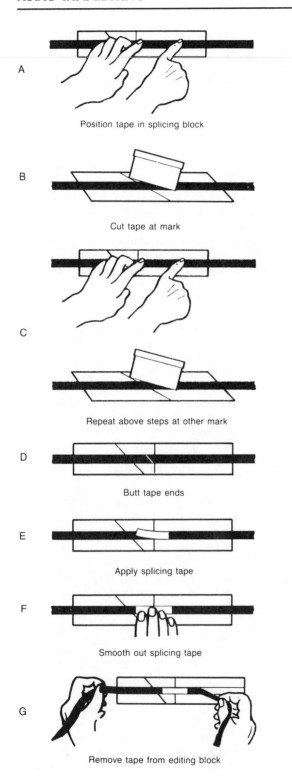

A

Position tape in splicing block

B

Cut tape at mark

C

Repeat above steps at other mark

D

Butt tape ends

E

Apply splicing tape

F

Smooth out splicing tape

G

Remove tape from editing block

FIGURE 7.5 Tape editing procedure. (Adapted from *Local Radio,* by Barry Redfern. Boston: Focal Press, 1981.)

that you don't butt them together directly over the cutting groove.

E. *Apply the splicing tape on the edit.* (See Figure 7.5E.) If you're using splicing tape from a roll, a piece about three-fourths of an inch in length is ample. Splicing tabs are precut at the appropriate length. The splicing tape should be centered at the edit. Make sure it is positioned straight along the channel of the splicing block. Remember the splicing tape is narrower than the audio tape so that it should not be over either edge of the audio tape.

F. *Smooth out the splicing tape.* (See Figure 7.5F.) Be sure to get air bubbles out from under the splicing tape for a strong bond. Rubbing your fingernail over the splice will usually take care of this.

G. *Remove the audio tape from the splicing block.* (See Figure 7.5G.) Never remove the audio tape from the splicing block by grasping one end and lifting. The lips on the edges of the channel will damage the audio tape. The proper procedure for removing audio tape from the splicing block is to grasp both ends of the tape just beyond the splicing block, apply slight pressure to the tape by pulling your hands in opposite directions, and lift straight up. The tape will pop out of the block and you will have completed your splice.

Thread the tape on your recorder and listen to the edited tape. If it came out as you wanted, you can discard the unwanted tape section. Sometimes you may find it necessary to shave a piece of the edit by splicing off one edge or another of the tape. If you've made a good edit mark, you'll rarely have to do this.

7.10 SPLICE DEFECTS

Beginning audio tape editors often encounter problems with their first few splices. These are usually overcome with practice and experience, but it is not uncommon to see splicing errors in manipulating the splicing tape itself and in manipulating the audio tape. (See Figure 7.6 for examples of common splicing problems.) One of the most common problems with splicing tape manipulation is using too much; a piece of splicing tape that is too long is difficult to position properly on the audio tape and makes the tape too stiff at the edit, which prevents proper contact with the tape recorder heads. On the other hand, a piece of splicing tape that is too short may not hold the audio tape together during normal use. Another cause of an edit not holding is that the splicing tape is poorly secured on the audio tape. For example, air bubbles or dirt or grease (from fingerprints or excessive marking with the grease pencil) may be under the splicing tape, preventing it from adhering to the audio tape. Other problems arise when the splicing tape is put on crooked; a portion of the splicing tape hangs over the edges of the audio tape, making it impossible for the tape to glide through the tape recorder transport properly.

One of the most common problems with audio tape

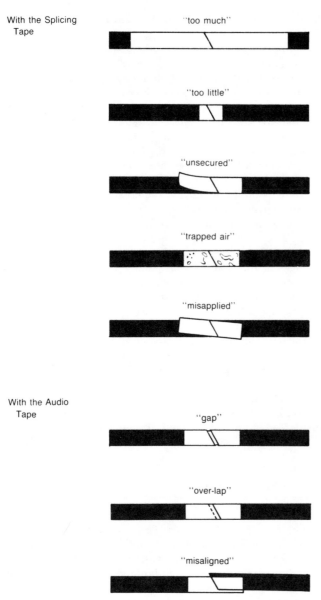

With the Splicing
Tape

"too much"

"too little"

"unsecured"

"trapped air"

"misapplied"

With the Audio
Tape

"gap"

"over-lap"

"misaligned"

FIGURE 7.6 Splicing problems. (Reprinted with permission from *Local Radio,* by Barry Redfern. Boston: Focal Press, 1981)

manipulation during the editing process is leaving a gap as you butt the two tape ends together. Obviously a gap at the edit point will be heard as an interruption of sound or too long a pause. On the other hand, if you overlap the two tape ends as you butt them together, you will get the same effect as if you had mismarked the edit point; in other words, the splice will not occur where you thought it would. A less common problem is lining up the pieces of audio tape incorrectly, so that one piece of tape is higher or lower than the other as you butt them. Obviously, if you are using a splicing block, the channel pre-

vents this from happening; some editing, however, is done without the benefit of the splicing block, and one can misalign the two pieces of tape. This prevents the tape from gliding through the tape transport properly.

7.11 LEADER TAPE

Leader tape is often used in the editing process. Leader tape is a plastic or paper tape that does *not* have a magnetic layer. It is sometimes clear plastic, but more often it is colored as well as marked, or timed, in 7 1/2-inch segments. This timing enables the operator to use leader tape to accurately cue up an audio tape. Leader tape is usually put at the beginning of an audio tape to mark the exact start of the recorded sound. (Unlike audio tape editing, leader tape is normally spliced onto audio tape using the ninety-degree cutting groove.)

The beginning of a tape is called the **head** (tape is normally wound on a reel "heads out") and white or green leader tape is commonly used to signify this. Another reason for putting leader tape at the beginning is to use the leader tape to thread the tape recorder and avoid wear and tear on the actual recorded portion of the audio tape. Leader tape can also be written on and titles or notes can be put at the beginning of a tape this way. The end of an audio tape is called the **tail,** and if leader tape is put on the end of a tape, it will usually be yellow or red (often the leader tape is actually white with the timing marks being the appropriate color). Some audio tape (especially that used for prerecorded programs) is stored on reels "tails out" or tails at the end of the recorded material. To play back a tape that is tails out, you would have to rewind the tape first.

In addition to being used at the beginning and end of an audio tape, leader tape is often used to separate various program segments. It is easier to cue up a tape when the operator can see the segments as they pass through the tape transport (even in fast forward) rather than to have to listen for pauses between the segments.

7.12 DUBBING

As mentioned in 7.6, **dubbing** is another form of audio tape editing. This electronic editing requires the use of two tape recorders. As you dub or copy from one to the other, the "master" tape recorder is in the play mode and the "slave" tape recorder is in the record mode. Using our previous example ("editing is really a two-step process"), you would dub "editing is" from the master to the slave tape recorder and then stop both. Next you'd cue up the master tape recorder past the word "really," and then dub "a two-step process" from the master to the slave tape recorder. Electronic editing requires a good deal of coordination, as you manipulate the two machines so that they start at the same time. Usually electronic editing produces a glitch at the edit point that can range from barely noticeable to terrible depending on the tape recorders used. If electronic editing becomes common with digital recording, it will be computer controlled like videotape editing; then audio tape dubbing can be precise.

Straight dubbing is frequently used in radio production work for reasons other than editing. Often a master tape is dubbed onto a working tape before splicing so that the original tape isn't cut during the editing process. You can dub from one tape format to another. For example, you may have a news tape that was recorded on cassette, but you want to put it on reel-to-reel so that you can edit it down or perhaps equalize it to improve quality. Finally,

dubbing can be used simply to make duplicate copies of any existing tape.

7.13 CONCLUSIONS

This chapter is an important one in your development as a radio production person. You might want to review it again before attempting the self-study or projects sections. Mainly, we have concentrated on the techniques of audio tape editing and not so much on the aesthetics. There are some important considerations in the aesthetics area and they can be developed after you've had time to master the basics.

Self-Study

■ QUESTIONS

1. Which layer of audio tape provides traction as the tape moves through the tape recorder transport?
   a) backing layer
   b) plastic base
   c) magnetic layer

2. Which of the following is the term for an unwanted effect of the magnetic signal involving adjacent layers of audio tape?
   a) tensilize
   b) print-through
   c) adhesion

3. Which type of audio tape is preferred by broadcasters?
   a) polyester
   b) acetate
   c) paper

4. Which thickness of audio tape is preferred by broadcasters?
   a) .5 mil
   b) 1.0 mil
   c) 1.5 mil

5. A tape problem that occurs when tape winds unevenly on a reel is called _____.
   a) cupping
   b) drop-out
   c) scattered wind

6. In addition to specially designed reels of splicing tape, audio tape editing can be accomplished with _____.
   a) cellophane tape
   b) splicing tabs
   c) masking tape

7. In most production situations, which type of edit is preferred?
   a) diagonal cut
   b) vertical cut
   c) horizontal cut

8. A razor blade should be replaced during a lengthy editing session as it can become magnetized after a period of time.
   a) true
   b) false

9. If you use splicing tape that is too long _____.
   a) it will be difficult to position it properly
   b) it will create a gap
   c) it will misalign the recording tape

10. Which term describes having the end of the material recorded on an audio tape at the outside of the reel?
   a) tails out
   b) tails in
   c) neither

11. Which describes a colored or clear plastic or paper tape that has the same dimensions as audio tape and is often used in audio tape editing?
   a) splicing tape
   b) scotch tape
   c) leader tape

12. Another term for electronic editing is _____.
   a) splicing
   b) dubbing
   c) curling

13. As a final test on editing, match the terms in the top list (1, 2, 3 . . .) with their definitions in the bottom list (e, r, t . . .) and then select the correct set of answers from the sequences shown in a, b, or c below.
   1. _____ print-through
   2. _____ drop-out
   3. _____ tensilize
   4. _____ scattered wind
   5. _____ polyester
   6. _____ splicing block
   7. _____ tails out
   8. _____ dubbing
   9. _____ grease pencil
   10. _____ cupping

   e. tape edges turning up
   r. a reel with the end of the tape at the beginning
   t. electronically transferring a signal from one tape to another
   s. to prestretch tape
   c. a crayonlike substance for marking edit points
   f. flaking of the oxide coating
   u. an uneven wind of tape
   p. the plastic base used to make most audio tape
   b. magnetic signal on one layer of tape bleeding onto another layer
   h. a device that holds tape for editing

   a) 1.b 2.f 3.s 4.u 5.p 6.h 7.r 8.t 9.c 10.e
   b) 1.f 2.b 3.s 4.e 5.p 6.h 7.r 8.t 9.c 10.u
   c) 1.f 2.s 3.b 4.t 5.c 6.e 7.p 8.h 9.u 10.r

■ ANSWERS

If you answered A:

1a. Right. It is the bottom layer of the tape sandwich.
2a. Wrong. To tensilize is to prestretch audio tape. Reread 7.2 and try again.
3a. Right. Polyester tape is preferred because it is strong and little affected by temperature and humidity.
4a. No. Thinner audio tape stretches too easily and is more susceptible to print-through. Reread 7.3 and try again.
5a. Wrong. This is when the edges of the tape turn up. Reread 7.4 and try again.
6a. Never. The adhesive material on cellophane tape will bleed through audio tape and gum up the heads of the tape recorder. Reread 7.7 and try again.
7a. Right. The diagonal cut or forty-five-degree cutting groove is used in audio tape editing because it gives a smoother sound transition and a stronger edit.
8a. Right. Since the metal razor blade cuts through the magnetic layer of audio tape, it becomes magnetized over a period of time and can degrade the audio signal at the point of the edit if not replaced.
9a. Right. Shorter tape will make for better edits.
10a. Right. The end of an audio tape is called the tail.
11a. Wrong. Splicing tape is used in audio tape editing, but it does not have the same dimensions as audio tape. Reread 7.7 and 7.11 and try again.
12a. Wrong. Splicing refers to physically cutting the audio tape during the editing process. Reread 7.6 and try again.
13a. Correct. You have finished the exercises for this chapter.

If you answered B:

1b. Wrong. This is the part that mainly provides strength. Reread 7.2 and try again.
2b. Right. Print-through occurs when the magnetic signal of one layer of audio tape affects an adjacent layer.
3b. Wrong. Acetate tape was once favored by broadcasters, but it breaks too often and is susceptible to temperature and humidity problems. Reread 7.2 and try again.
4b. You're close; 1.0 mil audio tape may be used by broadcasters, but it's not the best choice. Reread 7.3 and try again.
5b. Wrong. This is when the oxide flakes. Reread 7.4 and try again.
6b. Right. Splicing tabs are commercially available precut pieces of splicing tape on applicator strips specially designed for audio tape editing.
7b. No. The ninety-degree cut is only used when putting leader tape on an audio tape. Reread 7.7, 7.9, and 7.11 and try again.
8b. Wrong. Reread 7.9 and select the other response for this question.
9b. No. Length of splicing tape has nothing to do with this. Reread 7.10 and try again.
10b. Wrong. Reread 7.11 and try again.
11b. No. Scotch tape should never be used in audio tape editing. Reread 7.7 and 7.11 and try again.
12b. Right. Dubbing is often considered as electronic editing.
13b. No. You are confused about tape problems. Reread 7.2 and 7.4 and try again.

If you answered C:

1c. Wrong. This is where recording occurs. Reread 7.2 and try again.
2c. Wrong. Adhesion is a problem of tape layers sticking together, usually due to humidity. Reread 7.2 and 7.4 and try again.
3c. No. Paper tape would most likely be leader tape. Reread 7.2 and 7.11 and try again.
4c. Yes. Audio tape that is 1.5 mil thick is most often used by broadcasters.
5c. Right. This should be avoided because edges will be uneven.
6c. No. Office tapes should not be used for audio tape editing. Reread 7.7 and try again.
7c. No. You're way off base with this choice. Reread 7.7, 7.9, and 7.11 and try again.
9c. No. It shouldn't affect the position of the recording tape. Reread 7.10 and try again.
10c. Wrong. Reread 7.11 and try again.
11c. Right. This accurately describes leader tape.
12c. Wrong. Curling is a problem that can occur when there is a poor binding between the plastic base and the oxide coating of audio tape. Reread 7.4 and 7.6 and try again.
13c. You made many mistakes. Reread the entire chapter before trying again.

Projects

■ PROJECT 1

Make two edits in an audio tape on a reel-to-reel recorder.

Purpose

To enable you to feel comfortable editing a vocal audio tape.

Advice, Cautions, and Background

1. If you're not sure of what you are doing, ask the instructor for assistance. Don't take the chance of ruining the equipment.
2. Remember you are to do two edits, not just one.
3. You will be judged on the cleanness of your edits, so don't try to edit something that is too tight.

How To Do the Project

1. Read the Information section on audio tape editing.
2. Complete the Self-Study Questions on audio tape editing.
3. Familiarize yourself with the operation of the reel-to-reel tape recorder in your production studio. If you have questions, ask the instructor.
4. Assemble the editing tools and supplies that you will need, including splicing block, razor blades, grease pencil, and splicing tape.
5. You will either be given an audio tape by your instructor to edit, or you will be allowed to record your own. If you can record your own, select some news copy or a weathercast from your news wire service, or write something similar and record it on your tape.
6. Do your edits as follows:
   a. Press the play button and listen to what is recorded.
   b. Select something you wish to edit. Write down on a piece of paper the part you plan to edit with a few words before and after it. Put parentheses around what you plan to take out. For example: "Today's weather calls for (sunny skies and) a temperature of seventy degrees."
   c. Stop the tape recorder so it is at the exact place you wish to edit, in our example, just in front of "sunny."
   d. You are hearing the tape on the play head (remember ERP). Just right of dead center on the play head make your edit mark on the audio tape (remember AIM). Be careful not to get any grease pencil on the actual tape recorder heads.
   e. Then continue playing the tape until you get to the end of your edit, in our example, just before "a."
   f. Using the grease pencil, make your edit mark just as you did before.
   g. Spool out enough tape so that your edit marks can be positioned in the splicing block. Cut the audio tape at the first edit point according to proper splicing procedure. You might want to review Section 7.9 in the Information section for this chapter.
   h. Position the other edit mark in the splicing block and cut the tape as before. You should now have a loose piece of tape (the unwanted words "sunny skies and") and two pieces of tape with diagonal cuts that are both connected to the two tape reels.
   i. Butt the two tape ends and apply a proper amount of splicing tape. Make sure there are no twists in the audio tape.
   j. Rethread the tape in the recorder and rewind it a ways by hand. Push play and listen to your edit.
7. Repeat the above steps for your second edit.
8. Have the instructor listen to your edits so that you can get credit for them.

■ PROJECT 2

Dub from one audio tape recorder to another, making two edits to remove commercials.

Purpose

To enable you to feel comfortable with the type of electronic editing that can be done through dubbing.

Advice, Cautions, and Background

1. If you're not sure of what you are doing, ask the instructor for assistance. Don't take the chance of ruining the equipment.
2. The best way to do this exercise is to record something off the radio for the material you will be dubbing. Most radio studios have facilities for connecting a radio to an audio tape recorder electronically. If yours doesn't, you can hold a microphone in front of a radio and record onto a tape that way.
3. You may have trouble getting the machines to operate so that the edit occurs where you want it to. It is better to make the edit too loose than too tight because one that is loose is easier to correct. You simply need to record again, bringing in the material a little sooner. If your edit is too tight and cuts off the last part of what you had previously laid down, you will need to lay that part down again.
4. Make sure you have access to two tape recorders and two audio tapes.
5. Remember you are to do two edits, not just one.

How To Do the Project

1. Read the Information section on audio tape editing.
2. Complete the Self-Study Questions on audio tape editing.
3. Record something from the radio onto a cassette or reel tape, making sure there are at least two commercial breaks in the middle of what you record.
4. Connect one tape recorder to another so that the sound can be transferred electronically. You will need to take a cable from the audio output on the "master" tape recorder to the audio input on the "slave" tape recorder. If your studio is already set up for two tape recorders, you can just go on to the next step.
5. Dub a small portion of what you have on the master tape to the slave machine just to make sure everything is working correctly. You will need to put the master tape recorder in play and the slave tape recorder in record. Adjust levels so that both tape machines are about the same. If you have access to "tone," set the machine VU meters that way. (See the chapter on the audio console.)
6. Play back what you have just recorded and make any necessary adjustments. If everything recorded well, you are ready to start the actual dubbing.
7. Dub what you recorded off the radio from the master to the slave until you come to a commercial break. Hit the pause control on the slave machine right before the commercials begin, and hit pause on the master machine right after the commercials begin. It is better to let both machines run longer than you really want than to cut everything off too short.
8. Play the master tape until you get to the end of the commercial break. Listen carefully so that you know exactly where you want the edit of the program material to begin. Back up at least five seconds from your desired edit point and put the master machine in pause.
9. If you feel confident that the place where you pushed pause on the slave tape is where you want one portion of the program to stop and another to begin, leave it as it is. If you are not sure, listen to the tape again and find the correct point and put the machine in record and pause. Do not go past the point where you recorded or you will have an awkward period of no sound at all.
10. Play the master tape, and just as it gets to the spot where you want the edit to be, take the slave tape recorder out of pause. Let both recorders go until the next commercial break.
11. At that point, pause both machines as you did for the previous edit.
12. Go back and listen to the edit you just made on the slave machine. If it is what you want, proceed with the second edit. If not, redo it.
13. To do the second edit, cue the master tape at the end of the second commercial break and cue the slave tape close to where you stopped the recording, just as you did for the first edit.

14. Play the master recorder and take the slave recorder out of pause just as you did before. Continue recording for at least a minute or two, then stop both machines.
15. Listen to the edit you have just finished and make sure it was done correctly.
16. Have the instructor listen to your slave tape so that you can get credit for the electronic edits.

■ PROJECT 3

Do several audio tape splices *incorrectly*.

Purpose

To enable you to see what can happen if you do not splice correctly.

Advice, Cautions, and Background

1. You will be using the same equipment that you used for project 1, so you may want to do the two projects at the same time.
2. You can do all of these incorrect splices close together on one piece of tape. You will need to record something on the audio tape, but you can make up whatever you would like.

How To Do the Project

1. Read the Information section on audio tape editing, paying particular attention to the information and drawings of 7.10.
2. Complete the Self-Study Questions on audio tape editing.
3. Record something about two or three minutes long on a reel-to-reel audio tape recorder.
4. Listen to the tape, decide on editing points, mark them, and cut them just as you did for project 1. Cut about two inches of splicing tape and apply that—or try to. In all probability, it will be a bit crooked. Play it back and watch how it rides over the tape recorder heads. The sound may be a bit distorted because the long splice makes the tape too stiff for proper contact.
5. Make another edit just as you did for project 1, but this time apply a piece of splicing tape that is one-fourth of an inch long. Play the edit several times and rewind and fast forward past the edit point several times. In all likelihood the edit will come apart. If so, reapply another quarter-inch piece of splicing tape so you can complete this exercise.
6. Make another edit. This time use the proper amount of splicing tape, but purposely apply it crooked. Play the edit and you will notice that the crooked splicing tape sticks out above and below the level of the recording tape and does not ride properly over the head. Do not play this edit over and over because the sticky part of the splicing tape will gum up the heads.
7. Make a final edit, but while you have the recording tape in the splicing block, separate the two pieces of audio tape so that there is a slight gap between them. Put splicing tape over the edit, leaving this gap. Play back the edit and listen for the disturbance in the sound at the edit point.
8. Show the four incorrect edits to your instructor to receive credit for them.

CHAPTER EIGHT

Monitor Speakers

Information

8.1 INTRODUCTION

Monitor speakers are used to listen to the program (and also audition) sound in the radio studio (see Figure 8.1). They are often treated as passive devices that simply exist in the studio, but they are actually quite important. The sound that comes from them is the final product, so they are important in determining the quality of that product. What you hear on the monitor speakers is an accurate judge of what the listener will hear.

Speakers are **transducers.** They work in a manner opposite to that of microphones. Instead of converting sound waves into electrical energy, speakers produce sound from an electrical signal by converting the electrical signal into mechanical energy that produces an audible sound.

8.2 TYPES OF SPEAKERS

The most common type of monitor speaker found in the broadcast studio has a **dynamic** (or magnetic) construction. Its transducing element, called a ''driver,'' consists of a paper diaphragm, or cone, suspended in a metal frame. At the narrow end of the cone is attached a voice coil (a cylinder wound with a coil of wire), which is located between powerful circular magnets. When an electrical current is generated in the voice coil, it creates another magnetic force that moves the coil (and cone) in and out according to the electrical signal entering the coil. The cone vibration causes the surrounding air to move in a like manner, which our ears pick up as sound (see Figure 8.2).

Other speaker drivers (such as the **electrostatic** or **ribbon**) are considered too exotic for radio use and you are not likely to run across them in the production studio.

8.3 BASIC SPEAKER SYSTEM COMPONENTS

The basic components of the typical speaker system are the woofer, tweeter, crossover, and speaker enclosure (see Figure 8.3). **Woofer** and **tweeter** are names given to driv-ers or speakers used in a speaker system. Since no one speaker design can reproduce the entire frequency range adequately, different speakers were developed to handle different portions of it. A woofer is designed to be able to move a large volume of air that is necessary to reproduce lower frequencies. The cone must be large in size or be able to make large movements, and usually a woofer is a combination of both. However, this bulk prevents the speaker from adequately reproducing the higher frequencies that require rapid cone movement. The tweeter uses a lighter and smaller design; usually a convex dome replaces the cone. There are also midrange speakers, whose names describe the frequencies they reproduce.

An individual speaker is really a speaker system in that most modern speakers use at least a woofer and a tweeter driver. To divide the audio signal and send the proper frequencies to the proper driver, another element of the speaker is used—the **crossover.** A crossover is an electronic device that sends the low frequencies to the woofer and the high frequencies to the tweeter. Although there is no universal design for the crossover, most dividing points between the bass and treble frequencies are between five hundred and fifteen hundred hertz. A speaker that has just a woofer, a tweeter, and a crossover is a **two-way speaker system.** Speakers that employ another driver (such as a midrange) are **three-way systems.**

8.4 SPEAKER SYSTEM DESIGNS

The speaker drivers and crossover are enclosed in a box (enclosure) that also plays a role in how the speaker sounds. The two most widely used speaker enclosure designs are the acoustic suspension and bass reflex systems. The **acoustic suspension** design puts the speaker drivers (and crossover) in a tightly sealed enclosure that produces an accurate, natural sound with strong, tight bass. By absorbing it in the enclosure, the acoustic suspension prevents the sound wave generated from the rear of the cone from radiating and disrupting the main sound of the speaker. Acoustic suspension speakers are less efficient than some other designs and require a more powerful amplifier to drive them. The acoustic suspension design also

FIGURE 8.1 Typical production studio monitor speakers. (Courtesy of Electro-Voice)

main sound from the speaker. Some bass reflex design speakers have been criticized for not having quite as good tonal accuracy as the acoustic suspension design and even adding a boomy quality to the sound. These problems, however, are often the fault of a particular speaker's tuning and construction, rather than caused by the bass reflex design. Most bass reflex speakers produce clean, wide-ranging bass.

8.5 SPEAKER SOUND QUALITIES

There is a wide variety of speaker systems to choose from and, like some other radio production equipment, the differences between various models may be minimal. One of the important qualities that a good monitor speaker must have is excellent **frequency response.** We are able to hear sounds or frequencies in the range of twenty hertz to twenty kilohertz, although most of us do not hear quite that low or that high. Top line broadcast monitors often provide a frequency response range from forty-five hertz to twenty kilohertz. Increased use of CDs and DATs will make necessary speakers that produce as much of this range as possible.

Another quality important for the broadcast monitor speaker is its ability to produce a **flat frequency response.** The speaker should be able to reproduce low, midrange, and high frequencies equally well to produce a natural sound. The speaker itself should not add anything to the audio signal, such as a boosting of the highs.

Perhaps most important is merely how a speaker sounds. Among the combinations of driver types, speaker enclosure design, and crossover frequencies, there is no one speaker configuration that produces the ''best sound.'' It is agreed, however, that a good speaker sound does not just depend on the speaker itself. How a speaker sounds is also dependent on the program (what is being played through it), the dimensions and acoustic properties of the room in which the speakers are heard, the loca-

requires a rather large physical enclosure to insure accurate reproduction of the lowest bass notes.

On the other hand, the **bass reflex** design is quite efficient and produces a strong bass sound with less power required. The bass reflex speaker enclosure is designed with a vented port or opening that is tuned to allow some of the rear sound (the lower frequencies) to reinforce the

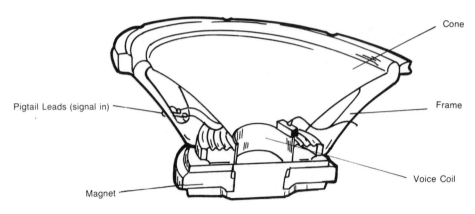

Cone

Pigtail Leads (signal in)

Frame

Magnet

Voice Coil

FIGURE 8.2 Dynamic speaker driver.

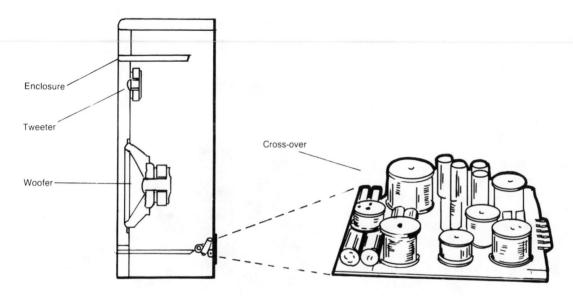

FIGURE 8.3 Basic elements of a speaker system.

tion of the speakers (in relation to the listener), and the listener.

8.6 SPEAKER PLACEMENT

In the radio production room, there may not be many options as to where the monitor speakers are located. Often they are positioned one on each side of the audio console. Sometimes the speakers may be just sitting on the counter (as the console is) and sometimes the speakers are hung from the ceiling or attached to the wall behind the audio console. How the sound spreads out from the speaker is somewhat dependent on the location of the speaker. For the best sound dispersion, the speakers should be hung in the upper corners of the production room. Keeping them close to the wall prevents a great deal of reflected sound and should produce a full, bass sound at a higher sound level than other possible positions. Hung speakers also keep counter space available for other production room equipment.

Where the operator is located in relation to the speakers also plays a role in how they sound, especially with stereo programming. Ideally, the operator is located directly between the two speakers and far enough back from them so that an equilateral triangle is formed if a line is drawn from speaker to speaker and from operator to speaker (see Figure 8.4). If the layout of the production room positions the operator closer to one speaker than the other, the source of all the sound appears to shift toward that one speaker. As a production person you may not have any control over the speaker placement, but it is important that you realize the effects of speaker placement on the sound you hear.

8.7 PHASE

The concept of **phase** was previously mentioned in the chapter on microphones. Miswiring monitor speakers can cause phase problems. Each speaker is fed its sound signal from the audio console monitor amp (and sometimes an external amp) by a positive and negative wire. If the wires are reversed on one of the speakers (i.e., the positive wire is connected to the negative terminal), the two speakers will be out of phase. As the driver moves the cone of one speaker in and out, the driver on the other speaker is moving out and in, so that the two speaker

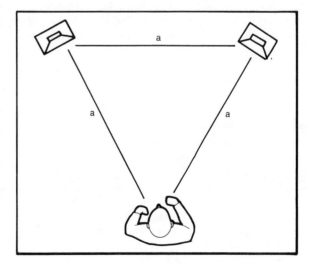

FIGURE 8.4 Speaker-to-listener relationship.

sounds are fighting each other and tend to cancel out individual sounds and diminish the overall sound quality. Since most speakers are wired by the station engineer, this should not be a problem for the radio production person.

8.8 MONITOR AMPLIFIERS

As you have previously learned, the audio console has an internal **monitor amp** that provides the signal to drive the monitor speakers. While this is adequate for many studio applications, some production rooms (and control rooms) are set up with external monitor amplifiers. This is merely a more powerful amplifier that provides higher volume levels and clearer reproduction of the sound signal. Remember, the volume of the monitor speakers is only for the pleasure of the operator and has no relationship to the volume of the signal being broadcast or recorded.

8.9 HEADPHONES

Headphones are another type of monitor in that they are tiny speakers encased in a headset (see Figure 8.5). Headphones are necessary in radio production because the studio monitor speakers are muted when the microphone is on and the operator must be able to hear sound sources that are also on. For example, if you are talking over the introduction of a song or reading a commercial over the background of a musical bed, headphones allow you to hear the other sound and the mic sound so that you can balance the two or hit appropriate cues. Headphones are also portable so that sounds can be monitored when an actual monitor speaker might not be available.

Like regular monitor speakers, headphones come in a variety of styles and price ranges. For best results in the radio production studio, look for headphones that feature large drivers and full (but comfortable) ear cushions and headband. Some headphones that fit in the ear but do not

FIGURE 8.5 Broadcast-quality headphones. (Courtesy of AKG Acoustics)

have ear cushions (usually called open air headphones) allow sound to leak out and cause feedback if operated at extremely loud levels.

8.10 CONCLUSIONS

Often, monitor speakers are given little or no thought. Some production people are only concerned with making sure sound comes out of them. But, as you can now understand, there are several variables that can affect how speakers sound, and the role of the monitor speaker in radio production is not as minor as one might initially believe.

Self-Study

■ QUESTIONS

1. A two-way speaker system consists of _____.
   a) a tweeter, a woofer, and a midrange speaker
   b) a tweeter, a woofer, and a crossover
   c) a tweeter and a woofer

2. The transducing element of a speaker is called _____.
   a) a driver
   b) a crossover
   c) a woofer

3. Which speaker enclosure design utilizes a tuned port to provide a highly efficient system with a full bass sound?
   a) acoustic suspension
   b) bass reflex
   c) bass boom

4. The individual speaker designed to reproduce higher frequencies is the _____.
   a) woofer
   b) crossover
   c) tweeter

5. For proper stereo sound, the listening angle formed between the speakers and the listener should be ninety degrees.
   a) true
   b) false

6. Good broadcast monitors have a frequency response of about _____.
   a) twenty hertz to two hundred hertz
   b) twenty hertz to two hundred kilohertz
   c) forty-five hertz to twenty kilohertz

7. The best place to locate monitor speakers in a production room is _____.
   a) in the upper corners close to the wall
   b) on the counter
   c) not in the room at all, but in an adjoining room

8. If two speakers are out of phase, _____.
   a) the bass sounds will be generated at the rear of the cones
   b) the cone of one speaker will be moving out while the cone of the other speaker will be moving in
   c) both positive wires will be connected to positive terminals

9. The best type of monitor to use when you need to use a mic in the control room to record a voice over music is _____.
   a) a headset
   b) a tweeter
   c) an acoustic suspension

10. As a review of monitors, match the items in the top list (1, 2, 3 . . .) with the choices in the bottom list (s, e, v . . .) and then select the correct set of answers from the sequences shown in a, b, or c on page 94.
   1. _____ acoustic suspension
   2. _____ bass reflex
   3. _____ crossover
   4. _____ driver
   5. _____ headphones
   6. _____ tweeter
   7. _____ woofer

   s. tiny speakers in a headset
   e. a transducing element for a speaker
   v. a speaker enclosure with a vented port
   t. a tightly sealed speaker enclosure
   l. reproduces lower frequencies

h. reproduces higher frequencies

f. sends the proper frequencies to the proper driver

a) 1. f 2. t 3. s 4. l 5. v 6. f 7. e

b) 1. v 2. t 3. f 4. e 5. s 6. l 7. h

c) 1. t 2. v 3. f 4. e 5. s 6. h 7. l

■ ANSWERS

If you answered A:

1a. No. This speaker complement would be in a three-way system. Reread 8.3 and try again.

2a. Yes. The driver transforms electrical signals into mechanical energy and thus audible sound.

3a. No. The acoustic suspension design is relatively inefficient. Reread 8.4 and try again.

4a. Wrong. The woofer is designed to reproduce the lower frequencies. Reread 8.3 and try again.

5a. No. This would put the listener directly in front of one of the speakers and all of the sound would appear to be coming out of that one speaker. Reread 8.6, check Figure 8.4, and select the other response.

6a. No, you are confusing this with the twenty hertz to twenty kilohertz hearing frequencies. Reread 8.5 and try again.

7a. Correct. This gives the operator the best sound.

8a. No, you are confusing this with speaker enclosures. Reread 8.4 and 8.7 and then try again.

9a. Right. A headset is needed to prevent feedback and to hear the music if the speakers are muted when the mic is on.

10a. You made many mistakes. Reread the entire chapter and try again.

If you answered B:

1b. Correct. These are the basic components of a two-way speaker system.

2b. Wrong. The crossover divides the electrical signals and sends them to the speaker drivers. Reread 8.2 and 8.3 and try again.

3b. Right. This answer is correct.

4b. No. The crossover is not a speaker but an electronic device for sending various frequencies to different speaker drivers. Reread 8.3 and try again.

5b. Correct. An angle of about sixty degrees should be formed between the listener and the speakers for the best stereo sound.

6b. No, you are confusing this with the twenty hertz to twenty kilohertz hearing frequencies. Reread 8.5 and try again.

7b. No, the sound isn't as good and the speaker takes up counter space that could be used for something else. Reread 8.6 and try again.

8b. Right. The sounds will be fighting each other when this happens.

9b. No, this is only part of a monitor speaker. Reread 8.9 and try again.

10b. No, you are confused about enclosures and tweeters and woofers. Reread 8.3 and 8.4 and try again.

If you answered C:

1c. No, but you're close. Reread 8.3 and try again.

2c. No. A woofer is a speaker designed to reproduce low frequencies. Reread 8.2 and 8.3 and then try again.

3c. There's no such enclosure design. Reread 8.4 and try again.

4c. Correct.

6c. Yes, you chose the correct range of frequencies.

7c. No, you couldn't hear it if it were in another room. Reread 8.6 and try again.

8c. No, one positive connected to a negative would put them out of phase. Reread 8.7 and try again.

9c. No, you are confusing this with enclosure designs. Reread 8.4 and 8.9 and try again.

10c. You are correct. You have now completed the section on monitor speakers.

Projects

■ PROJECT 1

Inventory the monitor speakers in your production room or studio.

Purpose

To familiarize you with the broadcast-quality speaker.

Advice, Cautions, and Background

1. Do not remove the grill cover from any speakers in your production room or studio without the approval of your engineer or instructor. If you need help, ask for it.
2. You will not be judged on your artistic ability, but try to make your drawing as clear as possible.

How To Do the Project

1. Read the Information section on monitor speakers.
2. Complete the Self-Study Questions on monitor speakers.
3. List the brand name and model of each monitor speaker at your production facility.
4. Sketch the front view of any one speaker (with the grill removed) and label the parts.
5. For the one speaker only, indicate if it is a two-way or three-way system or some other design.
6. If your engineer has a specifications sheet for this model speaker, borrow it and find out the frequency response of the speaker and its crossover frequency. Indicate these on your sketch.
7. Turn in your completed sketch and information to the instructor to receive credit for this project.

■ PROJECT 2

Listen to the sound coming from a speaker (or speakers) from different places in the production room.

Purpose

To make you aware of how sound can change as the relationship between speaker and listener changes.

Advice, Cautions, and Background

1. Your studio may be too small for you to hear any differences. If so, just indicate this.
2. The most important thing for your drawings will be to show the relative dimensions of the studio and the position of the speaker(s).

How To Do the Project

1. Read the Information section on monitor speakers.
2. Complete the Self-Study Questions on monitor speakers.
3. Make three sketches of your control room showing where the speaker(s) is (are) located.
4. On the first drawing, put an X where the production person usually sits. On the second drawing, put an X at another spot in the control room where you can stand to listen to the monitors. Do the same for the third drawing.
5. Play some music through the monitor speaker(s) and position yourself in each of the three places where you have placed Xs. Listen for any differences in the way the music sounds at the three locations.
6. Write a short report detailing how the music sounded at each position.
7. Give your drawings and your report to your instructor for credit for this project.

CHAPTER NINE

Cables, Connectors, and Accessories

Information

9.1 INTRODUCTION

The various pieces of equipment used in the radio production studio are all interconnected. This chapter looks at some of the **cables** and **connectors** used for this interconnection. It also discusses some of the accessories that make work in the production studio easier. Several accessories have already been mentioned: audio tape editing supplies, headphones, turntable stylus, microphone windscreen, and tape cartridges and cassettes, among others. You might also review those sections of previous chapters that discuss impedance and mic or line levels before beginning this chapter.

9.2 HARD WIRING AND PATCHING

Audio equipment in the production studio is connected together by two methods: **hard wiring** and **patching.** Hard wired connections are somewhat permanent (such as the turntable connection to the audio console) and are usually soldered or wired by the engineer. Equipment that may, from time to time, be moved from one production area to another (such as the audio tape recorder) is often connected by male and female connectors known as **plugs** and **jacks.**

Many pieces of audio equipment and even two different production studios are often connected together through the use of a **patch panel** (see Figure 9.1). The input and output of each piece of equipment is hard wired to the patch panel. Putting a patch cord into the correct holes in the panel allows you to interconnect the various pieces of equipment or studios.

For example, the inputs of a cassette recorder, a cart machine, and a reel-to-reel recorder might be hard wired into the first three positions of the top row of the patch bay. The outputs for those three recorders could be hard wired into the same positions of the bottom row. To enable sound from the cassette recorder to be recorded on the reel-to-reel, you would attach a patch cord from the cassette connection on the top row to the reel-to-reel connection on the bottom row. If you changed your mind and wanted to record the cassette on a cartridge, you would simply move the patch connector on the bottom row from the reel-to-reel position to the cartridge position.

In most broadcast situations, you will be dealing with four types of connectors: RCA, miniphone, phone, and XLR. In general, the female or receiving connectors are called jacks and the male connectors are called plugs, but often the terms plugs, jacks, and connectors are used interchangeably.

9.3 RCA CONNECTORS

The **RCA plug** is also known as the **phono** or **pin connector.** Notice that it is *phono*, not phone. Most home stereo equipment uses this type of connector. In broadcast production, this connector is often used to connect the turntable tone arm assembly to the turntable preamp. The RCA connector is always a mono connector, so two of them are needed to create stereo. That's why there is a left and right channel output on stereo audio equipment that uses this connection. The male plug consists of a thin outer sleeve and a short center shaft that plugs into the female jack (see Figure 9.2). Although there are female in-line jacks, the female end is most often enclosed in a piece of equipment (such as a tape recorder or preamp), so that the male end will just plug into the equipment. RCA connectors use two-conductor wire that sometimes picks up extraneous electrical noises such as switches.

9.4 MINIPHONE CONNECTORS

The **miniphone** connector (also called a **mini**) is most often required to connect portable cassette recorders to other pieces of production equipment. The output of many portable cassette recorders is a female mini jack. The male mini plug consists of a tip and a sleeve, which

FIGURE 9.1 Patch panel. (Courtesy of Gentner Electronics Corporation)

goes into the female jack. There are various sizes of mini-phone connectors, but the one used most in broadcast production is 3.5 millimeters. Mini connectors can be stereo or mono. Male mono plugs have one ring that separates the tip from the sleeve, and stereo plugs have two rings, which actually define the ring portion of the connector (see Figure 9.3). If the signal is stereo, both the female and male connectors should be stereo.

9.5 PHONE CONNECTORS

The **phone** connector is also known as the **quarter-inch phone.** Notice it is called *phone,* not phono. Most broadcast-quality headphones are connected to the audio console with a phone plug and most patch bays consist of female phone jacks into which phone connectors are

inserted. "Tip," "sleeve," and "ring" are names given to those parts of the male phone connector just like the miniphone (see Figure 9.4). Like the mini, the phone connector can be either mono or stereo. Again, the female end is often enclosed in a piece of equipment, but you can get in-line jacks if required.

9.6 XLR CONNECTORS

The **XLR connector** is also known as the **Cannon** connector or **three-pin** connector. It is the most common microphone connector in broadcast production use. This connector locks firmly and cannot be disconnected unless the connector lock is pressed. The three prongs of the male plug fit into the conductor inputs of the female jack. The guide pin on the female end fits into the slot for the guide pin on the male end so that the connector can not be put together improperly (see Figure 9.5). Like the RCA connector, the XLR connector is mono so that a stereo connection requires one XLR connector for the right channel and

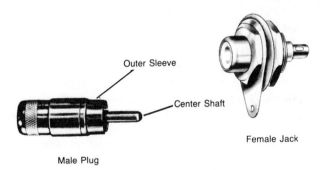

FIGURE 9.2 RCA connector. (Reprinted with permission of Switchcraft, Inc., a Raytheon Company)

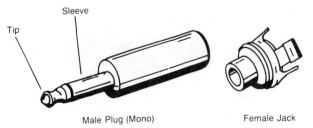

FIGURE 9.3 Mini connector.

Sleeve
Ring
Tip
Male Plug   Female Jack

FIGURE 9.4 Phone connector. (Reprinted with permission of Switchcraft, Inc., a Raytheon Company)

one for the left channel. The three-conductor wiring of the XLR connector makes this a high quality connection and it is often found on audio tape cart machines and reel-to-reels in addition to microphones.

9.7 CONNECTOR ADAPTERS

Something else in the connector realm that is very handy to have in a radio production studio is a supply of **connector adapters.** These enable you to change a connector from one form to another.

Let's say, for example, that you need to connect an RCA output to a phone connector input, but the only cable you can find has an RCA connector at each end. You can convert one RCA to a phone with an adapter. This is a single piece of metal, which in this case houses a female RCA input at one end and a male phone output at the other (see Figure 9.6). When the male RCA connector is placed into the female end of the adapter, the signal is transferred from the RCA connector to the phone connector and from there it can go to the phone input.

As another example, let's say you need a male phone to a male phone connection, but your only cables are male phone to female phone. You can remedy this situation with an adapter that has a male phone plug on each end. Simply place one end of the male adapter into the female jack.

Adapters usually come in most handy in emergency situations when some connecting cable fails, so having a variety of them around is good production practice.

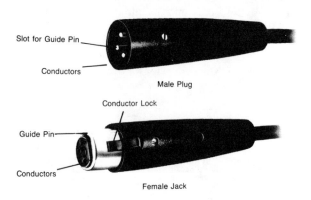

Slot for Guide Pin
Conductors
Male Plug

Conductor Lock
Guide Pin
Conductors
Female Jack

FIGURE 9.5 XLR Connector. (Reprinted with permission of Switchcraft, Inc., a Raytheon Company)

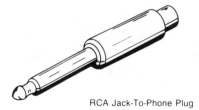

RCA Jack-To-Phone Plug

RCA Jack-To-RCA Jack
(In Line Connector)

FIGURE 9.6 Various connector adapters.

9.8 BALANCED AND UNBALANCED LINES

The cable most often used in broadcasting consists of two-stranded wire conductors that are encased in plastic insulation plus a third uninsulated wire, all encased in another plastic sheathing. For most wiring practices, the inner wires are designated ''+'' (red) and ''−'' (black); the uninsulated wire is the ground wire. The audio signal is carried on the positive and negative conductors. This type of cable is referred to as three-wire or **balanced cable** and often requires the XLR connector because that is the one designed to connect three wires.

Another type of cable is two-wire or **unbalanced.** In this configuration, the negative wire also acts as ground. An unbalanced cable is not as good as a balanced cable because unwanted audio interference, such as that created by a nearby electric motor, can creep into the two-wire system. Also, balanced cables can be longer than unbalanced cables without encountering degradation of the signal. Ideally, balanced and unbalanced cable should not be mixed in the same audio setup, but sometimes this cannot be avoided because different pieces of equipment are built for different cabling.

9.9 IMPEDANCE

Impedance is a complex way of looking at the total resistance in an audio circuit. The impedance of a particular piece of audio equipment is not obvious, but it can be either high or low. Most broadcast equipment is designed for low impedance because such a design gives less resistance to the signal. In general, a low impedance audio source operates into a low or high impedance input (although the low output/high input mismatch may not give the best quality results), but a high impedance source (output) should not be placed into a low impedance input because it will cause sound distortion. There are transformers that will match a high impedance to a low impedance and vice versa. But again, the best production practice is not to mix high and low impedances.

9.10 MIC, LINE, AND SPEAKER LEVELS

Equipment inputs and outputs can be one of three levels: mic, line, or speaker. You can think of these levels as very low for **mic level** (which usually must be preamplified to be used further), normal for **line level** (most equipment will use line levels), and very high for **speaker levels** (designed to drive a speaker only). Problems arise when various levels are mismatched. For example, if you tried to feed an audio tape recorder from a speaker level source, you would probably distort the recording, as the speaker level source is too loud and there is no control to turn it down. Another problem would occur if you fed a mic level signal into a line level input. In this case, the signal would be too low to be usable, as mic levels must be preamplified to a usable level. Most broadcast equipment inputs and outputs are clearly designated as mic, line, or speaker level, and good production practice only sends the proper output to the proper input.

Fortunately, most of the cabling of production room equipment has been done by the engineer and all the connections of various pieces of equipment have been worked out so that everything matches.

9.11 STUDIO TIMERS

Timers have already been mentioned because some audio consoles have built-in timers, but it is not uncommon to find a separate studio timer in the radio production room (see Figure 9.7). Since the timing of radio production work is so important, an accurate timing device is crucial. Most studio timers are digital, showing minutes and seconds, and include at least a start, stop, and reset control. Many studio timers can be interfaced with other equipment (such as tape recorders and turntables) so that they automatically reset to zero when that piece of equipment is started. Shorter timers (ten minutes) are usually adequate for radio production work, but twenty-four-hour timers are often found in the studio.

9.12 TAPE DEGAUSSERS

The audio tape **degausser** or **bulk eraser** is merely a strong electromagnet used to erase audio tape in the production studio. If you remember the information in the audio tape recorder chapter, you know audio tape cartridges must be bulk erased, and it's good production

FIGURE 9.7 Broadcast studio timer. (Courtesy of Radio Systems, Inc.)

practice to erase all audio tapes even though reel-to-reel and cassette tape machines have erase heads in them. Some bulk erasers are designed for tabletop use (see Figure 9.8), while others can be hand held.

Erasing tapes is a simple operation, but is often done improperly by beginning production people and studio pros alike. To erase an audio tape (reel-to-reel, in this example),

a. Extend the tape to be erased an arm's length away from the degausser and then turn the degausser on. (If the tape is already sitting on the degausser when you turn it on, the transient surge of turning the unit on will put a click on the audio tape that can not be erased by normal operation of the eraser).

b. Place the tape on the guide pin and rotate it two or three revolutions.

c. Turn the tape over and rotate it another two or three times.

d. Move the tape an arm's length away from the degausser and turn it off.

Cartridge and cassette tapes are erased in a similar manner. Using a hand-held degausser is similar except that the tape is held still and the degausser is moved. The important points to remember are to turn the degausser on and off with the tape away from it and to keep the degausser turned on as you turn the audio tape from one side to the other. Since the degausser is an electromagnet, it's a good idea to keep your watch out of close contact with it when erasing tapes. Also, keep tapes you do not want erased away from the degausser when it is operating. Once a tape is erased, it can not be restored except by rerecording the material.

FIGURE 9.8   Bulk eraser (degausser). (Courtesy of Audiolab Electronics, Inc.)

There is another type of cartridge eraser that resembles a cartridge machine in appearance. When a cart is inserted and the eraser is turned on, the electromagnet comes on gradually (to avoid a surge that would cause a click on the audio tape) and thoroughly erases the cartridge. This type of unit also finds the splice on the audio tape cartridge. As the tape runs in the machine, a sensor locates the splice (where the tape was joined together to form the endless loop) and stops the tape just past the splice, which is the point at which you would begin to record. This is important because you do not want to record over the splice.

9.13 ON-AIR LIGHT

On-air lights are usually located outside the radio production room or studio. Normally, they are wired so that whenever the microphone in that studio is turned on, the on-air light comes on. Since a lit on-air light indicates a live microphone, good production practice dictates that when an on-air light is on, you *never* enter that studio and, if you are in the vicinity of the studio, you are quiet.

9.14 CART RACKS AND OTHER ACCESSORIES

A few accessories concern audio tape cartridges. In the studio, carts are normally stored or kept in **cart racks.** These can be built into equipment racks, can be wall mounted, or can be of the lazy Susan style. Often some labeling system has been designed to keep carts of a similar length grouped together so you can easily find the proper length for your production work.

Although carts of various lengths can be purchased from broadcast suppliers, it is not uncommon for some facilities to wind their own. A **cart tape winder** allows the broadcaster to spool the proper length of tape from a bulk reel to the center reel of a cartridge. The tape ends are spliced together and the rest of the cartridge is assembled. Older cartridges can be refurbished in this manner and special length carts can be customized, usually at less expense than purchasing new carts. Empty cartridges, lubricated audio tape, and other cartridge supplies are available.

Cart lables aren't really broadcast accessories since they're usually purchased at the local office supply store and are nothing more than file folder labels. Special broadcast cartridge labels can be found, but they are not necessary. Cartridge labels are important in broadcasting, primarily because most stations have developed a color code and labeling system that makes it easy for the broadcast operator to have the right cart and know exactly what is on it. Color codes usually separate station promos, jingles, public service announcements (PSAs), program opens, and songs—all of which may be on carts. For example, promos may use blue labels and PSAs may be on red labels. The information contained on a cartridge label usually includes a number (for logging or categorizing purposes), a title (song title, organization PSA is for, etc.), a time (length of recorded material), a start/stop (whether the cart starts with music or voice and how it ends), and the end cue (the last few words on the cartridge so that the broadcaster knows how it ends). There is no universal system so you'll have to learn the convention that your facility uses to fully understand cart labels. These labels can, of course, be used for other things—cassettes, reel-to-reel tapes, records, and CDs.

9.15 COPY HOLDER

A **copy holder** is an often overlooked, but highly useful, radio production room accessory (see Figure 9.9). It is merely a small easel that can sit on the audio console. It usually has its own stand that is designed to hold a piece of paper (radio script) in front of you. Once you're doing production work, you'll see how important this is. Not only does it free your hands from holding the script as you often have to be turning a pot or throwing a switch with your hands as you're reading the script), but it posi-

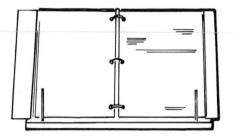

FIGURE 9.9 Copy holder.

tions the script where it should be for proper mic technique. Often broadcasters merely set the script on the counter in front of the audio console and read it from there; this, however, draws the head down toward the counter and script and away from speaking into the microphone. If your production facility doesn't have a copy holder, you'll find production work a lot easier if you suggest purchasing one.

9.16 CLEANING SUPPLIES

Cleaning supplies are common broadcast accessories. The basic supplies are cotton swabs and head cleaner, used to keep audio tape recorders clean. The swabs are not Q-Tips, but long wooden sticks with a cotton tip on one end. These are excellent for getting at hard-to-reach tape heads and getting off edit pencil grease, tape residue, and other dirt. Expensive head-cleaning solvents can be replaced by denatured alcohol, but because of its water content avoid using isopropyl, or rubbing alcohol.

Record-cleaning systems (such as the Discwasher), CD cleaners, tape demagnetizers, and stylus care systems are all useful aids in keeping the tools of audio production clean.

9.17 RECORD SLEEVES

Record sleeves or **shucks** are heavy paper jackets that are used to replace the flimsy record jackets that come with 45 RPM records. Not only do they better protect the record, but they are available in several colors so that records can be easily categorized. In a similar fashion, broadcast suppliers offer empty plastic "jewel cases" for CDs. Many promotional CDs come to radio stations in paper jackets, or the original case breaks, making replacement cases necessary.

9.18 CONCLUSIONS

Not every accessory used by the professional radio broadcaster has been mentioned in this chapter, but you have been introduced to the most common items used in the production studio, and you're less likely to run across something that makes you ask, "What's this for?"

Self-Study

■ QUESTIONS

1. Hard wiring is more permanent than patching.
    a) true
    b) false

2. Which broadcast connector has a guide pin?
    a) RCA
    b) phone
    c) XLR

3. Which broadcast connector has a sleeve and tip?
    a) RCA
    b) phone
    c) XLR

4. Which connector is most likely to be used for a patch bay?
   a) phone
   b) miniphone
   c) RCA

5. Which connector is always mono?
   a) phone
   b) miniphone
   c) RCA

6. A connector adapter is used _____.
   a) to transfer a signal in a patch bay
   b) to change a connector from one form to another
   c) to make a balanced line unbalanced

7. A balanced cable usually has _____.
   a) two wires
   b) three wires
   c) high impedance

8. Unbalanced cables are more susceptible to interference than balanced cables.
   a) true
   b) false

9. The normal inputs of an audio tape recorder are designed for which level of audio signal?
   a) mic
   b) line
   c) speaker

10. Which production room accessory is used to erase audio tapes?
   a) tape winder
   b) cart rack
   c) degausser

11. Which production room accessory is used to protect and help categorize records?
   a) Discwasher
   b) timer
   c) record shucks

12. When using a degausser, you should turn it on while holding the tape an arm's length away from it so that _____.
   a) you do not put a click on the tape
   b) you do not magnetize your watch
   c) you do not erase tapes that are in the vicinity

13. One of the advantages of a copy holder is _____.
   a) it frees your hands
   b) it magnifies the script
   c) it moves your head away from the mic

14. As a review of this chapter, match the pictures (1, 2, 3 . . .) on the next page with their names (p, x, m . . .) and then select the correct set of answers from the sequences shown in a, b, or c below.
   p. phone connector
   x. XLR connector
   m. mini connector
   r. RCA connector

c. copy holder
d. degausser
s. studio timer
b. patch bay

a) 1.m 2.p 3.r 4.x 5.d 6.b 7.s 8.c
b) 1.x 2.r 3.p 4.m 5.b 6.d 7.c 8.s
c) 1.x 2.r 3.m 4.p 5.d 6.b 7.s 8.c

1.

5.

2.

6.

3.

7.

4.

8.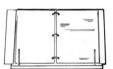

■ ANSWERS

If you answered A:

1a. Right. It is definitely more permanent.

2a. No. Review Figures 9.2–9.5, reread 9.3 and 9.6, and try again.

3a. No. The phono connector has an outer sleeve but no tip. Review Figures 9.2–9.5, reread 9.3–9.5, and then try again.

4a. Right. A male phone plug is the most likely connector to use with a patch bay.

5a. No, the ring on a phone connector makes it stereo. Review Figures 9.2–9.5 and reread 9.3–9.6 before trying again. Note: A phone connector can be mono, but also stereo.

6a. No. You would be very unlikely to use an adapter with a patch bay. Reread 9.7 and try again.

7a. No, you have it confused. Reread 9.8 and try again.

8a. Right. Because one wire conducts signal and also acts as ground, they are more likely to pick up unwanted noise.

9a. Wrong. A mic level might be fed into a tape recorder, but it must be preamplified to be usable. Reread 9.10 and try again.

10a. Wrong. This is used to custom-make audio tape cartridges. Reread 9.12 and 9.14 and try again.

11a. No. A record-cleaning system like Discwasher helps protect records, but it has nothing to do with categorizing them. Reread 9.16 and 9.17 and try again.

12a. Correct. Bring the tape in gradually to the degausser.

13a. Yes. In this way you are freer to operate the controls.

14a. No, you made many mistakes regarding connectors. Reread 9.3–9.6 and study the accompanying figures; then try again.

If you answered B:

1b. No. Reread 9.2 and choose the other answer.

2b. No. Review Figures 9.2–9.5 and reread 9.3–9.6. Then try again.

3b. Correct. (The miniphone connectors also have them.)

4b. No. You are warm but not correct. Reread 9.3–9.6 and try again.

5b. No, the ring on the miniphone connector makes it stereo. Review Figures 9.2–9.5 and reread 9.3–9.6 before trying again. Note: A miniphone connector can be mono, but also stereo.

6b. Correct. It transfers the signal so that another form of connector can be used.

7b. Right. There are three wires.

8b. Wrong. Reread 9.8 and choose the other answer.

9b. Right. Line level inputs and outputs are standard in broadcast production.

10b. No. Reread 9.12 and 9.14 and try again.

11b. No. This has nothing to do with records. Reread 9.11 and 9.17 and try again.

12b. No. You take the risk of magnetizing your watch regardless of how you turn it on. Reread 9.12 and try again.

13b. No. Reread 9.15 and try again.

14b. You made many mistakes. Reread the entire chapter and try again.

If you answered C:

2c. Right. The XLR jack has a guide pin that prevents it from being connected incorrectly.

3c. No. Review Figures 9.2–9.5 and reread 9.4–9.6. Then try again.

4c. No. Reread 9.3–9.6 and try again.

5c. Correct. You must use two RCA connectors, one for each channel.

6c. No. Adapters are not related to balance. Reread 9.7 and 9.8 and try again.

7c. No. If anything, balanced cable usually goes with low impedance, but the two are not necessarily connected. Reread 9.8 and 9.9 and try again.

9c. No. Speaker level is quite high and will usually distort if fed to the input of a recorder. Reread 9.10 and try again.

10c. Correct. The degausser erases.

11c. Yes. Record shucks are color-coded protective sleeves.

12c. No. Nearby tapes can be erased regardless of how you turn it on. Reread 9.12 and try again.

13c. No. If anything, it positions your head so that you have proper mic technique. Reread 9.15 and try again.

14c. Right. You have now completed the exercises for this chapter.

Projects

■ PROJECT 1

Inventory the broadcast accessories found in your production room or studio.

Purpose

To familiarize you with accessory items available.

Advice, Cautions, and Background

1. Use the Broadcast Accessories Inventory Form below to conduct your inventory.
2. You can use items in any production room or studio available at your facility. You will be asked to note the locations.

How To Do the Project

1. Read the Information section on connectors, cables and accessories.
2. Complete the Self-Study Questions on connectors, cables and accessories.
3. List the brand name and model of each item if possible.
4. Make sure you record the location of each item (e.g., Production Studio A, PDX 1).
5. Fill in all specifics on the form.
6. If your production facility does not have a particular item, indicate this on the form.
7. Turn in your Inventory Form to the instructor for credit for this project.

BROADCAST ACCESSORIES INVENTORY FORM

1. Item: Degausser   Location:
Brand Name & Model #:
[ ] Hand-held   [ ] Tabletop
2. Item: Studio timer   Location:
Brand Name & Model #:
Maximum length of time:
3. Item: Cart rack   Location:
Brand Name & Model #:
[ ] Wall-mount   [ ] Rack-mount
[ ] Lazy Susan
4. Item: Record cleaning system   Location:
Brand Name & Model #:
5. Item: Audio tape cartridge   Location:
Brand Name & Model #:
Length:
6. Item: Microphone windscreen   Location:
Brand Name & Model #:
7. Item: Copy holder   Location:
Brand Name & Model #:
8. Item: Editing block   Location:
Brand Name & Model #:
9. Item: Turntable stylus   Location:
Brand Name & Model #:
10. Item: Cart tape winder   Location:
Brand Name & Model #:

■ PROJECT 2

Degauss a tape.

Purpose

To make sure you know the proper procedure for bulk erasing audio tapes.

Advice, Cautions, and Background

1. This exercise is designed so that you can use either a table-mounted or hand-held degausser. If your facility has only a cartridge eraser, use that and modify the project to fit the operation of that type of degausser.
2. Remember to remove your watch, or be careful with it around the eraser so that it does not become magnetized.
3. Play the tape both before and after the degaussing.

How To Do the Project

1. Read the Information section on connectors, cables and accessories.
2. Complete the Self-Study Questions on connectors, cables and accessories.
3. Find a cassette or reel-to-reel tape that has material on it that is no longer needed. (Your instructor may provide you with one.)
4. Play a bit of the tape so you are sure something is on it.
5. Locate your facility's degausser.
6. Place the tape about an arm's length from the degausser and turn it on.
7. Gradually bring the tape to the degausser if you are using a table-mounted model, or bring the degausser to the tape if you are using the hand-held model.
8. For the table model, place the tape on or near the guide pin and rotate it two or three revolutions. For the hand-held model, move the degausser over the entire tape two or three times.
9. Turn the tape over. (Do not turn the degausser off.)
10. Repeat steps 7 and 8 for the other side of the tape.
11. Move the tape an arm's length from the degausser and turn it off.
12. Play part of the tape to make sure there are no clicks or remaining sounds.
13. Turn the erased tape in to your instructor for credit for this project.

■ PROJECT 3

Determine necessary connectors.

Purpose

To make sure you recognize different male and female connectors and know how to use them.

Advice, Cautions, and Background

1. You may find that you need some connectors that have not been discussed in this chapter. Occasionally equipment-manufacturing companies make equipment with unusual connectors in hopes that customers will buy only their brand of equipment so that they can connect it together easily. Usually this practice backfires and broadcasters avoid the equipment with oddball connections.
2. Some of your equipment may be equipped for video as well as audio. In this case, just ignore the video connections.
3. If your facility does not have a reel-to-reel and cassette recorder, use whatever two recorders are available.
4. Don't take connectors that are in use. Check with the instructor or the engineer as to which connectors you can use for this project.

5. You may not be able to find freestanding or in-line female examples for all the connectors. Just gather as many of the connectors as you can.
6. Make sure you return the recorders, microphone, and connectors to their appropriate places when you finish with the exercise.

How To Do the Project

1. Read the Information section on connectors, cables and accessories.
2. Complete the Self-Study Questions on connectors, cables and accessories.
3. Find a reel-to-reel recorder, a cassette recorder, and a microphone.
4. Draw a sketch of the panel(s) on each recorder where input and output connectors are placed. Draw a similar sketch of the connector at the end of the microphone.
5. Assemble male and female examples of the RCA, phone, miniphone, and XLR connectors.
6. Look at each input and output of the tape recorders and microphone and decide what kind of connector you think is needed. Plug in the appropriate connector to see if you are right.
7. Once you have determined all the proper connectors, write the names of the connectors on each sketch and draw arrows to all the inputs and outputs using each particular connector.
8. Turn the sketches in to your instructor to receive credit for this project.

CHAPTER TEN

Signal-Processing Equipment

Information

10.1 INTRODUCTION

Signal processing is nothing more than altering how something, such as an announcer's voice or a record, sounds. Usually it involves the manipulation of the frequency response, imaging, or dynamic range of the sound signal. **Frequency response** refers to the range of all frequencies that an audio component can reproduce, i.e., twenty hertz to twenty thousand hertz. **Imaging** refers to the perceived space between monitor speakers and how we hear individual sounds within that plane. **Dynamic range** refers to the audible distance between the softest sounds that can be heard over noise and the loudest sounds that can be produced before distortion is heard.

We've already seen some forms of audio processing in the equalization capabilities of some audio consoles and the bass roll-off of some microphones, but most signal processing is accomplished by the use of separate components. This chapter focuses on those electronic processors commonly used in radio; the amount of equipment available for signal processing in any one production facility, however, can vary widely from essentially none to a veritable smorgasbord of electronic black boxes.

10.2 PASSIVE AND ACTIVE EQUALIZERS

The most commonly used signal processor is the **equalizer.** An equalizer allows for manipulation of frequency response by adjustment of the volume of selected frequencies and can be thought of as a fancy **tone control.** You're familiar with bass and treble tone controls, as most home stereo systems have them. When you turn up the treble control, you increase the volume of higher frequencies. Unfortunately, a treble control turns up all the higher frequencies. An equalizer, on the other hand, offers greater flexibility and allows the operator, for example, to differentiate between lower-high frequencies and upper-high frequencies and make different adjustments to each.

Equalizers can be either passive or active. A **passive equalizer** has no amplification ability and therefore requires no power supply to operate. Many car stereo equalizers are passive, but it is unlikely that you will find a passive equalizer in the broadcast studio. A sound signal that passes through a passive equalizer's circuits suffers a slight loss of volume as it is processed. On the other hand, an **active equalizer** has a built-in amplifier and can compensate for any signal level loss during equalization and even boost the signal volume. Most equalizers found in the production studio are active equalizers.

10.3 THE GRAPHIC EQUALIZER

The two main kinds of equalizers found in radio production are the graphic equalizer and the parametric equalizer. The **graphic equalizer** is more common and derives its name from the rough graph of a sound's altered frequency response formed by the slider control settings on the equalizer's front faceplate (see Figure 10.1).

A graphic equalizer divides the frequency response range into separate bands, usually at one-third, one-half, or full octave intervals. If the first band of a full octave equalizer were at 60 hertz, the second would be at or near 120 hertz, the third at 240 hertz, and so on. Equalizers range from a mere five or six bands to over thirty bands. Obviously, the more bands you have to work with, the greater control you have, but it also becomes harder to correctly manipulate the equalizer. Most broadcast-quality graphic equalizers have ten bands. Each band has a slider volume control that is off in a middle position and can move up to increase, or down to attenuate, the volume at that particular frequency. The volume range varies, but ''+6'' to ''−6,'' or twelve decibels, is a common possibility. Figure 10.2 shows a basic five-band equalizer. Note how the slider setting would demark a frequency response graph indicating how the original sound was being manipulated. If we were playing a piece of music through this equalizer, the increase setting at sixty hertz would give the drums extra punch; cutting back at 250 hertz would help minimize bass boom; the increase at one kilohertz would add brilliance to the voices; the decrease

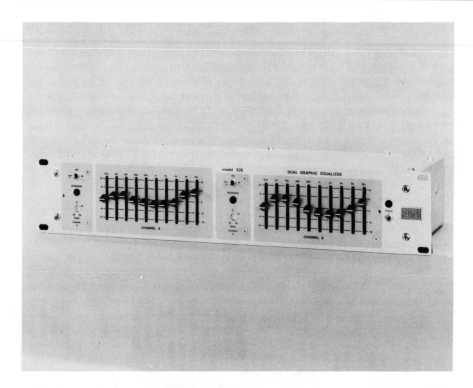

FIGURE 10.1   Ten-band graphic equalizer (stereo). (Courtesy of Urei, Inc.)

at four kilohertz would minimize the harshness of the sound; and the increase at eight kilohertz would add presence to the highs. There is no one correct setting for an equalizer, and we could have just as easily had all different settings yet produced an excellent sound. There are, however, settings that would make the sound very poor, and the production operator needs to beware of altering the sound too much.

10.4 THE PARAMETRIC EQUALIZER

The **parametric equalizer** gives the operator even greater control over the sound manipulation, as it allows not only volume control of specified frequencies, but control over the actual center frequency and bandwidth selected. For example, the five-band graphic equalizer mentioned above had a set center frequency band at 1 kilohertz, but

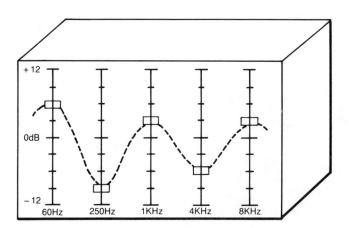

FIGURE 10.2   A simple five-band graphic equalizer.

a parametric equalizer allows us to choose an exact frequency (instead of 1000 hertz, maybe 925 hertz or 1200 hertz). If the graphic equalizer were increased at 1 kilohertz, not only would that frequency get a boost, but so would the adjacent frequencies (perhaps from 500–1500 hertz), according to a preset bandwidth determined by the manufacturer. Many parametric equalizers allow the operator to adjust that bandwidth. For example, still using the 1 kilohertz center frequency, the parametric equalizer operator could select a bandwidth of 800–1200 hertz or a narrower bandwidth of 950–1050 hertz to be equalized.

Most equalizers also have a switch that allows the sound signal to pass through the equalizer unaffected or unequalized. Figure 10.3 shows one type of parametric equalizer.

10.5 EQUALIZER USES

We've already said that the general use of an equalizer is to alter or change the sound character of an audio signal. The term "EQ" refers to the general process of equalization. Specifically, equalizers are used to cut down various forms of audio noise, alter recordings to suit individual taste, and create special effects.

The two most common forms of noise, especially in production work, are hiss and hum. **Hiss** describes a common high-frequency noise problem inherent in the recording process, and **hum** is a low-frequency problem associated with leakage of the sixty hertz AC power current into the audio signal. Although it is often impossible to entirely eliminate noise with an equalizer, careful adjustment can attenuate both hiss and hum to a less-noticeable level. (Remember, you also affect the program signal as you equalize, so EQ is usually a compromise between less noise and a still-discernible signal.)

Sometimes equalization is done to achieve a special effect. For example, cutting down most of the lower frequencies leaves a very tinny-sounding voice that might be perfect as a robot voice for a particular commercial or ra-

dio drama. Many effects are achieved by experimenting with various settings of the equalizer.

The equalizer is also used for altering the sound of records (or actually any music) to suit a particular listener. For some production work, you may need to accent the bass in a particular piece of background music, and the equalizer certainly could help do so. Equalizing anything is very subjective, and what sounds good to one listener may not to another. The key is to use any effect moderately and experiment to find just the right sound.

10.6 FILTERS

Filters are less likely to be found in the radio production room, but since they are a type of equalizer, a short discussion of them may prove useful. Instead of manipulating a specific frequency, filters affect a whole range of the audio signal. For example, a **low cut filter** cuts or eliminates all frequencies below a certain point, say 150 hertz. Instead of a normal frequency response of 20–20,000 hertz, once the signal goes through this filter, its response is 150–20,000 hertz. A **low pass filter** works in the same fashion but lets all frequencies below a certain point pass, or remain unaffected. In other words, a cut filter and a pass filter are opposites in their action. A **band pass filter** cuts all frequencies except a specified band. It has a low cut point (maybe 100 hertz) and a high cut point (maybe 10,000 hertz). When a signal is sent through this filter, only that portion of the signal between the two cut points is heard. A **band reject (or cut) filter** is just the opposite of the band pass filter in that it allows all frequencies to pass except a specified frequency range. A **notch filter** is a special filter that completely eliminates an extremely narrow range of frequencies or one individual frequency.

Usually filters are used to correct a specific problem. For example, a record may have a scratch that shows up around eleven kilohertz, and a notch filter is used to eliminate that frequency. Of course, filters eliminate both the problem *and* the actual program signal, so careful use is

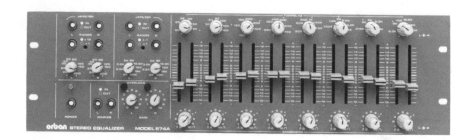

FIGURE 10.3 Quasi-parametric equalizer. (Courtesy of Orban Associates, Inc.)

necessary to maintain a good audio signal after filtering has taken place.

10.7 NOISE REDUCTION

We've mentioned the problem of noise inherent in the production process. Signal-processing devices known as noise reduction systems have been devised to help prevent noise. Note that these electronic devices can not get rid of noise that already exists; their job is to prevent noise from being added to a recording. The development of digital recording will make these systems obsolete as the noises they are meant to eliminate are ones inherent in the analog recording process. There are, however, two systems commonly found in broadcast use today: Dolby and dbx. Both are **companders**—their general operation is to compress (reduce the dynamic range of) an audio signal during recording and then expand the signal during playback—but they are not compatible systems.

10.8 DOLBY NOISE REDUCTION SYSTEMS

There are several **Dolby** systems in use—Dolby A, Dolby B, Dolby C, Dolby Stereo, and Dolby SR—in recording studios, broadcast stations, home stereo equipment, and movie theaters. The Dolby B and C systems and Dolby SR are most likely to be found in the production studio, often built into the electronics of audio tape recorders for radio production use.

The two-part Dolby process consists of increasing the volume of the program signal at certain frequencies (specifically at the upper end of the frequency spectrum where the signal is most likely to be lost to noise) before the recording begins. If the particular frequencies are not affected by noise, they are not altered by the Dolby encoding process. During playback, levels that were increased are decreased, but noise in the recording process was not boosted, so it seems lower in relation to the program level. Depending on the system employed, ten to twenty-five decibels of noise reduction can be attained using the Dolby process. Like all other signal-processing equipment, careful use is required to achieve the results the operator wants. Setting proper levels prior to recording with Dolby is important so that both encoding (recording) and decoding (playback) of the audio signal is at the same level.

Dolby SR (for spectral recording) is the newest and most sophisticated noise reduction system from the Dolby Laboratories. Employing both fixed and sliding band filters, Dolby SR carefully boosts the gain of portions of the audio signal at low levels to maintain a maximum recording level. At the same time, if a portion of the audio signal is already at a high level, it is attenuated, but only at that specific frequency and only by an amount necessary to prevent overload. Dolby SR circuits custom design the filtering required for encoding the signal at the highest level with the least amount of actual processing. During decoding, circuits are automatically created that are an exact mirror image of those used in the recording process to restore the original signal. Of course, noise introduced during recording is significantly reduced. A number of Dolby SR units are available to make conversion to this noise reduction system easy for any production studio.

10.9 dbx NOISE REDUCTION SYSTEMS

There are two dbx noise reduction systems: Type I and Type II. Type II is most often found in broadcasting, and there is no compatibility between the two dbx systems. Unlike Dolby, dbx compresses the signal over the entire frequency range during recording. Again, since the signal goes through the noise reduction unit before recording, is processed and recorded, and then is played back through the noise reduction unit, inherent recording noise is mostly covered up.

Noise reduction of forty decibels can be attained using the dbx system. The audio signal is compressed during recording by a two-to-one ratio (in other words, the dynamic range is cut in half), with the loud levels greatly reduced and the soft levels boosted by a carefully designed frequency response preemphasis. During playback, the signal is expanded by a one-to-two ratio, with deemphasis so that the original dynamic range is restored. Noise buildup usually introduced in the recording process is dramatically reduced; like all noise reduction systems, however, any noise present in the original audio signal is not reduced.

10.10 REVERBERATION

A signal processor that affects the imaging of sound is the **reverberation unit.** The three main types of reverb unit—plate, spring, and digital—all manipulate the sound signal to artificially produce the sound of different acoustic environments. As we've mentioned, reverb is reflected sound that has bounced off two or more surfaces. Sound heard (or produced) in a small studio sounds different than sound produced in a large hall or auditorium, and reverb is the main characteristic that audibly produces the difference.

A **plate reverb** unit consists of a large metal plate suspended within a frame (see Figure 10.4). A transducer at one end of the plate changes the audio signal into mechanical energy and vibrates the plate. A contact mic at the other end of the plate picks up the vibrations (reverb), and then sends the altered signal wherever it needs to go. Plate reverb systems are rather bulky and expensive and are not found in many production facilities.

Spring reverb units are less expensive and operate in a similar manner. A transducer at one end of a coiled spring

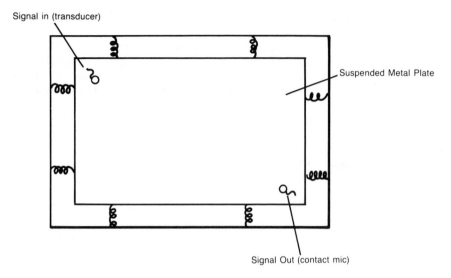

Signal in (transducer)

Suspended Metal Plate

Signal Out (contact mic)

FIGURE 10.4 Simplified internal structure of plate reverberation.

causes the spring to vibrate when a signal is sent through it (see Figure 10.5). A contact mic at the other end picks up the altered signal from the spring. The amount of reverb introduced into the signal can usually be controlled on both plate and spring reverb units.

The modern production studio is more likely to have a **digital reverb** unit. Rather than a mechanical-electrical device, the digital reverb is a pure electronic device (see Figure 10.6). The original signal is fed into the unit and is electronically processed to achieve the reverb effect; then the altered signal is sent out of the unit. Usually a greater number of effects can be produced with the digital units.

10.11 DIGITAL DELAY

A **digital delay** unit can be used in both the production studio and on-air control room. As its name implies, this signal processor actually takes the audio signal, holds it, and then releases it to allow the signal to be used further. The time the signal is held or delayed can be varied from fractions of a second to several seconds. While there are analog units, most delay systems are digital and the incoming signal is converted from its analog form to digital for processing and back to analog after processing.

In the on-air studio, a delay unit is often used in con-

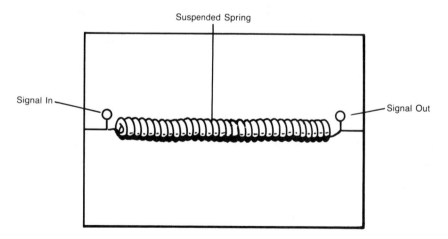

Suspended Spring

Signal In

Signal Out

FIGURE 10.5 Simplified internal structure of spring reverberation.

FIGURE 10.6 Digital reverb unit. (Courtesy of Yamaha Professional Audio Division)

junction with a telephone talk show. The program signal is sent through the delay unit to provide approximately a seven-second delay before it is sent to the transmitter. If something is said by a caller that should not be broadcast, the operator has time to ''kill'' the program before it is actually broadcast. (This is why callers are asked to turn their home radio down if they are talking to an announcer on-air, as the sound they hear on the radio is the delayed sound and not the words they are actually saying into the telephone. It's extremely difficult to carry on a conversation when you can hear both sounds.)

In the production studio, delay units are used to create special effects similar to reverb. Set for an extremely short delay, the units can create an effect that sounds like a doubled voice or even a chorus of voices.

10.12 COMPRESSORS

Two signal-processing devices, the compressor and the limiter, are used to affect the dynamic range of the audio signal. Although they are most often used to process the signal between the studio and the transmitter and therefore aren't pure production room devices, they were the first processing devices used in radio and virtually every radio station uses them. They are also occasionally used

in the production room to process the signal before it is sent to an audio tape recorder.

The **compressor** operates as an automatic volume control. If the audio signal is too loud, the compressor automatically lowers it, and if the signal is too soft, the compressor increases it. Several adjustments on the compressor determine its actual operation. The threshold of compression is the setting of the level of signal needed to turn on the compressor. As long as the audio signal stays below this point, the compressor does not do anything. Input level can be adjusted on the compressor, although this level is also determined by the output of the audio signal source. In any case, the compressor really needs to work only some of the time. If the input is too low, the threshold of compression will never be reached, and if the input is too high, the compressor will severely restrict the dynamic range. The compression ratio determines how hard the compressor works. A ratio of five-to-one means that if the level of the incoming signal increases ten times its current level, the output of that signal from the compressor will only double. Compressors also have settings for attack time (how quickly volume is reduced once it exceeds the threshold) and release time (how quickly a compressed signal is allowed to return to its original volume). The release time adjustment is very important, as too fast a setting can create an audible pumping sound as the compressor releases, especially if there is a loud sound immediately followed by a soft sound or a period of silence.

10.13 LIMITERS

A **limiter** is a form of compressor with a large compression ratio of ten-to-one or more. Once a threshold level is reached, a limiter doesn't allow the signal to increase any more. Regardless of how high the input signal becomes, the output remains at its preset level. If they are adjustable, attack and release times on limiters should be quite short.

Both the limiter and the compressor can be rather complicated to adjust properly. Too much compression of the dynamic range makes an audio signal that can be tiresome to listen to, and pauses or quiet passages in the audio signal are subject to the pumping problem mentioned earlier. Since they are often associated with the transmitter only, compressors and limiters are usually the domain of the engineer. If you do have access to them in the production facility, it may take some experimenting to get the kind of processing that you are looking for, as there are no standard settings for signal-processing devices. Figure 10.7 shows a system that combines both a compressor and limiter in a single unit.

10.14 OTHER SIGNAL PROCESSORS

A **flanger** is another processor for producing a specific special effect. This unit electronically combines an original signal with a slightly delayed signal in such a way as to cause an out-of-phase frequency response that creates a filtered swishing sound. A **de-esser** is an electronic processor designed to control the sibilant sounds without affecting other parts of the sound signal.

Currently there is a general trend to build signal-processing devices so that they perform more than one function, that is, to put more digital effects in one black box. For example, the **Harmonizer** continues to be a popular signal-processing tool in the production studio (see Figure 10.8). Manufactured by Eventide Clockworks, the Harmonizer offers a variety of audio effects in one unit. In addition to its ability to alter the pitch of an incoming audio signal, the harmonizer has time compression and expansion, delay, reverb effects, flanging, time reversal, and repeat capabilities. The operator should find it enjoyable to experiment with the variety of creative effects that can be produced with the Harmonizer.

As mentioned in chapter 5, there are black boxes capable of creating, mixing, and processing sounds, all in one unit. These digital audio workstations keep the sound in digital form throughout, so noise and distortion are not even introduced. Sometime in the not-too-distant future,

FIGURE 10.7 Compressor/limiter. (Courtesy of Urei, Inc.)

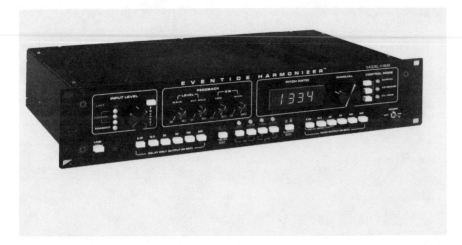

FIGURE 10.8 Harmonizer. (Courtesy of Eventide, Inc.)

radio stations may operate with inputs from CDs and DATs that are mixed and processed through one of these pieces of equipment and then sent to digitalized transmitters. This will result in signal quality that is much better than that possible today.

10.15 CONCLUSIONS

This chapter is not a complete guide to signal-processing equipment. There are other units available and in use in radio production facilities. Nor is this chapter intended to make you a professional operator of such equipment. What is intended is that you become aware of a number of the more common processors and that you have an understanding of their basic purpose. The actual operation of most of this equipment will take some trial and error work in your production facility. Above all, remember that one small effect used as part of a production can be very effective, but too many special effects in a production take away from their specialness. Use signal processing in moderation and remember that a lot of great radio production has been produced using no signal-processing equipment.

Self-Study

■ QUESTIONS

1. The equalizer processes an audio signal by altering which of the following?
   a) frequency response
   b) imaging
   c) dynamic range

2. Which type of equalizer has no amplification ability?
   a) active
   b) passive
   c) graphic

3. Which type of equalizer can select an exact center frequency and bandwidth as well as alter the volume at that frequency and bandwidth?
   a) graphic
   b) parametric
   c) dielectric

4. What type of filter would most likely be used to attenuate or eliminate a sixty-hertz hum in a recording?
   a) low pass filter
   b) band pass filter
   c) notch filter

5. The sixty-hertz hum mentioned in question 4 could also have been eliminated by the use of either Dolby or dbx noise reduction.
   a) true
   b) false

6. A signal processor that affects the imaging of a sound is the _____.
   a) equalizer
   b) noise reduction unit
   c) reverb unit

7. In order to create a tinny voice, you would _____.
   a) cut out most of the lower frequencies
   b) cut out most of the higher frequencies
   c) eliminate the EQ

8. The noise reduction system most likely to be found in the radio production studio is _____.
   a) Dolby A
   b) Dolby B
   c) Type I

9. In the Dolby system of noise reduction _____.
   a) volumes of certain frequencies are increased during recording and decreased during playback
   b) the dbx is increased with a calibrated tone so that it attains the level of thirty decibels
   c) all frequencies pass through except ones that have been preset by the notch filter

10. Which type of reverb has only electronic, not mechanical elements?
   a) plate
   b) spring
   c) digital

11. A compressor _____.
   a) usually has a compression ratio of ten-to-one
   b) lowers a signal that is too loud and raises one that is too soft
   c) does not operate unless it is connected to a digital delay unit

12. As a final test on signal processing, match the following pieces of equipment (1, 2, 3 . . .) with their primary functions (f, d, i . . .). (Letters may be used more than once.) Then select the correct set of answers from the sequences in a, b, or c at the top of page 117.
   1. _____ parametric equalizer
   2. _____ plate reverb unit
   3. _____ limiter
   4. _____ Dolby
   5. _____ digital reverb unit
   6. _____ dbx
   7. _____ compressor
   8. _____ notch filter

   f. manipulates the frequency response
   d. changes dynamic range
   i. deals with imaging
   n. reduces noise

a) 1.d   2.i   3.f   4.n   5.i   6.n   7.f   8.d
b) 1.f   2.i   3.d   4.n   5.i   6.n   7.d   8.f
c) 1.d   2.n   3.n   4.f   5.d   6.i   7.n   8.f

■ ANSWERS

If you answered A:

1a. Correct. Equalizers allow you to adjust selected frequency volumes and thus alter the audio signal's frequency response.

2a. No. An active equalizer has a built-in preamplifier. Reread 10.2 and try again.

3a. No. Center frequencies and bandwidths are preset on graphic equalizers. Reread 10.4 and try again.

4a. No. This type of filter allows lower frequencies to pass and would not eliminate noise at sixty hertz. Reread 10.6 and try again.

5a. No. Noise reduction units, regardless of brand name, can not eliminate noise that already exists in a recording. They only prevent noise during the recording process. Reread 10.7 and select the other response.

6a. No. Equalizers affect frequency response. Reread 10.2 and 10.10 and then try again.

7a. Correct. Cutting the bass will give a tinny sound.

8a. No. Reread 10.8 and 10.9 and try again.

9a. Correct. It is a two-step process.

10a. No. It has a transducer that changes the audio signal into mechanical energy. Reread 10.10 and try again.

11a. Wrong. That is a limiter. Reread 10.12 and 10.13 and try again.

12a. No. You are confusing frequency response and dynamic range. Reread 10.2–10.5, 10.12, and 10.13 and try again.

If you answered B:

1b. No. Imaging can be affected by other signal processors. Reread 10.1 and 10.2 and then try again.

2b. Correct. This is the best response.

3b. Yes. The parametric equalizer gives the operator the greatest control over the EQ process.

4b. No. This type of filter is usually used to allow a range of frequencies to pass, not to eliminate a single frequency. Reread 10.6 and try again.

5b. Yes, because you can't eliminate existing noise with noise reduction units.

6b. No. Noise reduction units affect dynamic range. Reread 10.7 and 10.10 and then try again.

7b. No. That is where the tinny sound would be. Reread 10.5 and try again.

8b. Correct. It is one of the common ones.

9b. No. Reread 10.8 and 10.9 and try again.

10b. No. It has a transducer that changes the audio signal into mechanical energy. Reread 10.10 and try again.

11b. Yes, it lowers and raises signals in that manner.

12b. Correct. You have now finished the section on signal processing.

If you answered C:

1c. No. Dynamic range can be affected by other signal processors. Reread 10.1 and 10.2 and then try again.

2c. Close, but not exactly correct. While some graphic equalizers do not have amplification, other graphic equalizers do. There's a better response. Reread 10.2 and try again.

3c. There's no such thing. Reread 10.3 and 10.4 and try again.

4c. Correct. This type of filter allows all frequencies to pass except a specified one, which we could specify at sixty hertz to eliminate the hum.

6c. Yes. This is what reverb units do by electronically changing the apparent acoustic environment in which we hear the sound.

7c. Wrong. That wouldn't really be possible. Reread 10.5 and try again.

8c. No. Reread 10.8 and 10.9 and try again.

9c. No, you are confusing this with filters. Reread 10.6 and 10.8 and try again.

10c. Correct. It has no mechanical elements.

11c. No, they have nothing to do with each other. Reread 10.12 and 10.13 and try again.

12c. You are either lost or you are guessing. Reread the entire chapter and try again.

Projects

■ PROJECT 1

Operate the signal-processing equipment in your facility.

Purpose

To familiarize you with the various functions of signal-processing equipment.

Advice, Cautions, and Background

1. You may not be able to do this entire project because of lack of equipment. Do it as best you can. If you do not have access to any signal-processing equipment, try to use equalizers that may be part of your audio console.
2. You can prepare the tape you will need for this at home if you have a mic, a turntable or CD, and a tape recorder.
3. Turn in both the original tape and the completed project tape so your instructor can compare them.
4. Feel free to review material in this book that deals with turntables, audio consoles, and tape recorders so that you can do this project properly.
5. You may need help from your instructor or engineer to arrange the signal-processing equipment.

How To Do the Project

1. Read the Information section on signal-processing equipment.
2. Complete the Self-Study Questions on signal processing.
3. Make a tape that consists of you talking for at least a minute, introducing a song, and the song itself. While you are recording the music, raise the volume at one point so that it is overmodulated, and then lower the volume at another point so that it is riding in the mud.
4. Rerecord this tape, using whatever signal processing you have available to accomplish the following:
   a. Change your voice for about fifteen seconds so that it sounds tinny.
   b. Accentuate the bass notes of the music for a brief period of time and then eliminate the bass notes.
   c. Lower the signal that is too loud and raise the signal that is too soft.
5. Clearly label and turn both the original tape and the rerecorded tape in to your instructor for credit for this project.

■ PROJECT 2

Visit a radio station to learn about the signal-processing equipment used there and write a report about what you learn.

Purpose

To give you more familiarity with signal-processing equipment.

Advice, Cautions, and Background

1. Find a place that has enough signal-processing equipment that your trip will be worthwhile. Your instructor may arrange a trip for the entire class to a radio station or recording studio.
2. Find someone at the facility who is willing to spend some time with you explaining how the equipment works.
3. Prepare questions that you want to ask so that you can guide the visit to some extent.
4. If possible, experiment with some of the equipment yourself. If the facility is unionized, you won't be able

to do this. Don't push on this particular point, as some people are very sensitive about who touches their equipment, but don't back away from the opportunity either.

5. Once you have made the appointment, keep it, and arrive on time.

How To Do the Project

1. Read the Information section on signal-processing equipment.
2. Complete the Self-Study Questions on signal processing.
3. Call various radio stations and recording studios until you find one that is willing to let you visit and one that has sufficient signal-processing equipment.
4. Visit the facility and talk with someone who can give you information for your report. Make a list of all the equipment you are shown and take notes regarding it. Some of the things you may want to find out are as follows:
   a. Is the equalizer passive or active, graphic or parametric?
   b. Do they have band pass or notch filters or both?
   c. Do they use Dolby or dbx and which system?
   d. Is the reverb system plate, spring, or digital?
   e. Is there a digital delay unit, and if so, how many seconds' delay does the station use?
   f. Do they have a compressor? A limiter?
   g. Do they have any of the more comprehensive signal-processing equipment, or are they considering buying it?
   h. What signal-processing equipment do they have that is not mentioned in this chapter, and what does it do?
5. As soon as you leave the facility, organize your notes so you remember the main points.
6. Write a report. It should be several pages long, preferably typed. Write your name and ''Signal-Processing Equipment Tour'' on a title page.
7. Turn the report in to your instructor for credit for this project.

CHAPTER ELEVEN

Production Situations

Information

11.1 INTRODUCTION

Throughout this text you have been introduced to various production principles and techniques: slip cueing a record, preventing multiple microphone interference, and editing audio tape, to mention a few. In this chapter, we will give some additional production tips that apply to particular types of radio programming, namely, music, news, commercials, public affairs programs, call-in talk shows, play-by-play sports, and drama. Entire books have been written about each of these types of programming, and this chapter will not give you the in-depth knowledge you need to perfect any of the program forms. It will, however, get you started in the right direction. Experience and advanced training can then propel you into more specialized skills. First we'll present some general production tips that are valid for many different production situations.

11.2 PRODUCTION SETUP

Before beginning any production work, set up the production studio. This means cleaning up any mess left behind from previous work in the studio. Theoretically, there should not be anything to clean up, because good production practice dictates that each person cleans up the production facility after each work session, but theory doesn't always work, so, if necessary, put away background music records, take old tapes off the recorders and counters, and clear some working space for yourself.

Set all audio console controls to a neutral position. In other words, turn on only those pieces of equipment that you are going to use. Not only is it easier to keep track of and manipulate the volumes for only the equipment you need, but it prevents any additional audio noise from being introduced into your production work from a piece of equipment that you are not using.

Clean all tape recorder heads. If editing has been done recently in the studio, some residual grease pencil may

have been left on the heads, and even normal use leaves some oxide material on or near the heads.

Bulk erase the tapes that you plan to use. In general, you do not need to worry about erasing anything that may be on these tapes already, because the custom in most studios is that any tape left in the production studio is up for grabs. If you want to save something that you've recorded, take the tape out of the production studio.

Take a look at the audio tape, too. If it is excessively worn or damaged in any way, throw it out. If you are using reel-to-reel tape, spool off a few feet from the front of the reel and throw it away. That part of the tape gets the wear and tear of threading and handling and will wear out before the rest of the tape.

If you are producing something that is very important or something that you know will be aired over and over, start with fresh tape.

If possible, use a tone generator to set levels to the tape recorders. (Remember, some audio consoles have a built-in tone generator for this purpose.) At the very least, read some copy into the mic and set a good level on the audio board and then balance that level with the input levels of the recorders. Do the same for the turntables and other sound sources you will be using.

These few minutes that you take to set up the studio will make the production go more smoothly and will actually save you time in the overall production process.

While you are doing your production work, keep notes. For example, if you are using any signal-processing equipment, note the settings for the effect you are producing so that you will be able to recreate it easily at another time. Also, write down the production music you use for music beds. That way you'll avoid using the same piece of music over and over. Make note of any sound effects or special recording techniques so that you can duplicate what you have produced at some future time, if need be.

Because much finished production work goes onto audio cartridges, make sure the cart has been erased and has been cued past the splice. After erasing and locating the splice, listen to the cart for a few seconds. Not only does this confirm that it is properly erased, but it helps prevent loose tape problems by playing it. (Take the cartridge out of the program mode on the audio board before recording onto it, or you'll get unwanted echo.)

Always listen to your finished production, at least once over the studio monitor speakers and once over the cue speaker. By listening in cue, you can tell if a stereo cartridge is out of phase, as you will be barely able to hear the out-of-phase part of the signal. Also listen for copy errors; make sure you said what the copy said. Of course, listen for overall quality. If the production didn't come out the way you thought it did, take the time to redo it.

As a radio production person, make time to experiment in the production studio. The best way to learn production is to do production, and the best way to create new effects is by production studio experimentation. If you create something of your own, it will be unique to your station and your production work.

11.3 MUSIC

Music constitutes the largest percent of radio station programming and is usually introduced and coordinated by a **disc jockey.** If you become a disc jockey, you will be spending most of your time in the on-air studio doing all your production work live. This is actually a more challenging production situation than that in the production studio, where you have the time and luxury of rerecording until you get things just the way you want. On-air broadcasting is fast-paced, pressure packed, and, for most people, fun.

Although the main element of the programming is music, the main duty of the disc jockey is talking. Much of this talk involves introducing music. For this, your announcing style must fit the format of the radio station. For example, fast-paced, high-energy, rapid-fire speech is not appropriate for a classical music or big band format, but may be required at a contemporary hit radio station.

Don't imitate announcers you've heard on radio, but rather develop your own personal style. A delivery similar to your normal conversational style is appropriate to begin with, and you'll find that it will develop into a radio voice with time. Try to think of something to say between records that makes a logical transition. Maybe two records have the same theme or are by two different artists who once worked together or have a similar instrumentation.

Have a variety of ways of getting into and out of the music. Many beginning announcers latch onto one record introduction and use it over and over ("Here's a classic from the Beatles . . . "; "Here's a classic from Bob Dylan . . . "; "Here's a classic from . . . "). If you have trouble thinking of clever material, read what is on the record jacket. This will often give you an idea for something to say that is unusual or informative.

Your station may have certain policies regarding what you say and how you say it. For example, some stations have a policy requiring you to talk over the beginning and ending of records in order to prevent people from recording whole songs off the air. Other stations have particular slogans ("your tops of the pops") that they want repeated at regular intervals.

As a disc jockey, you will also be talking about things other than music. For example, you may need to give the time, temperature, commercials, weather, news, or traffic. Or you may introduce other people, such as the newscaster, who will give some of this information. Station policy will probably dictate whether you must be very formal about these introductions or whether you are given the latitude to banter with the other person. At some stations, the good-natured joking between disc jockey and helicopter traffic reporter is part of what keeps listeners tuned in.

Regardless of what is going on within the live production situation, always assume the mic may be open. Don't say anything that you wouldn't want to go out over the air. This includes personal conversations and, of course, indecent language. Many studios have an on-air light inside the studio as well as the one outside the door. This inside light is to alert the announcer to the fact that the mic is live, but the best rule is to assume the mic is always on.

Obviously, as a disc jockey you need to be proficient at operating the equipment so that you can cue up and play records, tapes, CDs, etc. But this involves more than just equipment manipulation because you are normally operating equipment and talking. This means you have to plan ahead. For example, if you have to join a network, you must know exactly when and how to do it. If you aren't sure whether you've cued up a record or tape, redo it. You must have everything cued up and ready to go and have a routine for what you are doing. It's also good practice to have an alternative if something goes wrong. If the cartridge you want to play doesn't fire, have in mind what you will do immediately. A good announcer can overcome most miscues so that the listening audience does not even know that anything went wrong.

Make sure you have previewed the record, especially to know how it begins and ends. This will ensure that you avoid **walking over** (beginning to outro a song before it is really over) a false ending. Previewing also helps you know how much instrumentation there is at the beginning of the record before the vocal starts. In this way you can talk over the instrumental but not the vocal part of the beginning. Sometimes timing information is provided on the record or cartridge and this helps you with **voice-overs** on the intro and outro of the song. In any case, there is no excuse for a disc jockey playing a record on the air that he or she is not completely familiar with.

Plan how you will get from one piece of music to the next if you play them consecutively. You might want to review the sound transitions mentioned in the chapter on turntables. Remember to work for a variety of ways rather than using the same method time after time. Listen to the on-air monitor frequently, if not continuously. Most audio consoles allow the announcer to hear the program line, the audition line, or the on-air signal; only the on-air signal, however, allows you to hear exactly what the listener hears.

When your shift is over, clean up around the studio. It is also a nice idea to pull the first couple of songs or the first commercial break material for the next announcer so he or she can get off to a smooth start. Playing music on radio is a hectic but rewarding job. Disc jockeys are, in every sense of the word, production people. Not only do they have to manipulate all the broadcast equipment, but they must add the element of announcing and present it all live and within the fast pacing of the radio station's format.

11.4 NEWS

If you are involved with radio production, you are likely to do some news work at some point in your life. In some instances the disc jockey is expected to just **rip and read** from the news service on the hour or half hour. At the other extreme are all-news stations, which usually have separate on-air people for news, weather, sports, traffic, commentaries, business news, and the like. This is a complicated format that necessitates people who are very knowledgeable in their specialties and who have established themselves and their voices as personalities. Whatever situation you find yourself in, some knowledge about newscasting will prove useful.

Even if you are expected to just rip and read, you should give some time and thought to your news presentation. First, you must decide which news to present. Of course, you probably have a news format to follow, but you should also try to select those items that are most likely to be of interest to your listeners. You may find that you need to do some rewriting of the wire service news and write some transitions to take the listener from one story to the next.

Timing is important on a news break. Make sure you read your news copy in the time prescribed. Sometimes beginning newscasters run out of news to read before the newscast time is up. To prevent this, you should pad your newscast with some extra stories that you can cut if you have to but provide a cushion if you need extra material. You'll usually need to get commercials in at an appropriate time during a newscast, so make sure you know when this happens and are prepared for it.

Don't ever read a newscast cold. Read it over first so that you are familiar with the material. Rewrite anything that is not natural for you, such as tongue-twisting phrases that you might trip over. Also rewrite if there are long sentences that make you lose your breath before you finish them. Avoid too many numbers or facts jammed

into a single sentence. Whenever something is unclear, rewrite to make it simple and easy to understand. Remember, broadcast news should be conversational and written for the ear, not the eye.

When a news story includes the actual voice of the person in the news, such as the mayor commenting on the new city budget, that segment is an **actuality.** Most radio news operations strive to include many actualities within a newscast because these bring life to the news. It is more interesting to hear the mayor's comments than the voice of an announcer telling what the mayor said. Actualities are best reserved for opinion or reaction. Actual facts about the story can be given by the reporter and then the news maker can say what he or she thinks about the subject.

Obviously, many news actualities are gathered in the field with portable tape recorders; you can, however, also make use of the phone to gather them. Many small radio stations have one-person news departments, and in these cases the phone actuality is especially crucial. In some situations, newsroom phones are semipermanently hooked up to tape recorders. But if not, you can use **alligator clips** to tap into the phone signal. Remove the earpiece cover on the phone receiver, attach the clips to the two prongs within the earpiece, and send the signal to the input of your recorder. Another way to record from the phone is to use a contact mic that is specifically made to attach to the phone for this purpose. You must obtain permission to record someone for broadcast use, and your station newsroom probably has specific guidelines to follow for doing this.

Actualities generally need to be edited. For this, you should use all the editing techniques presented in chapter 7 and then add one very important rule: make sure that when you edit you don't change the meaning of what someone has said. Ethical news procedures dictate that a great deal of care be taken in this area because the elimination of a single word can greatly alter a news report. For example, ''The mayor did not agree with the city council's decision . . .'' could easily become just the opposite if the word ''not'' were edited out, ''The mayor did agree with the city council's decision. . . .''

When you are editing and need to eliminate part of what a person said, either because it is too long or it is irrelevant, try to match voice expressions where the statement leaves off and where a new one begins. Edits are usually best if made at the end of thoughts, because a person's voice drops into a concluding mode at that point. Be careful not to edit out all the breaths the person takes because this will destroy the natural rhythm. People do breathe, and actualities without any breathing sound unnatural. If an edit is going to be too tight because the person runs words together, add in a little background noise or add a breath from a different place on the tape. Either of these will make for a natural-sounding pace between two edit points.

Try to maintain a constant background level throughout the actuality. To do this, you may have to mix in background noise from one part of the tape to another part. If you mix narration with an actuality, make sure you maintain the same level for both, and try to have background noises that are similar, or at least not jarring.

When editing, cut loosely if in doubt of where you actually want to make the edits. It is much easier to take more out later than it is to put material back in once it has been edited out. But, in case you do need to put something back, save all outtakes until you are totally finished with the editing procedure.

Whether you're a disc jockey reading a few newscasts or a broadcast journalist at an all-news station, you may wish to consult one of several good books available on techniques and ethics of gathering, writing, editing, and presenting news. Several of these books are listed in the Suggested Reading section at the end of this book.

11.5 COMMERCIALS

Most radio production people are involved with producing commercials. At their simplest level, commercials are simply copy that the announcer reads over the air. At their most complex, they are highly produced vignettes that include several voices, sound effects, and music. In between are testimonials by famous people, an announcer followed by a cartridge, dialogue between two actors, and an announcer over music.

Commercials are usually exactly thirty seconds or exactly sixty seconds. Because they are inserted within other programming elements, they must have exact times. Otherwise part of the commercial will be cut off or there will be dead air. At some stations, commercials are brought on and taken off by computers, which are very unsympathetic to anything that is too long or too short.

Anyone reading commercial copy should use a natural, sincere style. Reading commercials in a condescending manner is definitely uncalled-for. Commercials pay station salaries and should be treated with respect. If you are to read commercial copy live, you should read it over ahead of time to minimize stumbling on words, just as you would do for the news. If the commercial involves both reading live and playing a cartridge, make sure you rehearse the transition between the two. Sometimes a cart sounds like it is ending, but actually has additional information—perhaps new store hours or a bargain price. If you are to read material after the cart ends, make sure you do not read over the top of the carted information.

Probably the most common form of commercial you will produce involves an announcer over music. The usual format for this is as follows:

a. music bed at full volume for a few seconds
b. music bed fades under and holds
c. voice-over read on top of music bed
d. music bed brought up to full volume at end of voice-over for a few seconds
e. music bed fades out

Although this seems simple enough, it will not come easily until you've practiced and accomplished it many times. Not only must you be concerned with timing, but you have to determine how much music to use to establish the spot, balance the levels between voice and music bed, select appropriate music, and correctly manipulate the broadcast equipment. Usually you do all of this at the same time, although it is possible to record the voice-over and mix it with music at a later time.

Highly produced spots usually take a relatively long time to prepare. Minidramas, which start with music and involve two people bantering to the accompaniment of sound effects, involve a great deal of preproduction, rehearsing, mixing, and editing. They are, however, among the most challenging, creative products a radio production person handles. Often different parts of them are recorded at different times. The talent will record their parts and then leave, especially if they are highly paid talent. Then the production person will mix the talent skit with music and sound effects.

Commercials create interesting production challenges—and also pay the bills.

11.6 PUBLIC AFFAIRS PROGRAMS

Public affairs programming usually consists of long programs that explore a news or community issue in-depth. Some public affairs programs take a lighter tone and profile an individual or group. The typical public affairs show is a half-hour interview or discussion between host and guest(s). Although some stations have a specific public affairs host, many stations delegate this responsibility to a news person or an announcer.

The key to good public affairs programming is proper preparation. The host needs to research the subject and the guest before doing the program. Not only will this provide background, but it should enable the host to make a list of questions to ask.

Asking the right questions really means asking good questions. For example, ask questions that require more than a simple yes or no answer. Don't ask, "Do you agree with the mayor's new policy regarding the police?" but rather, "What do you think of the mayor's new policy regarding the police?" Ask short, simple, and direct questions. The question, "Given the salaries of employees and the possible raises they will receive, what do you think the effects will be on the social security system and the GNP?" will most likely get a response of, "Huh?" Break complex questions down into a number of questions such as, "How do you think increasing salaries five percent will affect the GNP?" Ask questions that do not require long answers. Don't ask, "What would you do to improve the city?'' but, ''What is the first thing you would do to improve the city?''

Asking good questions also means knowing how to handle the answers you get. For example, if the answer is too wordy, ask the person to summarize the response. If the answer is muddy or unclear, ask the material over again in smaller parts. If the answer is evasive, come back to it later or ask it again from a different angle. If the response gets off track, redirect. And if the response goes on and on, interrupt politely and redirect.

Listen carefully to what the guest says so you can ask appropriate follow-up questions. Sometimes interviewers become so engrossed in thinking about the next question that they miss an important point the guest has made that could lead to something significant. Although you should write questions ahead of time so that you remember to cover all important points, don't stick slavishly to those questions. In all probability when you ask question one, the guest will also answer questions three and seven, so you must constantly flow with the conversation. The more you can lead off what the guest says, the more natural the interview will appear. But make sure you do get the information you want.

If you are going to be recording the program at a remote location, make sure all the equipment works before you leave the station. This also holds true for recording in the studio; check everything out before your guest arrives.

You may be using a single microphone, so talk at the same level as the interviewee. As a broadcast professional, your voice may be stronger than the interviewee's, in which case lower your voice or else keep the mic further away from yourself than from the guest. If you are talking with several guests, move the mic back and forth as each person talks. Also follow speakers if they move their heads. Never let the guest take the microphone. He or she probably won't know how to use it properly, and you will lose control of the conversation.

When you have a number of different guests, identify them frequently, because the listener has difficulty keeping track of the various voices. Even a single guest should be reintroduced during a thirty-minute program. Not only does this remind listeners who your guest is, but it introduces him or her to that part of the audience that joined the program in progress.

When you record at a remote location, listen to at least part of the tape before you leave to make sure you have actually recorded something. It's embarrassing to get back to the station and discover that you have nothing on the tape, and it might be impossible to rearrange the interview for another time. If you are doing the interview in the studio, make sure you have a recording before the guest leaves.

Many public affairs programs are aired live or ''as taped,'' but sometimes it is necessary to edit the tape. If you are going to be editing extensively, make a log of the material so that you know what is on the tape and where

it is. As you edit, keep in mind that your editing should be used to clarify or simplify what the guest has said and should be used to correct mistakes or verbal fluffs.

Public affairs shows are part of almost all broadcast stations' programming, and an understanding of the program concept and techniques, especially interviewing, will help you handle this production situation.

11.7 CALL-IN TALK SHOWS

Not everyone is cut out to handle hosting a call-in talk show. You must be fast on your feet and able to ad-lib in an entertaining and effective manner. For many programs, you're expected to have more than broadcast production knowledge. For example, a sports program or radio psychology show requires a host with some expertise in those areas. Usually the telephone talk show host has an engineer handling the equipment so that the host can concentrate on dealing with the callers, but this is not always the case, especially in smaller-market radio.

A telephone talk show host has to be able to handle people tactfully (or, in some cases, abrasively, if that is the style of the program). As when interviewing for public affairs programs, the host must remain in charge of the program. Many of the other principles of public affairs interviewing also apply to call-in shows.

If you have a guest that people are asking questions of, you should give information about the guest and redirect questions if they are not understandable. The host must be able to establish good communication, without the aid of body language.

11.8 PLAY-BY-PLAY SPORTS

Many announcers also handle some sports broadcasting duties, and **play-by-play (PBP)** announcing skills can be a valuable asset for anyone entering the radio business. As a radio sports announcer, you must keep up the chatter, and you must describe completely what is happening. Since the listeners do not have the video image of TV, you have to be their eyes. Sports announcers often work in a team of which one announcer provides the play-by-play while another offers color commentary along with game statistics.

The PBP sportscaster operates remote equipment designed for sports broadcasting. Most of it is similar to studio equipment but extremely portable. A small audio console and headset microphone make up the bulk of sports remote equipment. The headset mic arrangement allows the sportscaster the use of both hands and keeps the counter or tabletop free for equipment and stat sheets.

The signal is sent from a remote console to the station by phone line or **microwave.** You should also have some other way of communicating with the studio, such as a separate telephone line. This way you can talk with the station about production matters that should not be heard by the audience. For example, commercials are usually played from carts at the station, and you might need to coordinate when and how many will be played during a break in the action.

Pregame preparation is very important for sports broadcasting. Gather all the information and facts about the teams and players, make sure all the equipment is ready to go, and get to the game in plenty of time to check out the broadcast booth so you know everything is in order.

Sportscasting is one of the most glamorous aspects of radio production, but it is time-consuming and requires quick thinking and a thorough knowledge of the sport.

11.9 DRAMA

Drama is not produced very often on radio anymore, but when it is undertaken, it employs the use of many production skills, such as microphone techniques and the blending of sound effects and music into the production. The setting and action must be conveyed by the talent, sound effects, and music. Drama is best recorded with one microphone, but you may need to have people with louder voices position themselves a little further away from it. It is also important to keep perspective during a production. In other words, people who are coming toward the supposed location of the play should sound far away at first and then nearer. The best way to do this is for the talent to walk away or toward the mic. You can mark the studio floor as to where they should start or stop talking to be on mic or off mic.

Sometimes one actor performs several parts. The actor needs to be able to create distinctly different voices in order to do this. In fact, all voices used within a drama should be distinctively different because audience members have trouble distinguishing one character from another. Talent should avoid using an affected radio voice but rather talk in their character's natural, conversational style.

Sound effects can be simulated in the studio, usually on a different microphone than the talent is on. Or they can be prerecorded or taken from a sound effects album and edited into the production at a later time. They can be used to establish locale, tell time, establish mood, indicate entries and exits, and establish transitions. Music is also an effective way to establish mood and create transitions. Most radio dramas open and close with music that is appropriate to the overall theme of the drama.

11.10 CONCLUSIONS

Although music, news, commercials, public affairs programs, call-in talk shows, play-by-play sports, and drama are major forms of radio programming, other forms do exist. For example, some stations have children's programs and others occasionally produce documentaries. Others are no doubt open to new forms of programming that may become popular in the future.

Radio production is an exciting profession. The various types of programming allow for variety in the day-to-day work. Radio is a personal medium, and those working in it can justifiably feel that they are affecting the lives of many other people.

Self-Study

■ QUESTIONS

1. The production studio should be cleaned up by _____.
   a) each production person when he or she finishes a session
   b) the first person to use the facility in the morning
   c) the station receptionist

2. When you are working in the production studio, you should _____.
   a) turn on all the equipment even if you don't plan to use it
   b) use only fresh tape
   c) set levels using the tone generator

3. A fast-paced disc jockey talk style is most appropriate for a _____.
   a) rock format
   b) classical music format
   c) big band format

4. Some stations want disc jockeys to talk over the beginning and end of records so that _____.
   a) cueing mistakes will be minimized
   b) people can not record entire songs off-air
   c) there is more time for commercials

5. To walk over a false ending of a song is to _____.
   a) leave the mic open when it should be closed
   b) recue a cartridge
   c) give the outro of a song before it is really over

6. An actuality is _____.
   a) the voice of a person in the news
   b) a pad for a newscast
   c) wire service copy

7. Radio news copy should contain_____.
   a) as many facts and numbers as possible
   b) simple, easy-to-understand sentences
   c) tongue-twister phrases

8. News actualities should be edited to _____.
   a) change the meaning of what a person says
   b) cut out material that is irrelevant
   c) cut out breaths

9. Commercials with a music bed usually _____.
   a) are thirty-seven seconds long
   b) are read by a disc jockey
   c) have a voice-over read on top of the music bed

10. Which would be the best interview question?
   a) Do you favor capital punishment?
   b) What do you think will be the outcome of the present attempt to outlaw capital punishment?
   c) What do you think will happen regarding an amendment against capital punishment being added to the Constitution after it has been discussed by the state legislature in light of the case pending in Florida at the present time and the one recently decided in Illinois?

11. When you are interviewing, you should _____.
   a) ask follow-up questions based on what the interviewee says
   b) make sure you ask all your questions in the order you have written them
   c) let the interviewee hold the microphone

12. Play-by-play sports announcers
   a) are usually abrasive
   b) cue up commercials while the game is in progress
   c) usually work in teams

13. Radio drama is usually recorded_____.
   a) at a remote location
   b) with one microphone for the entire cast
   c) in violation of the rules of perspective

14. As a final review of this chapter, match the items in the top list (1, 2, 3 . . .) with the production situations (m, n, c . . .) that most appropriately fit them and then select the correct set of answers from the sequences shown in a, b, or c below.

   1. _____ most likely to be thirty seconds long
   2. _____ most likely to be thirty minutes long

   3. _____ most likely to be produced remotely
   4. _____ handled by a disc jockey
   5. _____ the least-common form of programming today
   6. _____ most likely to contain actualities
   7. _____ involves listeners calling the station

 m. music
 n. news
 c. commercials
 p. public affairs
 t. call-in talk shows
 s. play-by-play sports
 d. drama

 a) 1.c 2.p 3.s 4.m 5.d 6.n 7.t
 b) 1.p 2.c 3.s 4.m 5.t 6.d 7.n
 c) 1.c 2.p 3.t 4.m 5.d 6.n 7.s

■ ANSWERS

If you answered A:

 1a. Right. All production people are responsible for their own cleanup.
 2a. No. This can introduce unnecessary noise. Reread 11.2 and try again.
 3a. Right. Rock music is most likely to require a fast pace.
 4a. No. This would be a strange way to cover mistakes. Reread 11.3 and try again.
 5a. No. An open mic has nothing to do with a walk-over. Reread 11.3 and try again.
 6a. Right. Actualities are statements from the people involved.
 7a. No. Facts and numbers can be confusing when a person can not refer back to them. Reread 11.4 and try again.
 8a. Never. This is a definite ethics violation. Reread 11.4 very carefully and try again.
 9a. No. Music is included in the commercial's thirty-second length. Reread 11.5 and try again.
 10a. No. This can be answered yes or no. Reread 11.6 and try again.
 11a. Yes, you should listen and ask appropriate follow-up questions.
 12a. No. A few have been, but sports people are not generally abrasive; talk show hosts are more likely to have this demeanor. Reread 11.7 and 11.8 and try again.
 13a. No. It is best produced in the controlled environment of a studio. Reread 11.9 and try again.
 14a. Right. You have now completed this chapter.

If you answered B:

 1b. Wrong. No one would want to be first. Reread 11.2 and try again.
 2b. No. It is fine to reuse audio tapes if they are not excessively worn. Reread 11.2 and try again.
 3b. No. This should be more subdued. Reread 11.3 and try again.
 4b. Right. If people can not record the entire song, they are more likely to buy the record.
 5b. No. Carts have nothing to do with walk-overs. Reread 11.3 and try again.
 6b. No, a pad is extra stories. Reread 11.4 and try again.
 7b. Correct. Radio copy should be easily understood.
 8b. Right. This is one of several proper reasons.
 9b. No. Commercials with a music bed have usually been produced before they go on the air. Reread 11.5 and try again.
 10b. Yes, this is the best choice.
 11b. No. Your interview can become very stilted if you do that. Reread 11.6 and try again.
 12b. Wrong. Commercials are usually played from the studio. Reread 11.8 and try again.
 13b. Yes, one microphone is usually sufficient.
 14b. Wrong. This is an easy set of questions. Try again.

If you answered C:

 1c. Naturally not. Reread 11.2 and try again.
 2c. Yes. Setting levels with the tone generator is a good practice.

3c. No. This should be more subdued. Reread 11.3 and try again.

4c. No. This is not a valid reason and would not really gain much time. Reread 11.3 and try again.

5c. Right. This is what a walk-over is.

6c. Wrong. Reread 11.4 and try again.

7c. No. These are difficult for the newscaster to read. Reread 11.4 and try again.

8c. No. Breaths are natural and usually should be left in. Reread 11.4 and try again.

9c. Correct. That is how they are produced.

10c. No. This question is much too convoluted. Reread 11.6 and try again.

11c. No. You will lose control. Reread 11.6 and try again.

12c. Yes. One person does play-by-play and the other does color commentary.

13c. No. It utilizes perspective. Reread 11.9 and try again.

14c. Wrong. This is an easy set of questions. Try again.

Projects

■ PROJECT 1

Record a creative thirty-second or sixty-second commercial.

Purpose

To develop your skill in creating a commercial following the basic commercial format and to train you to work within a specific time limit.

Advice, Cautions, and Background

1. The commercial must be exactly thirty seconds or sixty seconds.
2. You can write the commercial either for an actual product or for something you make up.
3. Be creative in terms of the idea, the wording, and the special effects.
4. Keep in mind that the commercial is to sell a product or idea, and the creativity should enhance the subject and not detract from it.

How To Do the Project

1. Read the Information section on production situations.
2. Complete the Self-Study Questions on production situations.
3. Think up an idea for the commercial. Make sure your idea is producible, i.e., that you have all the people, music, effects, and equipment necessary to do it.
4. Write the commercial, making sure it is thirty or sixty seconds.
5. Do a practice recording of your material and listen to it. If it's good enough, give it to the instructor. If not, redo it until it is done well.
6. On the tape or tape box, write your name and ''Commercial Production Project.'' Turn in the completed tape to your instructor to receive credit for this project.

■ PROJECT 2

Record a fifteen-minute rock music, classical music, or country music disc jockey show.

Purpose

To enable you to develop disc jockey skills.

Advice, Cautions, and Background

1. You may do as many of these formats as you wish and get credit for each. In other words, you could do both a rock show and a classical show, but don't do two of the same type.
2. You will need different voice intonations for each style. For example, your talk on a rock show might be fast and bubbling, but for a classical show you would be more subdued.
3. Listen to several disc jockeys who do the type of show you are planning to do and pick up whatever ideas you can, but remember that you should not try to just copy what another disc jockey is doing.
4. Vary your pitch, volume, and tone so that your voice doesn't become monotonous. Remember that the listener can't see you, so facial expressions and gestures have no effect.
5. Try to establish a mood or theme for your fifteen-minute segment.
6. Make the program exactly fifteen minutes. This shouldn't be much of a problem, because you can fade out music or ad-lib at the end.

How To Do the Project

1. Read the Information section on production situations.
2. Complete the Self-Study Questions on production situations.
3. Select the music you wish to play and time it. You will be playing each piece in its entirety. Except for classical music, selections should not be over five minutes.
4. Plan and write any commercials, station breaks, or other breaks you wish to include. Think through how you will introduce the various music selections.
5. Make sure you have a total of approximately fifteen minutes of material including music and talk.
6. Do the program and tape it, ending at fifteen minutes. Use your own creativity and style. If it is good enough, give the tape to the instructor. If not, do it again until it is acceptable. Put your name and "Disc Jockey Project" on the tape or tape box.
7. Turn the completed tape in to the instructor to receive credit for this project.

■ PROJECT 3

With two other students, record a fifteen-minute news program.

Purpose

To further develop news skills.

Advice, Cautions, and Background

1. Begin work on this fairly early. Since it will be a team effort, you will need time for coordination.
2. Select for your news team reliable people who will not be dropping out of the project. It is annoying to have to change your format after you begin.
3. It is a good idea to select a producer who will handle coordination.
4. Be sure to work up transitions from one type of news to another, as this will probably be the most awkward part of the newscast. Also, plan the beginning and ending.

How To Do the Project

1. Read the Information section on production situations.
2. Complete the Self-Study Questions on production situations.
3. Decide what each person will do. There are many different ways of organizing this, all of which could probably be found at some radio station somewhere. Following are some things to consider:
   a. What program elements do you want to include, such as international news, national news, local news, sports, weather, editorial, commercials, human interest?
   b. How do you plan to handle transitions? For example, each person could introduce the next one or one anchor could introduce all the others.

   c. How do you plan to handle writing and announcing duties? Does each person write and read his or her own news or do some people write the news and others announce?
   d. How do you plan to handle engineering? One person could be responsible for levels, or each announcer could be responsible for his or her own levels, or you could preset levels and no one would be responsible during the actual newscast.
4. Decide on time allocations for the various segments of news so that you total fifteen minutes.
5. Check your organization and ideas with the instructor.
6. Set a definite date to do the taping.
7. Have a dry run of the program and be sure to check timing.
8. Tape the program and listen to it. If it is good enough, turn in the tape to your instructor. If not, redo it.
9. On the outside of the tape or tape box write ''Newscasting Project'' and list the names of those participating.
10. Give the instructor a separate sheet of paper that lists everyone's name and the duties each fulfilled for the production. Turn in this sheet and the completed tape to receive credit for this project.

■ PROJECT 4

Record a five-minute interview show in which you are the interviewer.

Purpose

To prepare you for this very common type of broadcasting situation.

Advice, Cautions, and Background

1. Your interview must be exactly five minutes. Making an exact time without having an awkward ending will probably be the hardest part of the project, but it is a lesson worth learning because broadcasting is built around time sequences.
2. Don't underprepare. Don't fall into the trap of feeling that you can wing this. In five minutes you must come up with the essence of something interesting, and you can not do this unless you have an organization of questions in mind. You will also only be able to record the interview once. You can not redo this project.
3. Don't overprepare. Don't write out the interview word for word. It will sound stilted and canned if you do.
4. Five minutes is actually a long time; you will be amazed at how much you can cover in this time.
5. As interviewer, don't talk too much. Remember the purpose is to get the ideas of your guest over to the audience, not your own ideas.

How To Do the Project

1. Read the Information section on production situations.
2. Complete the Self-Study Questions on production situations.
3. Select someone in class to interview. It's not mandatory to do this. You can interview a friend, but it will probably be easier to do it with someone in class.
4. Decide what the interview will be about. You may select any subject you wish. You could pretend the interviewee is a famous person. You could talk about some facet of a person's life or his or her views on some current subject.
5. Work up a list of questions. Make more than you think you will actually need just in case you run short.
6. Think of a structured beginning and ending for the show, as those will probably be the most awkward parts.
7. Discuss the interview organization with your guest so you are in accord as to what is to be discussed.
8. Tape the interview, making sure you stop at five minutes. Listen to it and check that it has recorded before your guest leaves. You are finished with the project once the interview is taped. Even if it did not come out as you hoped, do not redo this project.
9. On the tape or tape box write ''Interview Project'' and your name. Give the interview tape to your instructor to receive credit for this project.

■ PROJECT 5

Record a ten-minute play-by-play broadcast of some sports event.

Purpose

To allow those interested in doing sports broadcasts to develop skills in this area.

Advice, Cautions, and Background

1. This must be a real situation. Don't just pretend that you are seeing some sports event. You must actually do it from a sports event or else from a TV broadcast of a sports event.
2. Be sure to do your homework. Preparation is important so that you can keep announcing even during lulls in the action. Make sure you know enough about the sport and the players before you attempt the broadcast.
3. Make sure you can pronounce all the players' names correctly.
4. If you go to a game, try to situate yourself somewhere where there won't be too much crowd noise to interfere with your recording. If you do the project from a TV set, you will, of course, have to turn down the volume.
5. You may wish to rehearse silently or out loud or by recording several times before you actually do your ten-minute recording.

How To Do the Project

1. Read the Information section on production situations.
2. Complete the Self-Study Questions on production situations.
3. Select the sporting event you wish to use.
4. Attend the event and take a portable tape recorder, or turn the volume down on your TV set and get your equipment ready to do a play-by-play.
5. At some point, start your broadcast and continue recording it for about ten minutes. Try to start at some logical spot, such as the beginning of a quarter, inning, or round.
6. On the tape or tape box write your name and ''Play-By-Play Broadcast Project.'' Give the completed tape to your instructor to receive credit for this project.

■ PROJECT 6

With several other students, record a radio drama.

Purpose

To allow you to practice your dramatic abilities and to give you the experience of performing radio dramas.

Advice, Cautions, and Background

1. Make sure you have a group of congenial, dependable people. You don't want to start rehearsal and then have to switch cast members.
2. Sound effects will probably give you the most trouble. Make sure you have all that you need.
3. People can get credit for this assignment without being on-air. For example, you might want to have one person in charge of sound effects, one in charge of engineering, and one as director.
4. If you want to write a play rather than use one that is already written, this is fine.
5. One person can play more than one role in radio by changing voices.

How To Do the Project

1. Read the Information section on production situations.
2. Complete the Self-Study Questions on production situations.

3. Select the group and choose a director.
4. Have the director or the group select a play. Following are some books you may be able to find in a library that contain radio plays:
   a. *Radio Workshop Plays*
   b. *Creative Broadcasting*
   c. *Radio's Best Plays*
   d. *Radio Plays for Young People*
5. Decide what each person is going to do for the production.
6. Check with the instructor about what you are planning to do and what problems you expect to experience.
7. Make sure everyone gets a copy of the script. You can check with the instructor about ways to get the script duplicated.
8. Have set times to rehearse. Rehearse section by section both with and without microphones and then put the whole thing together. Rehearse music and effects as well as dialogue.
9. When the production is polished enough, record it. Listen to it and if it is good enough, give the tape to the instructor. If not, redo it.
10. On the tape or tape box write ''Radio Drama Project'' and the names of all the people who are involved.
11. On a sheet of paper, list the names of all involved and write what each did for the production. Give this sheet and the completed tape to the instructor to receive credit for this project.

Sound Signals

A.1 INTRODUCTION

When sound is naturally produced (for example, an announcer speaking into a microphone), we think of that sound as a **sound signal.** In radio production, when that sound signal is then recorded on audio tape, it is called an **audio signal.** Obviously, all radio production must start at some point with a sound signal, but during the actual production process we are often manipulating an audio signal. To further complicate things, these terms are often interchanged when people talk about various radio production processes. This appendix, by taking a brief look at sound, will help you understand many aspects of the production process, whether it involves a sound signal or an audio signal.

A.2 SOUND

When something vibrates, sound is generated. For example, plucking a single guitar string causes a mechanical vibration to occur, which we can easily see by looking at the string. Of course, we can also hear it. The vibrating string sets adjacent air molecules in motion, which in turn set neighboring air molecules in motion and on and on. Sound develops waves (like a stone dropped into water), which vibrate up and down and set the air molecules in a push (**compression**) and pull (**rarefaction**) motion. Figure A.1 shows a representation of sound being produced.

A.3 CHARACTERISTICS OF SOUND WAVES

A sound wave's **amplitude** relates to its **volume.** The loudness of a sound can be thought of as the height of the sound wave. The louder the sound, the higher the amplitude (see Figure A.2A). As a sound gets louder, more compression and rarefaction of air molecules takes place.

Frequency relates to the **pitch** of a sound wave. The number of times a sound wave vibrates (goes in an up-and-down cycle) per second determines its frequency, and how we hear these vibrations determines its pitch (see Figure A.2B). The faster something vibrates, or the more cycles per second, the higher the pitch of the sound. The **wavelength** is the distance between two compressions or two rarefactions. The higher pitched sounds have the shorter wavelength.

In radio jargon, cycles per second are known as **hertz (Hz).** A sound wave that vibrates at two thousand cycles per second is said to have a frequency of two thousand hertz. When the cycles per second get higher, for example twenty thousand hertz, the term **kilohertz (kHz)** is often used. It denotes one thousand cycles per second, so twenty thousand hertz could also be called twenty kilohertz.

A sound's **waveform** relates to the **tone** or **timbre** of the sound. It's the characteristic of sound that distinguishes one announcer's voice from another even though both may be saying the same thing at the same volume and pace. A graphic representation of a pure tone is shown as the shape of a sine wave, as in Figure A.2C. Each sound has one basic tone that is its **fundamental;** most sound, however, is a combination of many tones with different strengths at different frequencies, so the waveform is much more complex, as shown in Figure A.2D. These other pitches are either exact frequency multiples of the fundamental (known as **harmonics**) or pitches that are not exact multiples of the fundamental (known as **overtones**). The interaction of the fundamental, harmonics, and overtones creates the timbre of any particular sound.

A sound's **wave envelope** relates to its **duration,** or the change in volume of a sound over a period of time. Normally, a sound's wave envelope goes through three stages: **attack,** the time it takes an initial sound to build to full volume; **sustain,** the time the sound holds its full volume; and **decay,** the time it takes a sound to die out from full volume to silence.

A.4 FREQUENCY RESPONSE

In radio production, we frequently mention the **frequency response** of equipment or, for that matter, the frequency response range of human hearing. In very general terms, we can think of the human ear as able to hear frequencies within the range of twenty to twenty thousand cycles per second. For most of us, it's not quite so low nor quite so high. Therefore radio production equipment should be able to reproduce an audio signal in that range.

For example, a monitor speaker may have a frequency

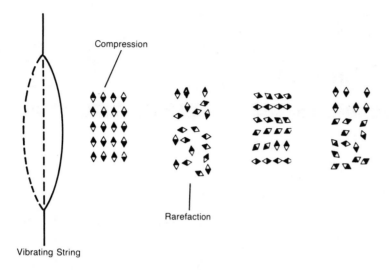

Compression

Rarefaction

Vibrating String

FIGURE A.1 The production of sound.

response of forty hertz to eighteen kilohertz, meaning that speaker can accurately reproduce all frequencies within that range. An inexpensive broadcast microphone may have a frequency response of only eighty hertz to thirteen kilohertz. It would not be able to pick up any of the higher frequencies above thirteen thousand hertz. This would not be a problem if the mic were used primarily to record speech, because the human voice usually falls in a frequency range of two hundred to three thousand hertz. Obviously, if you wanted to record a musical group (which often has sounds in the full range of frequencies), you would want to use a microphone with a wider frequency response.

Frequency response is often shown with a frequency response curve because some equipment may not pick up some frequencies as well as others. Since most broadcast equipment is designed to pick up all frequencies equally well, it is considered to have a flat frequency response curve.

Low frequencies (bass) are those below 350 hertz; midrange frequencies are those between 350 and 3500 hertz; and high frequencies (treble) are those over 3500 hertz. As frequencies change, we think in terms of the musical interval of the **octave,** or a change in pitch caused by doubling or halving the original frequency. For example, a sound going from bass to midrange to treble frequencies by octave intervals would go from 220 hertz to 440 hertz to 880 hertz to 1760 hertz to 3520 hertz to 7040 hertz and so on.

As humans, we are subject to an awkwardly named **equal loudness principle,** by which we hear midrange frequencies better than either high or low frequencies. In radio production (and other forms of sound or audio signal manipulation), we often compensate for this by equalization of the signal.

A.5 DYNAMIC RANGE

When we mention **dynamic range** in a radio production context, we're referring to the range of volumes of sound that broadcast equipment can handle. This intensity of a sound is measured in **decibels (dB).** One decibel represents the minimum difference in volume that we can hear, but a change of three decibels is often necessary before we actually hear a difference in volume.

The dynamic range goes from zero decibels, at the **threshold of hearing,** to 120 decibels, at the **threshold of pain.** A whisper is around 20 decibels, normal conversation is near 60 decibels, average music-listening levels are between 30 and 80 decibels, and some rock concerts have been measured above 110 decibels.

Dynamic range relates the volume of one signal to another, such as signal to noise. We should also note that dynamic range is measured on a logarithmic scale. For example, to hear one audio signal twice as loud as another, you would have to increase the volume of one by ten decibels in relation to the other.

A sixty-decibel dynamic range was once considered quite adequate for high-quality broadcast production equipment; today's digital equipment, however, offers an increased dynamic range and a ninety-decibel range is now common.

A.6 NOISE AND DISTORTION

Inherent in any electronic equipment is **noise.** Microphones can add noise to the audio signal if they employ an extremely long cable. Turntables and recorders can introduce noise from mechanical gears or just the electronics used in amplifying the signal. Any unwanted sound

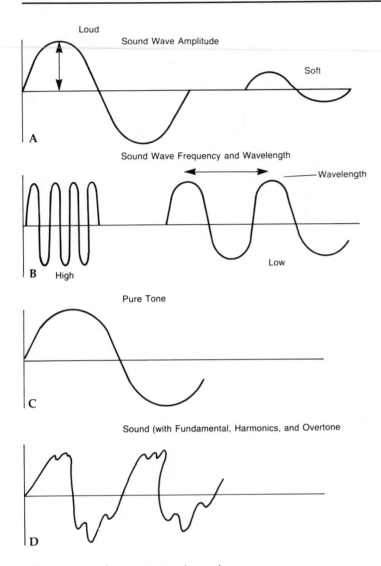

FIGURE A.2 Characteristics of sound waves.

element introduced in the production process that was not present in the original sound signal is thought of as noise.

In broadcast production, the noise level should be kept as low as possible. Most radio production equipment is designed to produce a **signal-to-noise ratio (S/N)** of at least sixty-to-one. In other words, when sixty decibels of sound signal are reproduced by the equipment, only one decibel of noise is introduced. Obviously, the higher the S/N ratio the better.

Distortion is an unwanted change in the audio signal due to inaccurate reproduction of the sound. One type of distortion is loudness distortion, which can occur when a signal is recorded at a level too loud for the equipment to handle. The overdriven signal sounds muddy and the reproduced signal does not have the same clarity or sharpness that the original signal did.

A.7 HISS AND HUM

Hiss is a very noticeable form of noise often associated with the tape recording process. Noise in the frequency range of two to eight kilohertz is heard by the human ear as hiss. **Hum** is a specific problem heard in any audio signal at sixty hertz. It is caused when the AC electrical current (which is sixty hertz) leaks into the audio signal. A poor or broken ground in any part of the electrical circuit can cause hum. Both hiss and hum sound exactly as their names imply.

A.8 WOW AND FLUTTER

A common problem with both turntables and tape recorders is improper playback speed, which results in a distorted, off-pitch sound of the original sound signal. **Wow** refers to slow changes in pitch caused by slow, regular variations in the playback speed. On the other hand, **flutter** is rapid variations in pitch and volume caused by rapid, regular changes in the playback speed. Again, both names are somewhat descriptive of the sounds heard.

A.9 STEREO

Most modern radio production is done in **stereo.** Stereo merely attempts to recreate the acoustic environment as we actually hear it. When we hear any sound, all of the sound enters both our right and left ears; the orientation of the sound, however, is slightly different for the sound entering the right ear than it is for the sound entering the left ear. In its simplest form, stereo is composed of two monaural systems—sound is picked up by two microphones and is recorded on two channels of an audio tape recorder. Although both microphones hear the total sound, the mic placed toward the right of the sound source will "hear" the sound differently than the mic placed to the left of the sound. The right and left channels indicate an orientation of the total sound.

Additional Production Projects

■ PROJECT 1

Record an air check tape.

Purpose

To instruct those interested in doing on-air broadcasting how to make an audition tape, something usually required when applying for a job.

Advice, Cautions, and Background

1. To apply for on-air jobs in broadcasting, you will send your resume and an air check tape to many stations. An air check tape is an audio tape of five to ten minutes that you record to show how you handle on-air broadcast situations.
2. Ideally, an audition tape is an edited-down sample of your actual on-air work, but if you are not on-air on a regular basis, a simulated air check can be put together in the production studio.
3. Try to make the tape as general as possible so that it could be sent to several different types of stations.
4. Put those things you do best at the beginning of the tape. Many potential employers don't have time to listen past the first few minutes and will rule you out if they don't like the beginning. Don't structure the tape so that it builds to a climax because probably no one will listen that far.
5. Feel free to use things you've done for other projects for your audition tape.
6. Keep the pace of the tape moving. Don't do any one thing for too long.
7. It is assumed that you have completed this entire text before you attempt this project.

How To Do the Project

1. Plan what you intend to include in your tape. An air check format might include ad-lib introductions to a few songs (either fade out the music after a few seconds or edit to the end of the songs so that the listener doesn't have to hear the whole song), a short newscast, some more song introductions, and a commercial or public service announcement. If you can do play-by-play, you might want to put a short sportscast at the end. There is no standard format so do whatever showcases your talent best.
2. Plan the order of your tape. Make it sound like a continuous radio show as much as possible.
3. Record your tape and listen to it. Redo it if it doesn't present good broadcast skills. If it's good enough, give it to the instructor.
4. On the tape or tape box, write your name and ''Air Check Project.'' Turn the completed tape in to the instructor for credit for this project.

■ PROJECT 2

Record a thirty-minute original radio program.

Purpose

To give you experience with more complicated production, to sharpen skills learned in other projects, and to utilize your creative ideas.

Advice, Cautions, and Background

1. You are to produce something that can be done on radio but isn't done very often. Therefore this can not be a regular disc jockey show. It must be an original idea.
2. Start working on this right away, as your preproduction time will probably be lengthy.
3. Check with the instructor frequently about your ideas, problems, and progress.
4. Don't get in over your head. Think up an unusual idea but make sure it is something you can actually complete.
5. Remember this is to be done so that it could be broadcast and therefore must comply with all FCC rules about profanity and indecent language.
6. Make sure the technical quality of the project is good.
7. It is assumed that you have completed this entire text before you attempt this project.

How To Do the Project

1. Think up an idea of some sort of program that could be aired on radio and isn't being done to any great extent. You can pretend the program is part of a series or that it is a single program. Ideas that have been used by students in the past include a narrative of advice about hitchhiking, a composite of humorous material, and an interview with several six-year-olds.
2. Check your ideas with the instructor.
3. Begin putting the program together in whatever way your particular idea demands.
4. Check with the instructor before you do the final taping and at any other times when you need help or advice.
5. Tape and edit (if necessary) so that you have a finished program that is thirty minutes in length.
6. On the tape box write your name, the program title, the exact time of the program, and a very brief summary of the content.
7. Give the completed tape to the instructor for credit for this project.

Glossary

Absorbed sound Sound that goes into walls, ceilings, and floors of a studio.

Acoustic suspension A speaker enclosure design that consists of a tightly sealed box that prevents rear sounds from disrupting main speaker sounds.

Active equalizer A device for adjusting frequencies that has an amplifier.

Actuality A voice report from a person in the news rather than from the reporter or newscaster.

Adhesion A condition that occurs when one layer of audio tape sticks to another.

Alignment The relationship between the audio tape and the position of the tape recorder head.

Alligator clips Metal connectors that can be used to transfer sound from a phone to a tape recorder.

Amplifier A piece of equipment that boosts volume.

Amplify To make louder.

Amplitude The strength or height of a sound wave or radio wave.

Analog A situation wherein the output continuously varies in a manner that is the same shape as the sound wave input.

Attack The time it takes an initial sound to build up to full volume.

Audio console The piece of equipment that mixes, amplifies, and routes sound.

Audio signal A sound signal that has been processed into an electromagnetic form.

Audio tape recorder A device that rearranges particles on magnetic tape in order to store sound.

Automatic music sensor A button on a digital audio tape recorder that allows the operator to skip forward or backward to the start of a new song.

Azimuth A tape alignment problem in which the tape recorder head leans to one side or the other.

Backing layer The back side of audio tape; the side that does not have magnetic oxide.

Balanced cable A cable with three wires—plus, minus, and ground.

Band pass filter A filter that cuts all frequencies outside of a specified range.

Band reject filter A filter that allows all frequencies to pass except a specified frequency range.

Bass reflex A speaker enclosure design that has a vented port to allow rear sounds to reinforce main speaker sounds.

Bass roll-off switch A switch that turns down bass frequencies to counter the proximity effect.

Belt drive turntable A system in which the turntable motor is coupled with the platter by a thin rubber belt.

Bias A high-frequency signal that improves frequency response of a recording and cuts down distortion.

Bidirectional Picking up sound from two directions; usually refers to a microphone pickup pattern.

Binary A number system that uses two digits, 1 and 0.

Blast filter See pop filter.

Boom stand A stand that can be placed away from an announcer; usually it consists of one vertical pipe with a horizontal pipe at the top of it.

Bulk eraser See degausser.

Cable Wire that carries audio signals.

Cannon See XLR.

Capacitor mic Another name for a condenser mic.

Capstan A metal shaft that controls the speed of a tape recorder.

Carbon mic An early form of microphone not used for radio anymore.

Cardioid Picking up sound in a heart-shaped pattern; usually refers to a mic pickup pattern.

Cartridge A device that converts the vibrations from the turntable stylus into variations in voltage; also, the tape for a cartridge tape recorder.

Cart labels Pieces of paper with adhesive backing that describe what is on a cartridge tape.

Cart racks Shelves for storing audio cartridges.

Cartridge recorder A tape recorder that uses tape that is in an endless loop.

Cart tape winder A machine for spooling a length of tape into a cartridge.

Cassette recorder A tape recorder that uses one-eighth-inch tape housed in a plastic case.

Ceramic mic A type of mic often used for inexpensive consumer-quality tape recorders.

Channel   The route an audio signal follows; also, the grouping of controls on an audio console associated with one input.

Clock   See timer.

Combo   The working procedure by which the announcer is also the equipment operator.

Compact disc (CD)   A recordlike piece of equipment onto which sound is recorded digitally and read by a laser.

Companders   Devices that compress dynamic range during recording and expand it during playback.

Compression   A sound wave characteristic that occurs when the air molecules are pushed close together.

Compressor   A volume control usually associated with the transmitter that boosts signals that are too soft and lowers signals that are too loud.

Condenser mic   A mic that uses a capacitor, usually powered by a battery, to respond to sound. It has a wide frequency response, so it is often used in radio.

Connector adapters   Freestanding connector parts that allow one connector form to be changed to another.

Connectors   Metal devices to attach one piece of audio equipment to another.

Contact   See penetration.

Control board   See audio console.

Copyholder   A small easel that sits on the audio console and frees the reader's hands to operate equipment.

Cross-fade   To bring up one sound and take down another in such a way that both are heard for a short period of time.

Crossover   An electronic device that sends low frequencies to the speaker woofer and high frequencies to the tweeter.

Cross talk   The picking up on a tape track of the signal from another track.

Crystal mic   A type of mic often used for inexpensive consumer-quality tape recorders.

Cue   To preview an input (such as a record or audiotape) before it goes over the air; also, to set up an audio source to the point at which it is to start.

Cue burn   Damage to the outer grooves of a record caused by backtracking the record.

Cue tone   A noise that cannot be heard that is put on a cartridge tape to stop it automatically.

Cue wheel   Part of a CD player that allows the operator to find the exact starting point of the music.

Cupping   The turning up of the edges of audio tape.

Curling   The twisting of a tape from front to back.

dbx   A noise reduction system that compresses both loud and soft parts of a signal during recording and then expands them during playback.

Dead air   A long pause when no sound is heard.

Dead roll   To play music with the volume turned down at first, to shorten the piece's duration.

Dead sound   Sound with very little echo or reverberation.

Decay   The time it takes a sound to go from full volume to silence.

Decibel (dB)   A measurement to indicate the loudness of sound.

De-esser   A processor that gets rid of sibilant sounds without affecting other parts of the signal.

Degausser   A magnetic unit that erases tapes.

Demagnetizer   A device to remove magnetic buildup on a tape recorder head.

Desk stand   A mic stand for a person in a seated position.

Digital   A situation wherein the output varies in discrete on-off binary steps that are sampled.

Digital audio stationary head (DASH)   A digital recording system that records horizontally, used for two-track and multitrack reel-to-reel systems.

Digital audio tape (DAT)   High-quality tape that can be dubbed many times without degradation because of the sampling process of its recording method.

Digital audio workstation (DAW)   A computer-based system that can create, store, edit, mix, and send out sound in a variety of ways all within one basic unit.

Digital delay   A unit that holds a signal temporarily and then allows it to leave the unit.

Digital reverb   A unit that produces reverberation electronically.

Direct drive turntable   A turntable platter that sits on top of the motor.

Direct sound   Sound that goes straight from a source to a microphone.

Disc jockey   A person who introduces and plays music for a radio station. The term arose because the person plays recorded discs and rides gain on the audio board.

Distortion   A blurring or sound caused by overamplification or other inaccurate reproduction of sound.

Dolby   A noise reduction system that raises the volume of the program signal most likely to be affected by noise during recording and then lowers it again during playback, so that the noise seems lower in relation to the program level.

Drop-out A flaking off of oxide coating from audio tape so that the total signal is not recorded.

Dubbing Electronically copying material from one tape to another.

Duration The time during which a sound builds up, remains at full volume, and dies out.

Dynamic mic A mic that consists of a diaphragm, a magnet, and coils. It is extremely rugged and has good frequency response, so it is used often in radio.

Dynamic range The volume changes from loud to soft within a series of sounds; also, the amount of volume change a piece of equipment can handle effectively.

Dynamic speaker A speaker with a cone attached to a voice coil. Electrical current in the voice coil creates a magnetic force that moves the cone.

Echo Sound that bounces off one surface.

Editing Splicing or dubbing material to rearrange or eliminate portions of it.

Electrostatic speaker A rarely used type of monitor speaker.

Equalization (EQ) The adjustment of the amplification given to a specific range of frequencies.

Equalizer The unit that adjusts the amount of amplification given to a specific range of frequencies.

Equal loudness principle The hearing of midrange frequencies better than high or low frequencies.

Fade To gradually increase or decrease the volume of music to or from silence.

Fade-in To bring sound up from silence to full volume.

Fade-out To take sound from full volume to silence.

Fader Part of an audio console that moves up and down to control volume.

Feedback A howling noise created when the output of a sound (usually from a speaker) is returned to the input (usually a mic).

Feed reel See supply reel.

Filter A unit that cuts out a particular frequency range of the audio signal.

Flanger A device that electronically combines an original signal with a slightly delayed one.

Flat Quality of a frequency curve wherein all frequencies are reproduced equally well.

Floor stand A mic stand for a person in a standing position.

Flutter Fast variations in sound speed.

Four-track recording Four signals on a tape all going the same direction.

Frequency The number of cycles a sound wave or radio wave completes in one second.

Frequency response The range of highs and lows that a piece of equipment reproduces.

Full-track A recording method that uses the whole tape for one monophonic signal.

Fundamental A basic tone and frequency that each sound has.

Gain control See volume control.

General Radiotelephone Operator License A license given by the FCC that requires thorough knowledge of engineering and broadcast law. A test is required to obtain this license.

Graphic equalizer An equalizer that divides frequency responses into bands that can then be raised or lowered in volume.

Grease pencil A crayonlike substance used to mark edit points on tape.

Guard bands Small portions of empty tape between each track and at the edges of the tape.

Half-track mono The recording of two separate mono signals on a tape, one going to the left and one going to the right.

Half-track stereo The recording of two tracks on one tape, both going the same direction to produce stereo.

Hand signals A method of communication that radio production people use when a live mic prohibits talk or when they are in separate rooms.

Hard wiring Connecting equipment in a fairly permanent manner, usually by soldering.

Harmonics Exact frequency multiples of a fundamental tone.

Harmonizer A signal processor that performs a number of functions including pitch alteration, compression/expansion, delay, reverb effects, flanging, and repeat.

Head An electromagnet that rearranges iron particles on tape; also, the beginning of an audio tape.

Headphones Tiny speakers encased in a headset.

Height A tape alignment problem in which the tape head is too high or too low.

Hertz   A measurement of frequency based on cycles of sound waves per second.

Hiss   A high-frequency noise problem inherent in the recording process.

Hum   A low-frequency noise problem caused by leaking of the sixty-cycle AC power current into the audio signal.

Idler wheel turntable   A system in which the turntable motor shaft drives a rubber disc that drives the platter.

Idler arm   A tension part of a reel-to-reel tape recorder that will stop the recorder if the tape breaks.

Imaging   The apparent space between speakers and how sounds are heard within the plane of the speakers.

Impedance   The total opposition a circuit offers to the flow of alternating current.

Input selectors   Switches that are used to choose mic or line positions on an audio board.

Jacks   Female connectors.

Kilohertz   A thousand cycles per second.

Laser   An acronym for light amplification by simulated emission of radiation; a narrow, intense beam in a compact disc that reads encoded audio data.

Laser diode   A semiconductor with positive and negative electrons that converts electrical input into optical output.

Leader tape   Plastic tape that does not contain iron particles to record. It is used primarily before and after the recording tape so that the tape can be threaded.

Limiter   A compressor with a large compression ratio that won't allow a signal to increase beyond a specified point.

Line level   An input that has already been preamplified.

Live sound   Sound with a great deal of echo and reverberation.

Low cut filter   A filter that eliminates all frequencies below a certain point.

Low pass filter   A filter that allows all frequencies below a certain point to go through unaffected.

Magnetic layer   The part of the tape that contains the iron oxide coating.

Master fader   The control that determines the volume of the signal being sent from the audio console.

Megahertz   A million cycles per second.

Microphone   A transducer that changes sound energy into electrical energy.

Microwave   Radio waves that can carry audio signals for fairly long distances.

Mic level   An input that has not been preamplified.

Mini   See miniphone plug.

Miniphone plug   A small connector with a sleeve and a tip.

Monaural   One channel of sound coming from one direction.

Monitor speaker   A piece of equipment that plays back sound.

Moving-coil mic   Another name for a dynamic mic.

Multiplay   A type of CD player that can hold up to one hundred CDs and access material on them according to a prescribed pattern.

Multiple microphone interference   Uneven frequency response caused when microphones that are too close together are fed into the same mixer.

Noise   Unwanted sound in the electronic equipment itself.

Noise reduction   Methods of eliminating unwanted sound from a signal.

Nondirectional   Another word for omnidirectional.

Notch filter   A filter that eliminates a narrow range of frequencies or one individual frequency.

Octave   A sound that doubles in frequency; for example, sounds at 220 hertz and 440 hertz are an octave apart.

Omnidirectional   Picking up sound from all directions; usually refers to a microphone pickup pattern.

On-air light   A signal that comes on to indicate a live mic is on in the studio.

On-air studio   The studio from which programming is broadcast.

Open air   Headphones that fit into the ear.

Output selectors   Buttons that determine where a sound goes as it leaves the audio console.

Overtones   Pitches that are not exact frequency multiples of a fundamental tone.

Pan knob   The part of an audio board that controls how much sound goes to the right channel of a stereo system and how much goes to the left channel.

Parametric equalizer   An equalizer that can control the center frequency and the bandwidth that will have its volume raised or lowered.

Passive equalizer   An equalizer that does not have an amplifier.

Patching   Connecting equipment together through the use of jacks and plugs.

Patch panel   A board that contains jacks that can be used to make connections with plugs.

PBP   See play-by-play.

Peaking in the red   Modulating a signal so that it reads above 100% on the VU meter.

Pegging the meter   Operating sound so loudly that the needle of the VU meter hits the metal peg beyond the red area.

Penetration   A tape alignment problem in which the tape head is too far forward or too far back.

Performance studio   A studio used primarily by actors or musicians that has microphones but not other production equipment.

Phase   The up and down position of one sound or radio wave in relation to another.

Phone plug   A connector with a sleeve and a tip.

Phono plug   See RCA plug.

Pickup pattern   The area around a mic where it "hears" best.

Pinch roller   A rubber wheel that holds tape against the capstan.

Plastic base   The middle part of audio tape, usually made of polyester.

Plate reverb   A unit consisting of a large metal plate suspended in a frame that vibrates when a transducer changes an audio signal to mechanical energy. A mic then picks up the vibrations as reverberation.

Play-by-play   A term designating sports broadcasting from the scene.

Plugs   Male connectors.

Polar pattern   A two-dimensional drawing of a mic's pickup pattern.

Pop filters   Ball-shaped accessories placed over the microphone to reduce plosive sounds.

Pot   See potentiometer.

Potentiometer   A round knob that controls volume.

Preamplification   The initial stage of amplification.

Pressure mic   Another name for a dynamic mic.

Pressure pads   Small, soft elements that keep cartridge tape pressed against the tape heads.

Print-through   The bleeding through of the magnetic signal of one layer of tape to an adjacent layer of tape.

Production studio   The place where material for radio is produced before it is aired.

Program/audition switch   A switch that determines whether sound is sent to the transmitter or kept in the control room.

Proximity effect   A boosting of basses as a sound source gets closer to a condenser mic.

Quarter-inch phone   See phone plug.

Quarter-track stereo   The recording of two stereo signals on one tape in which two signals go to the left and two go to the right.

Rarefaction   A sound wave characteristic that occurs when the air molecules are pulled apart.

RCA plug   A connector with an outer sleeve and a center shaft.

Record player   A unit that spins a record, picks up a signal, and amplifies the sound through a speaker.

Reel-to-reel recorder   A tape recorder that uses open reels of tape placed on a feed reel and a take-up reel.

Reflected sound   Sound that bounces back to the original source.

Reinforced sound   Sound that causes objects to vibrate at the same frequency as the original sound.

Remote start switches   Buttons that enable a piece of equipment to be operated from a distance.

Restricted Radiotelephone Operator Permit   A license that the FCC gives to people who need to operate equipment and keep a station on the air. No test is required.

Reverberation   Sound that bounces off two or more surfaces.

Reverb ring   The time it takes for a sound to go from full volume to silence.

Reverb route   The path a sound takes from a source to a reflective surface and back again.

Ribbon drive speaker   A rarely used type of monitor speaker.

Ribbon mic   A mic that consists of a metallic ribbon, a magnet, and a coil. Because it is bulky, heavy, and fragile, it is rarely used in radio anymore.

Riding in the mud   Operating volume consistently below 20% on the VU meter.

Riding the gain   Adjusting volume during production.

Rip and read   To read news copy from the wire service machine with very little editing.

Rotary head digital audio tape (R-DAT)   Another name for digital audio tape.

Rotation   See tangency.

RPM   Revolutions per minute.

Sampling   In digital technology, the process of taking from the original sound source to convert to binary data.

Scattered wind   When tape does not spool up evenly on a reel.

Segue   To cut from one sound at full volume to another sound at full volume.

Sel sync   Selective synchronization, a feature that makes a record head act as a play head.

Sensitivity   A mic's efficiency in terms of volume.

Shock mount   A mic stand that isolates the mic from mechanical vibrations.

Shuck   A heavy paper record jacket.

Signal processing   Manipulating elements of sound, such as frequency response and dynamic range, so that the resulting sound is different than the original sound.

Signal-to-noise ratio (S/N)   The relationship of desired sound to inherent unwanted electronic sound. The higher the S/N ratio, the purer the sound.

Slider   See fader.

Slip cueing   Preparing a record to play by having the motor on and holding the edge of it until it should be played.

Solo switch   A button that allows one particular audio board sound to be heard on the monitor.

Soundproofing   Methods of keeping wanted sound in the studio and unwanted sound out of it.

Sound signal   A noise that has not been processed into an electromagnetic form.

Source/tape switch   A switch that allows someone to monitor either the input or the output of a tape recorder.

Speaker   A transducer that converts electrical energy into sound energy.

Speaker level   An input that has been amplified several times in order to drive a speaker.

Speed selector switch   On a turntable, the control that determines whether the record plays at 33 1/3 RPM, 45 RPM, or 78 RPM.

Splicing   The physical cutting of audio tape.

Splicing block   The device that holds audio tape during editing.

Splicing tape   Special tape used for holding together audio tape in the editing process.

Spring reverb   A coiled spring that vibrates when a transducer sends an audio signal through it. A mic then picks up the vibrations as reverberation.

Stereo   Sound recording and reproduction that uses two channels coming from right and left to imitate live sound as closely as possible.

Stylus   A small, compliant strip of metal that vibrates in record grooves.

Supply reel   The reel on the left-hand side of a reel-to-reel or cassette tape recorder that holds the tape before it is recorded or played.

Sustain   The amount of time a sound is at full volume.

Tail   The end of an audio tape.

Take-up reel   The reel on the right-hand side of a reel-to-reel or cassette tape recorder that holds the tape after it is recorded or played.

Tangency   A tape alignment problem in which the head is not pointed straight ahead.

Tape guide   A stationary pin that leads tape through the transport system of a reel-to-reel recorder.

Tape transport   The part of a reel-to-reel tape recorder that moves the tape from the supply reel to the take-up reel.

Tensilize   To prestretch an audio tape.

Tension arm   A moveable guide for tape on a reel-to-reel recorder.

Three-pin connecter   See XLR.

Threshold of hearing   The softest sound the human ear can hear, noted as zero decibels.

Threshold of pain   The loudness level at which the ear begins to hurt, usually about 120 decibels.

Tilt   See zenith.

Timbre   The distinctive quality of tone that each voice or musical instrument has.

Timer   A mechanism with a series of numbers that can be used to indicate how long something is recorded.

Tone arm   The device that holds the turntable cartridge and stylus.

Tone control   A control that increases the volume of the high frequencies or the low frequencies.

Tone generator   An element in an audio board or other piece of equipment that produces a hum that can be set to one hundred percent to calibrate equipment.

Tracking force gauge   A device used to adjust the weight of a tone arm.

Transducer   A device that converts one form of energy into another.

Tray   The area where the CD sits so that it can spin and be read by the laser.

Trim   A knob to fine-tune the volume of each input on an audio board.

Tuner   The part of the radio receiver that makes it possible to receive one particular radio station.

Turntable   A device for spinning a record and converting its vibrations into electrical energy.

Tweeter   The part of a speaker that produces high frequencies.

Unbalanced cable   Cable with two wires, of which one is positive and the other is combined negative and ground.

Unidirectional   Picking up sound from one direction; usually refers to a mic pickup pattern.

Variable resistor   A device that controls the amount of signal that gets through the audio console and thereby controls the volume.

Voice-over   Speech over something else, such as music.

Volume control   A knob or fader that makes sound louder or softer.

VU meter   A unit that gives a visual indication of the level of volume.

Watts   Units of power.

Wave envelope   A representation of a total sound, including its attack, sustain, and decay.

Waveform   The shape of an electromagnetic wave.

Wavelength   The distance between two crests of a radio or sound wave.

Well   See tray.

Windscreen   See pop filter.

Woofer   The part of the speaker that produces low frequencies.

Wow   Slow variations in sound speed.

Wrap   See penetration.

XLR   A connector with three prongs.

Zenith   A tape alignment problem in which the head is tilted too far forward or backward.

Suggested Reading

Allin, Glyn. *Sound Recording and Reproduction*. Boston and London: Focal Press, 1981.

Alten, Stanley R. *Audio in Media*. Belmont, Calif.: Wadsworth Publishing Company, 1986.

Blume, Dan. *Making It in Radio*. Hartford, Conn.: Continental Media Company, 1983.

Book, Albert C., Norman D. Cary, and Stanley I. Tannenbaum. *The Radio and Television Commercial*. 2d ed. Chicago: Crain Books, 1984.

Busby, Linda, and Donald Parker. *The Art and Science of Radio*. Newton, Mass.: Allyn and Bacon, 1985.

Clifford, Martin. *Microphones*. Blue Ridge Summit, Pa.: Tab Books, 1986.

Dudek, Lee J. *Professional Broadcast Announcing*. Boston: Allyn and Bacon, 1982.

Hasling, John. *Fundamentals of Radio Broadcasting*. New York: McGraw-Hill Book Company, 1980.

Hewitt, John. *Air Words: Writing for Broadcast News*. Mountain View, Calif.: Mayfield Publishing Company, 1988.

Hilliard, Robert L. *Radio Broadcasting*. New York: Longman, 1985.

Hunter, Julius K., and Lynne S. Gross. *Broadcast News: The Inside Out*. St. Louis: C. V. Mosby Company, 1980.

Keith, Michael C. *Broadcast Voice Performance*. Boston and London: Focal Press, 1989.

Keith, Michael C., and Joseph M. Krause. *The Radio Station*. 2d ed. Boston and London: Focal Press, 1989.

MacDonald, R. H. *A Broadcast News Manual of Style*. New York: Longman, 1987.

McLeish, Robert. *The Technique of Radio Production*. Boston and London: Focal Press, 1988.

Nisbett, Alex. *The Technique of the Sound System*. Stoneham, Mass.: Focal Press, 1979.

——. *The Use of Microphones*. Stoneham, Mass.: Focal Press, 1983.

O'Donnell, Lewis B., Philip Benoit, and Carl Hausman. *Modern Radio Production*. Belmont, Calif.: Wadsworth Publishing Company, 1986.

——. *Radio Station Operations*. Belmont, Calif.: Wadsworth Publishing Company, 1989.

Oringel, Robert S. *Audio Control Handbook*. 6th ed. Boston and London: Focal Press, 1989.

Stephens, Mitchell. *Broadcast News*. New York: Holt, Rinehart, and Winston, 1980.

Thom, Randy. *Audio Craft: An Introduction to the Techniques of Audio Production*. Washington, D.C.: National Federation of Community Broadcasters, 1982.

Walters, Roger L. *Broadcast Writing: Principles and Practice*. New York: Random House, 1988.

Zeiss, P. Anthony, and Noel T. Smith. *Broadcast Announcing: A Practical Approach*. Killeen, Tex.: Central Texas College Press, 1982.